Manifest Destiny and

Mission in American History

MANIFEST DESTINY *AND* MISSION *IN* AMERICAN HISTORY

A REINTERPRETATION

BY

Frederick Merk

WITH THE COLLABORATION OF

LOIS BANNISTER MERK

VINTAGE BOOKS

A Division of Random House

NEW YORK

TO
My Harvard
and Radcliffe Students
Always an Inspiration

VINTAGE EDITION, FEBRUARY, 1966

VINTAGE BOOKS

are published by Alfred A. Knopf, Inc.
and Random House, Inc.

MANUFACTURED IN THE UNITED STATES OF AMERICA

Preface

THIS BOOK is a study in public opinion. It appraises American opinion regarding expansionist projects in the United States in the nineteenth century. It has for one of its themes the desire of some imaginative elements in American society to see the boundaries of the nation coincide with the rim of the North American continent. A loud expression of that desire was heard during the Polk administration. It was accompanied by an unprecedented growth in the territorial possessions of the nation. In those years the annexation of Texas was completed, the Oregon Country up to the 49th parallel was acquired, and the vast Mexican cession was obtained. When Polk entered office the national domain had not been enlarged in a quarter century; its area had remained fixed at 1,788,000 square miles. During Polk's term it was increased by 1,204,000 square miles. Those years were the era of the surge to the Pacific. The relationship between the agitation for expansion and this surge is one of the subjects of this study.

In the Polk era expansionist agitation at two levels can be discerned. One was the level of acquisition of the entire continent. The other was acquisition merely to the shore of the Pacific. The two are differentiated here perhaps more sharply than the agitators of the 1840's would have approved. The agitators found a lack of differentiation advantageous, and may have relied on it. It won votes among those who, though attracted by Oregon and California, might have been scared off by vistas more remote.

Agitation for expansion occurred again a half century after Polk. This time it was directed to insular objectives and culminated in a new prize—an overseas empire. That episode and its ultimate outcome are described here partly for their own sake and partly to offer the reader helpful comparisons.

Preface

Throughout history expansionism has varied in intensity from individual to individual, from nation to nation, and from period to period. In antiquity it was an obsession of some rulers; it did not interest others at all. In oligarchic and democratic societies it has had a like history. Indeed, in some societies, alternations of expansionism and retreat from it have been distinct phenomena.

Alternations of this kind can be studied to special advantage in a democratic society such as the United States. In this type of society the forces producing expansionism are more visible than in a closed society. Data for studying them are abundant—embarrassingly so. There is a plenitude of newspapers and these represent wide divergences of interest. They represent sections of the nation far apart in desires; also, metropolitan communities as against rural; and political parties in clash, internally and with each other. Subterranean pressures which erupt into expansionism are detectable and measurable in the United States. They may be social or economic, generated by inventions or by the emergence of new classes or sections to political power. They may be emotional or intellectual, drawn to the surface by winds of world sentiment or enlightenment. Where governments resort to creation of sentiment under cover as the Polk government did, this is sooner or later ascertained in a free society. The locating and measuring by the historian of underground sources of expansionism is especially facilitated where newspapers are free, where diaries and private correspondence have become open to examination on a large scale, and where masses of public archives and court cases are made accessible by guides and indexes and microfilming. In America expansionism is examinable as under a microscope or seismometer. A process—world-wide and age-old—may be seen repeating itself in varying forms as in a test tube.

Expansionism is usually associated with crusading ideologies. In the case of Arab expansionism it was Islam; in Spanish expansionism, Catholicism; in Napoleonic expansionism, revolutionary liberalism; in Russian and Chinese expansionism, Marxian communism. The equivalent of these ideologies in the case of the United States was "Manifest Destiny." This was a mixture of republicanism, democracy, freedom of religion, Anglo-Saxonism, and a number of other ingredients. It was harnessed to the cause of continentalism in the 1840's and, strangely enough, to insular expansionism a half century later, which is one of the curiosities of history.

Ideas are spread by propaganda. This has always been so, and, with improvement in the means of communication, has become increasingly so. The manufacture and dissemination of propaganda has been a major industry throughout history, and it looms large in this study. Propaganda becomes ammunition in politics. It is fired in barrages to win the public mind. In turn, it meets barrages of counter propaganda. In these battles the outcome, whether of victory or defeat, is registered on such public-opinion indicators as party platforms, results of national elections, and votes cast on measures in Congress and in state legislatures. These are recordings of a climate of opinion produced by propaganda, and the historian cannot ignore them except at his peril.

To a greater degree than normal, this study makes use of quotations from editorials of the press, speeches in Congress, and orations on the hustings. Language found there is more indicative of public opinion and is fresher than any generalized phrases of a historian of a later day could be. These raw materials are set before the reader for reasons of prudence also. They contain views which even by the present generation may not be read with equanimity. If they should unhappily lead to high feeling, better by far that the clash be among politicians and editors of a bygone age than among the living in an epoch sufficiently disturbed.

Expansionism is an exciting study. It does not, however, always leave the spirit of the reader uplifted. It involves elbowing owners of property rudely to one side and making away with their possessions. This aspect of the study may prove at times oppressive. If so, let the reader recall an observation made by George Santayana in his *Life of Reason:* "Those who cannot remember the past are condemned to repeat it."

In preparing this book I have had generous help from many persons and institutions. I wish I could express my thanks by name to each of the friends who assisted me. But space does not permit it. I must express my gratitude to them as a group. I have had more than ordinary courtesy from the staff of the following libraries: the British Museum, the Public Records Office in Chancery Lane, London, the Library of Congress, the National Archives, the New York Public Library, the New York Genealogical and Biographical Society, the New York State Library, the Boston Public Library, the Massachusetts State Library, the Massachusetts Historical Society, the Boston Athenaeum, the Congregational Library of Boston, the American Antiquarian Society, the New Hampshire Historical Society, the Pennsylvania Historical Society, the Wisconsin State Historical Society, the Indiana State Historical Society, the Historical and Philosophical Society of Ohio, and the libraries of Harvard, Yale, Columbia, Duke, Chicago, and California at Berkeley. I am indebted to my publisher, Alfred A. Knopf, and to his staff, for saving me from many an inadequacy and infelicity of writing. More than to any other person or group I am indebted to my wife, Dr. Lois Bannister Merk, collaborator in this research, constant contributor to my thought and clarifier of it, and a penetrating critic of my English.

F. M.

Cambridge, Massachusetts
May 1962

Contents

Chapter I

Prologue

A SENSE OF MISSION to redeem the Old World by high example was generated in pioneers of idealistic spirit on their arrival in the New World. It was generated by the potentialities of a new earth for building a new heaven. It appeared thereafter in successive generations of Americans, with changes in the type of mission, but with the sense of mission unaltered. At Plymouth and at Boston the type was religious liberty, the right to worship in a church that was pure and free of heresies, in covenant with God, and organized on a congregational basis. By 1776 mission had come to cover a principle of government—government independent, based on the consent of the governed, republican in character, and free of the excrescences of a hereditary aristocracy. By the time of the Constitutional Convention and the first Congress, it included a federal type of government, careful balances of powers, and, presently, a Bill of Rights protecting the individual against congressional intrusion upon equality of religion, freedom of speech, of the press, and of assembly, and all the other basic rights brought by Englishmen to America. By the time of the Jeffersonian revolution it was protection against federal encroachment on rights reserved to the states, and safety for the freedoms guaranteed in the Bill of Rights. By the time of Andrew Jackson it included a concept of democracy greatly widened. By the time of Lincoln it embraced freedom for the slaves and a determination that government of the people, by the people, for the people should not perish from the earth. By Woodrow Wilson's day it meant the Fourteen Points, and by the time of the second Roosevelt, the Four Freedoms. In all these enlargements of mission the Goddess of Liberty holding aloft her light to the world seemed to Americans to be, in reality, themselves.

The Goddess of Liberty faced eastward. But America faced westward. In the wilderness new societies were constantly arising as population flowed to the interior. These societies formed governments by means of compacts, as Frederick Jackson Turner pointed out in one of the greatest of his early essays, "Western State-Making in the Revolutionary Era." [1] The compacts were the agreements of men entering unsurveyed, often uncharted land, who found themselves outside recognized legal limits and undertook to abide by the common will. In the realm of government, compacts meant what covenants with God meant in the realm of the spirit. Their prototype was the Mayflower Compact entered into by the Pilgrims off the shores of Plymouth in 1620. Within a century and a half, by 1772, the compacts had made their way to "Western waters," where, on the upper courses of the Tennessee, frontiersmen from North Carolina, on learning that they were beyond the line drawn by the Indian treaties of 1768, protected themselves against eviction by forming the Watauga Compact, once characterized by the historian Theodore Roosevelt, somewhat grandiloquently, as the first written constitution adopted west of the Appalachian Mountains.[2] The same procedure was carried to the region of West Virginia, where pioneers, in 1776, sent a petition to Congress asking to be organized as the state of Westsylvania. It was used again in 1780, in the Cumberland Compact of the Nashville basin; and in 1784, in the attempt of settlers in what is now eastern Tennessee to win recognition as the state of Franklin. In these western proceedings south of the Ohio, pioneers resorted to concepts of social covenant—agreements to abide by the common will—for their self-preservation.

In the area north of the Ohio the concepts employed in setting up

[1] Frederick J. Turner: "Western State-Making in the Revolutionary Era," *American Historical Review*, I (1895–6), 70, 251.

[2] Theodore Roosevelt: *The Winning of the West* in *Works of Theodore Roosevelt* (New York, 1926), X, 171.

governments were more legalistic. They were concepts forged in a decade of controversy with the British Parliament in 1765–75. They were the work of men east of the mountains, philosophical radicals seeking protection against Parliamentary legislation, especially of the sort contained in the Coercive Acts of 1774. Parliament had passed these acts under the constitutional theory that the empire is unitary, with authority centering in London, and that this authority possessed a right to impose decisions on the overseas dominions. The radicals proceeded on the theory that the empire is federal, that the overseas dominions are autonomous, that colonial legislatures are co-ordinate with Parliament under the King, and that subjects of the King are not bound by acts of Parliament unless they give consent. These differences were not reconcilable. They led to war in which the concept of autonomy was carried to its culmination in American independence. The concept was applied, soon after, by the Congress of the Confederation, to the trans-Allegheny West. It became the basis for the Northwest Ordinance of 1787, in which new communities arising in the West obtained increasing autonomy as they qualified for it by growth of population and ultimately achieved admission to the governing union as equal states.

Under the Constitution the Northwest Ordinance became part of the federal framework of the Union. It became the mode used most frequently for enlarging the Union. It was one of a great series of charters for expansion that included the Land Ordinance of 1785, which provided for the orderly sale of land and safe title to it, and the Bill of Rights of 1791, which guaranteed individual and states' rights.[3] These charters constitute a veritable flowering of genius—a genius for converting revolutionary idealism into practical devices of government for both the older communities of the East and the newer ones of the West. They were brought to flower by the heat of controversy with Parliament, by a spirit of reform bred in the war, and by the thrilling prospect, opened by victory, of an expanding republican society. They were a response, too, to the urgency of great problems demanding solution. All of them became part of an

[3] A convenient collection of these documents is Henry S. Commager: *Documents of American History* (6th ed., New York, 1958).

image of American freedom expanding into the wilderness. But older modes of state making were not forgotten in acceptance of the new. Compact was used for special purposes in the advance of civilization westward.

After the Revolution population in an unprecedented rush went over the Appalachian Mountains. It went into Kentucky and Tennessee, drawn by easy terms of land acquisition, by lax administration, and by speculative fever; it went into western New York and eastern Ohio; it thrust out, within a quarter century, a great wedge of settlement to the Mississippi River, the tip of which touched the river at St. Louis, the base of which lay in the upper waters of the Ohio and the Tennessee. Beyond the Mississippi, in the Louisiana Purchase area, lay the Territory of Orleans, which had a population, by 1812, large enough to win elevation to statehood. On the periphery of these settlements lay others that were growing rapidly. In West Florida, at Baton Rouge—Spanish in 1810 still—an American society was arising, to the apprehension of the authorities at Mobile. At the St. Marys River in Georgia an American population eyed Spanish lands across the river in East Florida—lands ill administered, ill defended, and open to seizure.

All this flooding of frontiersmen westward and southward represented forces that had been dammed up by war and had won release. From Cumberland Gap the old trail had been improved; the Ohio River had been rendered safe for travel by the defeat of the Northwest Indians at the Battle of Fallen Timbers; the Southwest Indians had been cowed by a succession of defeats, followed in each case by immense cessions of land; the Mississippi had been made by diplomacy to flow free to the sea. Frontier restlessness accounted for the rest. The new population brought new states into the Union. Some of them—Kentucky and Vermont—came by right of compact as a principle of state making. Others—Tennessee, Ohio, and Louisiana—came by right of the principles enunciated in the Northwest Ordinance of 1787.

Upon the Spanish borderlands, rising populations were under temptation to experiment with a special kind of state making—state making at the expense of a foreign power. Experiment of that sort was not altogether new, for in the trans-Appalachian West fur traders and settlers had made early incursions into New France, and in 1763 had helped to win it. The temptation to repeat the process in New Spain was fostered by disintegration of Spanish authority, which was, in turn, the result of a struggle at home between the supporters of Ferdinand VII and those of Joseph Bonaparte, a struggle that culminated in the Peninsular War. Moreover, West Florida—like Texas—was claimed by the United States as part of the Louisiana Purchase. Such conditions were congenial climate for frontier state making, and here seeds of a process tested elsewhere came to new flower. In West Florida a settlers' rising occurred in 1810. A miniature republic, under a "lone star" flag, was formed, and annexation to the United States was awaited. Annexation, as a state, failed. The ripe fruit was too promptly gathered as a territory by the Madison government, which simply seized and made it part of the Louisiana Purchase. Also, in East Florida and in Texas, Southern pioneers experimented with familiar concepts of state making. In East Florida, in 1812, several hundred "patriots," partly settlers, partly adventurers, crossed the St. Marys River from Georgia, staged an uprising, formed the Republic of Florida, organized a provisional government, and took possession of Fernandina and St. Augustine. Their leader, General George Mathews, an American army officer, was, however, in the end disavowed by his government, and the project failed.[4] In Texas—at Nacogdoches—a handful of American squatters, joining an expeditionary force from Natchez under the command of James Long, a former army officer under Andrew Jackson, staged an uprising of "patriots" against the Spanish in 1819 and organized the Republic of Texas, with Long as President. This project was premature also. The patriots were routed by Spanish forces and the Republic collapsed.[5]

State making at the expense of foreign governments intrigued

[4] Julius W. Pratt: *Expansionists of 1812* (New York, 1925), chs. 2, 5.

[5] *Niles' Register,* XVII (1819–20), 31; Hubert H. Bancroft: *North Mexican States and Texas* in *Works of Hubert Howe Bancroft* (San Francisco, 1886–9), XVI, 49–51.

Thomas Jefferson and James Madison, as well as the frontiersmen. It interested them in the two Floridas especially. Control of West Florida seemed desirable because it meant, as did control of New Orleans, command of the Mississippi. Control of East Florida seemed necessary to prevent a transfer of it to hands stronger than Spain's. The two Canadas, upper and lower, were of mild interest also. They were of more than mild interest to Western war hawks, especially after 1810. But all hopes of acquiring these territories, except for West Florida, came to naught as a result of the disappointing course of the War of 1812 and the peace negotiations at Ghent.

Jefferson and his disciples were not interested in state making in the trans-Rocky Mountain West on behalf of the United States. They actually were opposed to such an idea. That territory lay at a forbidding distance. It lay, measured in travel time, at the far corner of the world. It took the Lewis and Clark expedition eighteen months to travel from St. Louis to the Pacific. The Astorian Robert Stuart, returning home via the South Pass cut-off, took ten months. Sea communication between the eastern tidewater and the Pacific Northwest was a matter of six or eight months, depending on the weather. The voyage was often made by circumnavigating the globe. Jefferson expected that any society formed on the Pacific shore would consist of Americans. As such, it ought not be governed as a colony of the United States. Colonialism was contrary to the genius of American institutions. If attempted, it would subvert the liberties of the Republic itself. Any American state formed west of the mountains ought to take, Jefferson believed, the same course the American colonies had taken in 1776 and the Spanish colonies were in the process of taking. It ought to become an independent republic.[6]

Regarding the Spanish regions south and west of the Rio Grande, Jefferson had like views. Those regions seemed out of bounds to him, in a double sense, because of their immense distance and also because of the undesirability of their population.

[6] Frederick Merk: *Albert Gallatin and the Oregon Problem* (Cambridge, 1950), 12.

Central America and South America had a population nine-tenths Indian or Negroid. Brazil contained a large number of slaves brought in by the Portuguese. Central America would eventually be taken over, doubtless by Americans; and, perhaps, even South America. The United States seemed to Jefferson a "nest" from which the two Americas, North and South, would someday be peopled. These continents should be reserved, therefore, for that future.[7] In 1801 he wrote James Monroe, who had asked for advice about areas to which freed Negroes from the South could be removed, that none of the western possessions of the United States, nor those of continental South America, nor those of British North America, should be considered for Negro colonization.

> However our present interests may restrain us within our own limits, it is impossible not to look forward to distant times when our rapid multiplication will expand itself beyond those limits, and cover the whole northern, if not the southern continent, with a people speaking the same language, governed in similar forms, and by similar laws; nor can we contemplate with satisfaction either blot or mixture on that surface.[8]

Nothing was more certainly written in the book of fate, Jefferson believed, than that the people of the United States, north and south, would free their slaves. Nor was it any less certain that the two races, white and black, each equally free, could not live in the same government. "Nature, habit, opinion, has drawn indelible lines of distinction between them."[9] Freed Negroes should be colonized, Jefferson suggested, in the West Indies, and should not become further a blot on the fair pages of Central and South America, confusing the future of the white republics which would rise there. As for the republic of the "nest," it should not be extended beyond the color line of the Rio Grande, any more than beyond the high

[7] Thomas Jefferson to Archibald Stuart, January 25, 1786, in Paul L. Ford (ed.): *Works of Thomas Jefferson* (10 vols., New York, 1892–9), V, 73. Eagles would fly from the nest carrying principles of freedom, but with no strings tying them to the Confederacy.

[8] Jefferson to James Monroe, November 24, 1801, in Ford (ed.): *Works of Jefferson,* IX, 315–19. The correspondence took place after Gabriel's uprising of 1800.

[9] Ford (ed.): *Works of Jefferson,* I, 77. This is an extract from the "Autobiography," dated February 7, 1779.

line of the Stony [Rocky] Mountains. Concepts such as these shaped not only Jefferson's thinking but that of his disciples. As late as 1846 Albert Gallatin believed that the Oregon Country was destined to become an independent republic.[10]

Other elements of Jefferson's thinking were that republics should be kept to reasonable size and that, within republics, rights of states should be maintained inviolate. These were prerequisites of freedom, especially in a nation already as large as the United States. In such a nation power commensurate with the needs of maintaining law and order must go to the rulers. But power is corrupting, and only if limitations on it are rigorously maintained is it kept wholesome. In the Confederation period Kentucky, separated from Virginia by mountains, seemed a natural state, which should be organized under its own state government.[11] States of the Confederation should transfer some of their powers, Jefferson conceded in 1787, to the Union. But the extent of the transfer actually made at the Constitutional Convention left him uneasy, and, writing to friends in North Carolina from Paris, he made clear that he would be content if they held off ratification until assurances had been given of the addition of a bill of rights to the Constitution. As Vice-President in 1798 and 1799, Jefferson believed resistance to a consolidation of power by the Federalists vital to freedom, and this accounts for his clash with Hamilton and for the Virginia and Kentucky Resolutions. His wish to maintain limits on the size of republics and to preserve carefully, in the interests of freedom, the rights of states, would have been denied by few opponents of his. The only difference would have been in definitions of terms. No difference would have arisen over an insistence that remote territory should form completely independent governments.[12]

Federalists considered additions of even neighboring territory, in most cases, undesirable. Many objected to the Louisiana Purchase. They denounced maneuvers to acquire the Floridas. They raged at proposals of war hawks to conquer the Canadas. These

[10] Merk: *Albert Gallatin and the Oregon Problem*, 84.
[11] Ford (ed.): *Works of Jefferson*, V, 73.
[12] Ibid., XI, 181 ff.

objections were partly a matter of constitutional scruple. They expressed, also, fears of the consequences an expansion would bring —unsettling of sectional balances built into the Constitution, diminution of the East's control of power, increase of power of the wild West, the possibility of military clashes with England and with England's ally, Spain (the intended victims of the expansion), and, finally, distaste for sitting down to hotchpot with mixed races in Louisiana and in the Floridas, a distaste well expressed by Fisher Ames. "Otters in the wilderness," he wrote, would as soon obey and give effect to right principles "as the Gallo-Hispano-Indian *omnium gatherum* of savages and adventurers" in those western lands.[13] Much of Federalist feeling was unredeemed partisanship. So rancorous was the composite of these feelings that when, in the War of 1812, a British force approached New Orleans, Timothy Pickering communicated to a Federalist confidant a hope that the city might be captured, which would induce the trans-Appalachian West to cast its lot with the victors, and would restore the good old union of the thirteen original states in which New England would exercise her rightful influence.[14] In such a climate of opinion Federalists found no difficulty at all in joining Jeffersonians in resistance to ideas of extending the Union beyond the crest of the Rockies. As for any concept of hegemony by the United States over all the continent, Federalists and Jeffersonians would have been at one in repudiating it as unthinkable.

Yet in both parties prior to the War of 1812 there were individuals with imaginations stronger than their means of controlling them, or partisan tempers that deprived them of use of their minds, who did express a belief in the destiny of the United States to establish hegemony over the continent. Early in 1803, after news arrived that Spain had withdrawn from the United States, at Napoleon's request apparently, the right of deposit at New Orleans, the Federalist editor of the *New York Evening Post*, William Cole-

[13] Fisher Ames to Thomas Dwight, October 31, 1803, in *Works of Fisher Ames* (Boston, 1809), 484.

[14] Henry Adams (ed.): *Documents Relating to New England Federalism* (Boston, 1877), 414–18.

man, seized the opportunity to lash the back of Napoleon's dupe, Jefferson, with it. He maintained that regulation of the "destiny of *North America*" belongs of right to the United States. "The country is *ours,* ours is the right to the rivers and to all the sources of future opulence, power and happiness, which lay scattered at our feet; and we shall be the scorn and derision of the world if we suffer them to be wrested from us by the intrigues of France." [15] Coleman and his Federalist friends were ready to go to war with France over the issue.

Yet when the news arrived a few months later of Jefferson's astonishing fortune in acquiring Louisiana peaceably, and with it, control of the Mississippi, the discomfited editor had breath left only to explain that Britain, not Jefferson, deserved credit for what had happened, in that she had forced the hand of Napoleon; that the price paid for the province was far too high; that the territory itself was of little value except as a means of future barter with Spain for the two Floridas, which were obviously of far greater value; that the vast undefined Louisiana was beyond any of the nation's needs for years, if not centuries, to come; that, in the meantime, it was an actual threat to the nation in the attractions it offered to the unwise to settle in it, with a consequent too wide dispersion of population; and, indeed, that "by adding to the great weight of the western part of our territory, [it] must hasten the dismemberment of a large portion of our country, or a dissolution of the Government." [16] Yet Coleman's initial defiance of Napoleon is cited unwarily as evidence of early American liking for continentalist expansion.[17]

Other early sentiments of continentalism were uttered, probably with tongue in cheek also. In 1804 Charles Brockton Brown, romanticist and novelist, permitted his imagination to be carried, by enthusiasm over the acquisition of Louisiana, into "excursions

[15] *New York Evening Post,* January 28, 1803.
[16] Ibid., July 5, 21, 1803.
[17] Albert K. Weinberg: *Manifest Destiny; a Study of Nationalist Expansionism in American History* (Baltimore, 1935), 31.

into futurity." Instead of anticipating the "extension of this empire merely to the sea on the south, and to the *great river* [the St. Lawrence] on the north, we may be sure that, in no long time, it will stretch east and west from sea to sea, and from the north pole to the Isthmus of Panama." [18] In the same year an obscure patriot in Maine predicted in a Fourth of July oration that the national boundary would eventually be extended to the Isthmus.[19] Early in 1812, a war hawk, John A. Harper, assured the House of Representatives that the Author of Nature had "marked our limits in the south, by the Gulf of Mexico; and on the north by the regions of eternal frost." [20] But the more sober-minded elements in both political parties in the period prior to the War of 1812 consigned such revealers of God's purpose to the outer edges of the lunatic fringe.

On the Northwest coast lay genuine potentialities for expansion to the western sea. But they stirred little enthusiasm, prior to the War of 1812, either among the public or in the government. The discovery by Robert Gray of the mouth of the Columbia River in 1792 was belatedly announced in the United States. The earliest public reference to it seems to have been Captain George Vancouver's, in his narrative of a voyage to the North Pacific, printed in 1798.[21] The first detailed report of the Lewis and Clark expedition appeared only in 1807.[22] Astoria was a venture of private capital. It was designed to gain for John Jacob Astor control of the fur trade of the Columbia Valley and of the vast area eastward to the Great Lakes, which was partly British, partly American. In 1813, before news of the fall of Astoria had reached the East, Jefferson responded to a progress report sent him by Astor, expressing pleas-

[18] Brown made his prediction in a footnote added to his translation of C. F. C. Volney's *View of the Soil and Climate of the United States* (Philadelphia, 1804).

[19] Joseph Chandler: *An Oration Delivered on the Fourth of July 1804* (Portland, 1804), 11.

[20] *Annals of Congress,* 12 Cong., 1 Sess., 657 (January 4, 1812).

[21] Captain George Vancouver: *A Voyage of Discovery to the North Pacific Ocean and Round the World* (3 vols., London, 1798), I, 415.

[22] Patrick Gass: *A Journal of the Voyages and Travels of a Corps of Discovery* (Pittsburgh, 1807).

ure and romantically characterizing the venture as "the germ of a great, free and independent empire on that side of our continent." He further expressed the hope that if Astoria should fall to the British in the war, the American government would seek to obtain a convention with them at the peace conference providing for the "independence" of that country and acknowledging our right of "patronizing them in all cases of injury from foreign nations." [23] This was pallid interest in Astoria.

In the peace settlement at Ghent no enlargements of American territory were realized. The Canadas remained British. East Florida was not acquired. In the Far West, Astoria had fallen to a British naval force piloted by an Anglo-Canadian rival of Astor in the fur trade—the North West Company. The American peace commissioners at Ghent, confronted with the fact that American soil and positions were in British hands, did well, by exhibiting great hardihood, in obtaining even a treaty of mutual restoration of conquests.

Yet the peace did raise for Jeffersonians an issue of pride. Astoria had been lost in the war. It must be recovered. Federalists had been trumpeting the charge that the war was unnecessary, aggressive, ruinous. If its outcome proved to be a loss on the Pacific, Jeffersonians would suffer. In 1817 James Monroe became President. He was an expansionist with regard to territory east of the Rocky Mountains, though quite willing to see an independent republic rise west of the mountains. His Secretary of State was John Quincy Adams. Adams wanted everything east, west, north, and south of the mountains. He embodied the spirit of nationalism that was sweeping the country after the war. He was a Hamiltonian by instinct rather than a Jeffersonian, without any of Hamilton's predilections, however, for the British. In methods of diplomacy, as in aims, he was an imperialist.[24]

[23] Frederick Merk: "Genesis of the Oregon Question," *Mississippi Valley Historical Review*, XXXVI (1949–50), 596–7.

[24] Hamilton indulged in dreams of imperialism during the naval war with France. In 1799 he was inclined not merely to "look to the possession of the Floridas and Louisiana" but to "squint at South America," in collaboration apparently with the English fleet. His close associate, Gouverneur Morris, exhibited

One of his early assignments was to restore Astoria by diplomacy to its prewar status. He fulfilled it. He more than fulfilled it. He detected a technical error made by the British in the ceremony of restoration and put it in storage for subsequent use.[25] He obtained in 1818 an agreement of joint occupation of the Oregon Country which gave England a temporary commercial advantage but gained for the United States the great ultimate advantage of holding the region open to occupation by American pioneers.

With Spain, Adams dealt more summarily. By means of thinly veiled threats—threats to seize East Florida (already seized in part by Andrew Jackson), threats to seize Texas by right of a shadowy American claim and to recognize the revolted colonies of Spain in Latin America, and threats to have a showdown on the claims for damages suffered by American citizens at the hands of Spain—he extracted a treaty, the Adams-Onís treaty of 1819. The treaty ceded East Florida to the United States, gave recognition to an American seizure of West Florida, and transferred Spanish claims to the Pacific Northwest north of the line of 42° to the United States. In return the United States relinquished all claim to Texas and assumed the unpaid damage claims of its citizens to the extent of $5,000,000.[26]

In these triumphs President Monroe shared. Indeed he diligently collaborated in the work of acquiring Spanish claims north of 42° on the Pacific. He seemed to be succumbing to the temptations of imperialism and abandoning the republican virtues of his old leader. But he was not. He conceived of the United States as a trustee, merely, in seeking the Northwest coast and saving it from the British. He expected that the trustee would pass it on, at the right time, to a new republic which would grow up there. He hoped in the meantime, as did others, that Astoria would become

---

at the time of the Louisiana Purchase a curious mixture of imperialism and doubt about expansionism. Henry C. Lodge (ed.): *Works of Alexander Hamilton* (12 vols., New York, 1904), VII, 97; Anne C. Morris (ed.): *Diary and Letters of Gouverneur Morris* (2 vols., New York, 1888), II, 441–5.

[25] Merk: "Genesis of the Oregon Question," 606 ff.

[26] Samuel F. Bemis: *John Quincy Adams and the Foundations of American Foreign Policy* (New York, 1949), ch. 16.

an outlying naval base or a commercial base for the United States on the Pacific.[27]

Adams indicated, in instructions to ministers abroad and in conversations recorded in his famous diary, that he did not see eye to eye with his chief in these matters. In an instruction issued to Richard Rush, the American minister at London, on May 20, 1818, in regard to the unannounced sending of the warship *Ontario* to reclaim Astoria, which had raised a storm in London, Adams directed Rush to reassure the British as to the peacefulness of the mission. He directed the minister informally to advert to the "minuteness" of the present interests of the two nations in that country. At the same time he told the minister to suggest delicately that, if these interests should ever become an object of importance to the United States, Great Britain ought not to oppose American possession. If the United States left Britain all her holds upon Europe, Asia, Africa, and America, Britain ought not to view with eyes of jealousy and alarm every possibility of our extension "to our natural dominion in North America." [28]

"Our natural dominion" was spelled out by Adams a year and a half later at a cabinet meeting in a discussion of delays made by Spain in ratifying the Adams-Onís treaty. All Spanish possessions on the southern border of the United States, and all British on the northern, would come, Adams thought, to the United States before centuries had passed. Most Spanish possessions had already come by purchase.

> This rendered it still more unavoidable that the remainder of the continent should ultimately be ours. But it is very lately that we have distinctly seen this ourselves; very lately that we have avowed the pretension of extending to the South Sea; and until Europe shall find it a settled geographical element that the United States and North America are identical, any effort on our part to reason the world out of a belief that we are ambitious will have no other effect than to convince them that we add to our ambition hypocrisy. Crawford spoke of an article in the last Edinburgh Review defend-

[27] Merk: *Albert Gallatin and the Oregon Problem,* ch. 2.

[28] Adams to Richard Rush, May 20, 1818, in *House Docs.,* 17 Cong., 1 Sess. (Serial 68), No. 112, pp. 12–13.

> ing us against this charge of ambition; but if the world do not hold us for Romans they will take us for Jews and of the two vices I would rather be charged with that which has greatness mingled in its composition.[29]

The President, however, remained true to Jeffersonian precepts. He made this clear at a cabinet conference as late as 1824. He read to the Cabinet a draft of a message he proposed sending to Congress recommending the establishment of military posts, one high up the Missouri, another at the mouth of the Columbia or at the Juan de Fuca Strait. He included in the draft, however, "a strong argument against making any territorial settlement[s] on the Pacific, with a decided expression of an opinion that they would necessarily soon separate from this Union." Adams expressed doubts as to the expediency of sending such a communication to Congress. These were reinforced by Calhoun, who thought no such separation would ever occur; "the passion for aggrandizement was the law paramount of man in society," and "there was no example in history of the disruption of a nation from itself by voluntary separation." That opinion was also held by Samuel L. Southard, Secretary of the Navy, and the President, overborne by his advisers, withheld the message.

The vision of Adams of acquisition by his country of the entire continent had not been considered in the Cabinet during the formulation of the famous Monroe message of 1823. It might have been, for the concept of non-colonization by Europe in the message, was a related concept, even if not an opposite face of the same coin. Non-colonization had been Adams's brain child in 1823. He had written it into the message of that year without any consultation of the Cabinet at all, strange as this may seem now to students of American history.

The method by which the continent was to be acquired was also Adams's suggestion. The method was to be federation—federation of the constitutional type. In the 1824 discussion, above described, Adams expressed the opinion that "a government by federation

[29] Charles F. Adams (ed): *Memoirs of John Quincy Adams* (12 vols., Philadelphia, 1874–7), IV, 438–9.

would be found practicable upon a territory as extensive as this continent." [30]

Although neither the public nor Congress was interested in abstractions, both were interested in concrete issues of expansionism. A concrete issue relating to the Oregon Country appeared in the Senate in 1818 in the form of the joint occupation treaty; it came up in both houses in the form of perennial bills for the military occupation of the mouth of the Columbia; and in 1827, in the Senate, in the form of renewal of the occupation treaty. Information needed for the debates was supplied by spokesmen of the fur trade, overland and overseas, by such men as Thomas H. Benton and William S. Sturgis, the merchant prince of Boston, or by spokesmen of the New England whaling interests, such as Francis Baylies, or by diplomats such as Albert Gallatin, whose dispatches describing his negotiations were published promptly by Congress. Misinformation, also, was plentiful, provided by zealots such as John Floyd, and by politicians with little knowledge of the subject but with obligations to show activity to constituents. Benton's writings as a St. Louis editor and his speeches in the Senate and the public letters of Sturgis revealed the persistence of the Jeffersonian concept of ultimate independence of the Pacific Northwest, though with reservations about an outlying naval or commercial station at the mouth of the Columbia, which was Monroe's idea. A theme developed by Benton at great length in editorials and in speeches was that, at the mouth of the Columbia, a modern Tyre would rise, deflecting, by way of the Columbia and the Missouri, the commerce of the Orient to St. Louis. Easterners, objecting to all forms of transmountain expansionism, answered this by describing such terrors as the shifting sand bar at the mouth of the Columbia, the mountains separating the waters of the Columbia and the Missouri, and the savages lying in wait on the banks of both streams for opportunities to plunder passers-by.

A heavy interlarding of ignorance and unreality appeared in all these discussions. The region was a savage wilderness, known, even to explorers and trappers, only at its highways, and was at an

[30] Ibid., VI, 250–1.

immense distance from civilization. Confusion of the public was the chief outcome of the debates. The confusion was heightened by the lack of agreement among members of the government on the possibility of holding Oregon indefinitely. For tactical reasons, negotiations with the British had been carried on as if no doubt existed about the intent of the government to acquire dominion in Oregon. Yet to informed persons it was evident that members of the government held differing views in the matter. Zealots and politicians made capital among voters by urging military measures for the occupation of Oregon. Responsible persons, however, cited Gallatin's warnings of counter measures by the British if the United States should enter upon a policy of adventure. The Oregon issue remained, therefore, relatively stalemated in the period of the late 1820's and 1830's.[31]

The Adams-Onís treaty was given a mixed reception by the public. The Florida provision was universally acclaimed. Florida was near home. The loss of Texas, however, was a tragedy, and the acquisition of Spanish rights on the remote Pacific shore a poor setoff to it. The author of the treaty had no doubts at all about the value of the transcontinental provision. On the day the treaty was signed he exulted over it, and over his own part in bringing it to pass, to the extent of several pages in his diary. He wrote that Spain's acknowledgment of the American line to the Pacific marked a new "epocha" in our history, and that he, and he alone, was responsible for the initial proposal of it in the negotiations.[32] However, Thomas Benton, who considered the Rocky Mountains the ultimate American limit, was inconsolable about the loss of Texas, and he disliked, besides, the growing tendency in American politics to view a Secretary of State as heir apparent to the throne. He kept denouncing the Texas provision as a colossal blunder. The surrender of Texas seemed to him, and to all Westerners of like mind, a betrayal of the nation, a tearing apart of the valley of the Mississippi, an exchange of inner-valley unity for a slice of outer

[31] The foregoing account rests on Merk: *Albert Gallatin and the Oregon Problem,* ch. 2.

[32] Adams (ed.): *Memoirs of John Quincy Adams,* IV, 273–6.

space. Such feeling was especially strong in the rising new Southern center of the cotton kingdom, Natchez, and this was the city which sent the James Long expedition of 1819 to Texas to try to rectify the New Englander's lamentable error.

In the late 1820's and 1830's relative quiet fell on the whole western expansionist front. This was the era of absorption of the energies and emotions of the restless on the Northeastern front, in Maine. In Oregon the fur trade of Americans went into a decline. It almost disappeared as a result of depletion of the furs and cutthroat competition by the Hudson's Bay Company for what remained. Whalers lost interest in the Northwest coast as their fleet made its base in far-off Hawaii. Gallatin's warnings of the consequences of an American military adventure in Oregon had a sobering effect. As for Texas, the Mexican republic opened the province to peaceful occupation. Land, fabulously rich, was offered to Americans cost-free. A surge of Americans flowed there, accelerated by Mexican colonizers, the so-called *empresarios,* who had contracts to fulfill.

This flow of Americans to Texas aroused, after a time, uneasiness in Mexico. It was not according to plan. The plan had envisaged migration of Americans, Europeans, and native Mexicans in relatively equal numbers. That would have been safe enough. But a flow preponderantly American, a flow of rough frontiersmen in overwhelming numbers, had occurred instead. In 1828 a fact-finding commission—the Tèran Commission—was sent to Texas to study the situation. After a lengthy investigation it rendered a report on the number and temper of Americans in Texas. The report was an alarming document. On the basis of it, Lucas Alamán, Secretary of Foreign Relations, sent a warning to his Congress, in which the historic techniques of American frontiersmen, including the meshing of their aims and those of the American government, were fully revealed:

> They commence by introducing themselves into the territory which they covet, upon pretence of commercial negotiations, or of the establishment of colonies, with or without the assent of the Government to which it belongs. These colonies grow, multiply, become

> the predominant party in the population; and as soon as a support is found in this manner, they begin to set up rights which it is impossible to sustain in a serious discussion. . . . These pioneers excite, by degrees, movements which disturb the political state of the country . . . and then follow discontents and dissatisfaction, calculated to fatigue the patience of the legitimate owner, and to diminish the usefulness of the administration and of the exercise of authority. When things have come to this pass, which is precisely the present state of things in Texas, the diplomatic management commences: the inquietude they have excited in the territory, . . . the interests of the colonists therein established, the insurrections of adventurers, and savages instigated by them, and the pertinacity with which the opinion is set up as to their right of possession, become the subjects of notes, full of expressions of justice and moderation, until, with the aid of other incidents, which are never wanting in the course of diplomatic relations, the desired end is attained of concluding an arrangement as onerous for one party as it is advantageous to the other. Sometimes more direct means are resorted to; and taking advantage of the enfeebled state, or domestic difficulties, of the possessor of the soil, they proceed, upon the most extraordinary pretexts, to make themselves masters of the country, as was the case in the Floridas; leaving the question to be decided afterwards as to the legality of the possession, which force alone could take from them.[33]

In response to this warning the Mexican Congress in 1830 adopted a new colonization law, which was designed to cut off further American settlement. It was, however, not effectively implemented. Migration went on as before. The chief effect of the law was to produce friction with Americans already in Texas. This flared into an uprising in 1835, into a compact in the form of a declaration of independence, into war, and, finally, into a request for admission into the American Union. The Alamán thesis of a conspiracy maintained by the American government with frontiersmen sent abroad seemed to be confirmed.

To John Quincy Adams too, conspiracy seemed to be the unifying thread of recent events in Texas. It was a Southern conspiracy, planned and pressed by Southern slaveholders for the purpose of extending slavery, and it included the government of the United States, especially that of Andrew Jackson. Migrants sent out by

[33] *House Exec. Docs.*, 25 Cong., 2 Sess. (Serial 332), No. 351, pp. 313–14.

the conspirators to Texas incited the revolution and then pressed annexation on Congress. Imbued with such ideas, Adams led the fight in Congress and throughout the nation against annexation. In 1843, when the drive for annexation was in its final phase, he drafted and published an address to the nation, signed by himself and twelve others, in which he warned, after a reiteration of the conspiracy thesis, that annexation would be identical, if achieved, with dissolution of the Union.[34]

Charges of conspiracy, whether by Mexicans or by Adams, were distortions of the truth. What had happened was merely a repetition, on a grander scale than usual, of the old frontier process of state making at the expense of a foreign government—state making through migration and compact. Replying to the charges of conspiracy, the *New York Morning News,* in the spring of 1845, wrote an editorial entitled "The Popular Movement," which was sound history:

> From the time that the Pilgrim Fathers landed on these shores to the present moment, the older settlements have been constantly throwing off a hardy, restless and lawless pioneer population, which has kept in advance, subduing the wilderness and preparing the way for more orderly settlers who tread rapidly upon their footsteps. It is but a short time since Western Massachusetts, Connecticut and Rhode Island, although now proverbially the land of "steady habits" and good morals, presented a population no ways superior socially to that of Texas at the present day. As their numbers increased, law and order obtained control, and those unable to bear constraint sought new homes. Those latter have rolled forward in advance of civilization, like the surf on an advancing wave, indicative of its resistless approach. This is the natural, unchangeable effect of our position upon this continent, and it must continue until the waves of the Pacific have hemmed in and restrained the onward movement.
>
> To say that the settlement of a fertile and unappropriated soil by right of individual purchase is the aggression of a government is absurd. Equally ridiculous is it to suppose that when a band of hardy settlers have reclaimed the wilderness, multiplied in numbers, built up a community and organized a government, that they have not the right to claim the confederation of that society of

[34] *Niles' Register,* LXIV (1843), 173–5.

> States from the bosom of which they emanated. An inalienable right of man is to institute for themselves that form of government which suits them best, and to change it when they please. On this continent communities grow up mostly by immigration from the United States. Such communities therefore inevitably establish the same form of government which they left behind and *demand* of them that they *come* into the Union. Mexico is a government professedly of the people. If that people choose to change its form they have the right to do so. They have already done so with the approbation of the world. If therefore Mexico, in whole or in part, becomes so settled by the Anglo-Saxon race that they have a majority and decide to alter the system to that of the United States model, and ask for admittance into the Union, the same inalienable right will exist and who will deny it? [35]

If Adams "denied it," it was because he had changed his mind since he had written, a quarter century earlier, of our extension "to our natural dominion in North America." He had come to realize by 1843 that slavery as well as freedom might be extended by compact over the continent.

[35] *New York Morning News,* May 24, 1845.

Chapter II

Manifest Destiny

IN THE mid-1840's a form of expansionism novel in name, appeal, and theory made its appearance in the United States. It was "Manifest Destiny." The term was not wholly new. Phrases like it had been used before, but this precise combination of words was novel and right for a mood, and it became part of the language.[1] It meant expansion, prearranged by Heaven, over an area not clearly defined. In some minds it meant expansion over the region to the Pacific; in others, over the North American continent; in others, over the hemisphere. Its appeal to the public, whatever the sense, was greater than its counterpart had been in the days of Adams's vision. It attracted enough persons by the mid-1840's to constitute a movement. Its theory was more idealistic than Adams's had been. It was less acquisitive, more an opportunity for neighboring peoples to reach self-realization. It meant opportunity to gain admission to the American Union. Any neighboring peoples, established in self-government by compact or by successful revolution, would be permitted to apply. If properly qualified, they would be admitted. Some—the Mexican, for example—might have to undergo schooling for a time in the meaning and methods of freedom before they were let in.[2] A century might be necessary to complete the structure of the great American nation of the future.

[1] Julius W. Pratt: "John L. O'Sullivan and Manifest Destiny," *New York History*, XIV (1933), 213.

[2] *Democratic Review* (New York), XVII (October 1845), 243–8.

Any hurried admission to the temple of freedom would be unwise; any forced admission would be a contradiction in terms, unthinkable, revolting.[3] But a duty lay on the people of the United States to admit all qualified applicants freely. The doors to the temple must be wide open to peoples who were panting for freedom. Any

[3] The admission of Texas was considered a pattern which would be followed in all future cases. It was not aggression, as zealous Britishers maintained; it was the opposite. This was made clear in the *New York Morning News* in an editorial on October 13, 1845:

> It is looked upon as aggression, and all the bad and odious features which the habits of thought of Europeans associate with aggressive deeds, are attributed to it. . . . But what has Belgium, Silesia, Poland or Bengal in common with Texas? It is surely not necessary to insist that acquisitions of territory in America, even if accomplished by force of arms, are not to be viewed in the same light as the invasions and conquests of the States of the old world. No American aggression can stab the patriot to the heart, nerve the arm of a Kosciusko, or point the declamation of a Burke; our way lies, not over trampled nations, but through desert wastes, to be brought by our industry and energy within the domain of art and civilization. We are contiguous to a vast portion of the globe, untrodden save by the savage and the beast, and we are conscious of our power to render it tributary to man. This is a position which must give existence to a public law, the axioms of which a Pufendorf or Vattel had no occasion to discuss. So far as the disposition to disregard mere conventional claims is taken into account, the acquisition of Texas, commencing with the earliest settlements under Austin down to the last conclusive act, may be admitted at once, to be aggressive. But what then? It has been laid down and acted upon, that the solitudes of America are the property of the immigrant children of Europe and their offspring. Not only has this been said and reiterated, but it is actually, although perhaps, not heretofore dwelt upon with sufficient distinctness, the basis of public law in America. Public sentiment with us repudiates possession without use, and this sentiment is gradually acquiring the force of established public law. It has sent our adventurous pioneers to the plains of Texas, will carry them to the Rio del Norte, and even that boundary, purely nominal and conventional as it is, will not stay them on their march to the Pacific, the limit which nature has provided. In like manner it will come to pass that the confederated democracies of the Anglo American race will give this great continent as an inheritance to man. Rapacity and spoliation cannot be the features of this magnificent enterprise, not perhaps, because we are above and beyond the influence of such views, but because circumstances do not admit of their operation. We take from no man; the reverse rather—we give to man. This national policy, necessity or destiny, we know to be just and beneficent, and we can, therefore, afford to scorn the invective and imputations of rival nations. With the valleys of the Rocky Mountains converted into pastures and sheep-folds, we may with propriety turn to the world and ask, whom have we injured?

Other striking expressions of such views are in the New York *Sun*, May 30, 1845, and the Washington *Globe*, April 28, 1845. Senator Levi Woodbury had the same views; *Cong. Globe*, 28 Cong., 2 Sess., App. 233 (February 17, 1845).

shrinking from admitting them, out of selfish disinclination to share with others the blessings of American freedom, would be disgraceful. If it grew out of fear of the consequences, "we should meekly take the badge of dishonor and pin it to our front." [4]

The architecture of the temple of freedom was ideal for accommodating neighboring peoples. Its dominant feature was federalism, which left control of local affairs—such as slavery—to the states, and entrusted to the central government control over only such extra-local functions as foreign affairs, interstate and foreign commerce, coinage, and taxation for federal purposes. Federalism permitted a spreading of the domain of the Union almost indefinitely without any danger that a central tyranny would emerge such as had disfigured the Roman and the British empires. Already in the era following the War of 1812 the excellence of this basic principle of the Constitution for purposes of territorial expansion was apparent to such nationalists as Adams and John C. Calhoun.

The safeguards of the original Constitution in assuring freedom to peoples entering the temple had been reinforced by constitutional interpretation. Madison's and Jefferson's Virginia and Kentucky Resolutions of 1798, the South Carolina Exposition of 1828, and the Fort Hill Letter of 1832 of the mature Calhoun had been especially helpful.[5] These gave complete guarantees of safety to any neighbors of the United States who were contemplating entrance into the temple. They showed the Constitution to be a compact. Under it the parties to the compact—the states—reserve all governmental powers not delegated to the Union. If any dispute should arise over the reserved powers, and no satisfactory solution to it should emerge from the courts, the people of the separate states would be the final judges of what they had reserved. They would possess the right even to leave the Union if necessary to preserve

[4] *New York Morning News,* November 15, 1845. For the conception that it was selfish to withhold the blessings of freedom from other peoples, see *Kendall's Expositor,* IV, Nos. 10 and 11 (May 21, 1844), 167–72; *New York Morning News,* December 1, 1845; *Illinois State Register,* December 10, 1847.

[5] Richard K. Crallé (ed.): *Works of John C. Calhoun* (6 vols., New York, 1853–5), VI, 1, 59.

their freedom.[6] The peoples possessing these rights were not only the original thirteen but all that subsequently entered the Union. States' rights was a protective mantle that wrapped itself about any people entering the temple. Such was the attractive form in which expounders of Manifest Destiny presented it to the public in the mid-1840's.

Expounders appeared in the press, in Congress, and on the hustings. In the press one of the most influential was John L. O'Sullivan. He was the theoretician of the doctrine. He was a mixture of visionary, literary artist, scholar, adventurer, and politician. Born of American parents in Europe in 1813, he took his early schooling in French and English schools and, in 1831, received an A.B. degree with distinction from Columbia College and an M.A. a few years later. He was read in the law and practiced it intermittently in New York City. In 1837 he was co-founder of the *Democratic Review* and, in 1844, co-founder, with Samuel J. Tilden, of the *New York Morning News.* He edited both until 1846. His *Democratic Review* was a literary journal, Democratic in complexion, and contributed to by major writers—Hawthorne, Poe, Whittier, Alexander H. Everett, and others. He was a major contributor himself. He was author of the potent phrase "Manifest Destiny," coined in an editorial on the Texas issue in the *Democratic Review* for July and August 1845. He was described by Julian Hawthorne as "one of the most charming companions in the world . . . always full of grand and world-embracing schemes, which seemed to him, and which he made to appear to others, vastly practicable and alluring; but which invariably miscarried by reason of some oversight which had escaped notice for the very reason that it was so fundamental a one." He became in 1846 a regent of the University of New York. At the same time he was active in filibustering adventures to Cuba which led to his arrest and trial. In Polk circles he stood well, and in the Pierce

[6] *Democratic Review,* XIV (April 1844), 423; XV (September 1844), 219; XXI (October 1847), 285; Washington *Union,* October 7, 1845; *New York Morning News,* November 29, December 27, 1845; *New York Herald,* September 23, 1845.

administration became American minister to Portugal. During the Civil War he became publicly a Confederate sympathizer and exiled himself in England. After the war he returned to New York City, where he remained in obscurity until his death in 1895.[7]

But some members of Congress were more adept at giving succinct formulation to principles of Manifest Destiny. They were at their best in connection with the admission of Texas into the Union. An Illinois congressman, John Wentworth, for example, spoke on the eve of the adoption of the joint resolution of annexation:

> Many of this body would live to hear the sound from the Speaker's chair, "the gentleman from Texas." He wanted them also to hear "the gentleman from Oregon." He would even go further, and have "the gentleman from Nova Scotia, the gentleman from Canada, the gentleman from Cuba, the gentleman from Mexico, aye, even the gentleman from Patagonia." He did not believe the God of Heaven, when he crowned the American arms with success [in the Revolutionary War], designed that the original States should be the only abode of liberty on earth. On the contrary, he only designed them as the great center from which civilization, religion, and liberty should radiate and radiate until the whole continent shall bask in their blessing.[8]

The same ideas were expressed in Congress a few days later by a fellow Illinoisan, Stephen A. Douglas, who sought to make evident that he was really a moderate in the matter.

> He would blot out the lines on the map which now marked our national boundaries on this continent, and make the area of liberty as broad as the continent itself. He would not suffer petty rival republics to grow up here, engendering jealousy at each other, and interfering with each other's domestic affairs, and continually endangering their peace. He did not wish to go beyond the great ocean—beyond those boundaries which the God of nature had marked out.[9]

[7] Pratt: "John L. O'Sullivan and Manifest Destiny"; Julian Hawthorne, *Nathaniel Hawthorne and His Wife* (2 vols., Boston, 1885), I, 160; *New York Morning News,* December 1, 1845.

[8] *Cong. Globe,* 28 Cong., 2 Sess., 200 (January 27, 1845).

[9] Ibid., 227 (January 31, 1845).

Another formulation was by Andrew Kennedy, of Indiana, speaking in the House early in 1846 in the debate on the Oregon issue.

> Go to the West and see a young man with his mate of eighteen; and [after] a lapse of thirty years, visit him again, and instead of two, you will find twenty-two. That is what I call the American multiplication table. We are now twenty millions strong; and how long, under this process of multiplication, will it take to cover the continent with our posterity, from the Isthmus of Darien to Behring's straits? [10]

Daniel S. Dickinson, of New York, gave the Senate, early in 1848, when the terms of peace with Mexico were under consideration, the same general formulation:

> But the tide of emigration and the course of empire have since been westward. Cities and towns have sprung up upon the shores of the Pacific. . . . Nor have we yet fulfilled the destiny allotted to us. New territory is spread out for us to subdue and fertilize; new races are presented for us to civilize, educate and absorb; new triumphs for us to achieve for the cause of freedom. North America presents to the eye one great geographical system . . . ; it is soon to become the commercial center of the world. And the period is by no means remote, when man . . . , yielding to . . . laws more potent than those which prescribe artificial boundaries, will ordain that it [North America] shall be united . . . in one political system, and that, a free, confederated, self governed Republic.[11]

A free, confederated, self-governed republic on a continental scale—this was Manifest Destiny. It was republicanism resting on a base of confederated states. Republicanism by definition meant freedom. It meant government by the people, or, rather, by the people's representatives popularly elected. It meant more. It was government of a classless society, as contrasted with that in a monarchy, which was dominated by an arrogant aristocracy and headed by a hereditary king. It meant, moreover, freedom from established churches headed by monarchs. Under American Republicanism religious denominations were equals. Among equals the most worthy were, perhaps, the Protestant denominations—

[10] Ibid., 29 Cong., 1 Sess., 180 (January 10, 1846).
[11] Ibid., 30 Cong., 1 Sess., App. 86–7 (January 12, 1848).

at least this was the view of much of rural America. But in the larger cities, especially those with a growing Irish and German population, Roman Catholicism was given its due by editors of Democratic journals. Religious freedom was stressed as a feature of the American Arcadia increasingly as California and Mexico (which were Catholic) came within range of expansionist hopes. Journalistic emphasis on equality of religions was attractive especially to readers with memories of the disabilities suffered by themselves or their forebears in a Europe where kings fixed the religion of their subjects.

Democracy was another element in American freedom emphasized in the 1840's more than earlier. Democracy meant many things. It meant political democracy, with wide suffrage, frequent elections, and a hoped-for limit of presidential tenure to a single term. It also meant economic democracy, especially democracy of land ownership, which, in turn, meant ease of land acquisition. Low price of land, prospective pre-emption of government land under the act of 1841, were referred to happily; free homesteads, as urged by George H. Evans in the *Working Man's Advocate,* seemed in prospect. By contrast was described, with indignation, the shocking state of affairs in Europe, where land was engrossed by landlords, where people were excluded from possession, where famine was endemic. The chief evil of Europe, the *Democratic Review* pointed out, the blight which especially "oppresses England and destroys Ireland, is the exclusion of the people from the soil. England, with a population larger than our Union, has but thirty-two thousand proprietors of the soil. That which constitutes the strength of the Union, the wealth and independence of the people, is the boundless expanse of territory laid open to their possession." [12] This was rapidly being overrun by needy settlers. Business democracy, also, was stressed, the absence particularly of legalized

[12] *Democratic Review,* XXI (October 1847), 291–2. Pre-emption and the prospects of graduation and donation in the future were all discussed as part of the image of land democracy in the United States. Examples of such discussion are Washington *Union,* October 23, 1845; *New York Morning News,* June 13, 1846; *Illinois State Register,* October 1, 1847; *Cong. Globe,* 30 Cong., 1 Sess., App. 128 (January 19, 1848).

monopolies. Free trade was glorified, especially when the Walker Tariff of 1846 had been achieved. Thus an admission as a state to the American Union was admission to a temple whose furnishings were steadily being made more attractive.

An especial value, promised to people admitted to the temple, was the beneficial use, with American help, of their natural resources. The use made by European monarchs of the resources of the wilderness was a negation of the kindly intentions of Providence. In the case of the Oregon Country, the contrast was pointed out by Adams in upholding the American claim to 54° 40′:

> We claim that country—for what? To make the wilderness blossom as the rose, to establish laws, to increase, multiply, and subdue the earth, which we are commanded to do by the first behest of God Almighty. . . . She [England] claims to keep it open for navigation, for her hunters to hunt wild beasts; and of course she claims for the benefit of the wild beasts as well as of the savage nations. There is the difference between our claims.[13]

Mexico's failure to improve California, a land of Eden, was attributed to an incompetent local bureaucracy, degenerating into a state of anarchy, and to a slothful population. The same was true of the agricultural and mining potentialities of Mexico proper. If those areas were brought into the American confederation, the people would be taught the value of their blessings and trained to develop them for the good of mankind.[14]

For lands in dispute with a foreign state, as the Oregon Country was, the theme was stressed that a true title is acquired only by actual occupation. Occupation was the moral force which should, and would, move territory into the American orbit. This was graphically phrased by O'Sullivan in the *New York Morning News,* at the end of 1845, in an editorial headed "The True Title." According to O'Sullivan, the legal title of the United States to all Oregon is perfect, but:

> Away, away with all these cobweb tissues of rights of discovery, exploration, settlement, contiguity, etc. . . . [The American

[13] *Cong. Globe,* 29 Cong., 1 Sess., 342 (February 9, 1846).
[14] Hartford *Times,* July 24, 1845.

claim] is by the right of our manifest destiny to overspread and to possess the whole of the continent which Providence has given us for the development of the great experiment of liberty and federative self government entrusted to us. It is a right such as that of the tree to the space of air and earth suitable for the full expansion of its principle and destiny of growth—such as that of the stream to the channel required for the still accumulating volume of its flow. It is in our future far more than in our past, or in the past history of Spanish exploration or French colonial rights, that our True Title is to be found. [American population is growing at a mighty pace. In little more than a lifetime it will number three hundred million souls.] Oregon can never be to [England] or for her, any thing but a mere hunting ground for furs and peltries. . . . Nor can she ever colonize it with any sort of transplanted population of her own. It is far too remote and too ungenial for any such purpose. . . . In our hands . . . it must fast fill in with a population destined to establish within the life of the existing generation, a noble young empire of the Pacific, vying in all the elements of greatness with that already overspreading the Atlantic and the great Mississippi valley.[15]

A "noble young empire" of Oregon, vying with the United States for greatness, would be outside the United States in the beginning, of course. But needless to say, in its own good time, it would present itself at the portals of the temple.

By enlargement of the boundaries of Arcadia, room would be made for the oppressed of the Old World, as well as for the blest of the New. A refuge would be created for those fleeing the tyrannies of monarchical Europe. An Alabama congressman expressed that view early in 1845, in urging the annexation of Texas in terms differing from those of hundreds of others only in being more poetic.

Long may our country prove itself the asylum of the oppressed. Let its institutions and its people be extended far and wide, and when the waters of despotism shall have inundated other portions of the globe, and the votary of liberty be compelled to betake himself to his ark, let this government be the Ararat on which it shall rest.[16]

The extent to which the land of refuge for the oppressed should be enlarged occasioned little debate. The Republic would be, and

[15] *New York Morning News,* December 27, 1845.
[16] *Cong. Globe,* 28 Cong., 2 Sess., App. 43 (January 3, 1845).

should be, extended to its natural boundaries. Natural boundaries were a concept as old as the nation itself. Definitions had changed, however, from generation to generation. The natural boundaries at the west had been, in the closing years of the American Revolution, the Mississippi. In 1803 they had become, for Jeffersonians, the Rocky Mountains. In the 1840's they had become, for those who had vision, the Pacific Ocean; and for many, the continent, indeed, the hemisphere. Whatever the natural boundaries, they ought to be wide enough to ensure peace. If petty rival republics were allowed to grow up in North America, they not only would engender, as Douglas pointed out, "jealousies at each other" and interferences with each other's domestic affairs—with questions of slavery, for instance—but would offer tempting opportunities to European despots to create divisions in the New World and to harass the republican institutions of the United States. If natural limits were accepted as boundaries for the confederacy, the people of the continent would be at peace.

One other text was part of the gospel of Manifest Destiny—the duty of the United States to regenerate backward peoples of the continent. This was a concept tardy in arriving. It acquired importance only when Mexico moved, in the mid-1840's, into the focus of American expansionism. Regeneration had not been part of the thinking of the American government in dealing with the red man of the wilderness. The Indian was a heathen whose land title passed, according to canon well established, to the Christian prince and his heirs who had discovered or conquered him. Natives retained only rights of occupancy in their lands. Numbering but a few hundred thousand in the latitudes of the United States, they were provided for by concentration on reservations. Even Jefferson was content to dispose of them thus. Federalists preferred to deal with them, and with the scatterings of French and Spanish elements among them, simply by keeping their skirts clear of them. The "Gallo-Hispano-Indian *omnium gatherum* of savages and adventurers" was something respectable elements in the East did not wish to get near to. But Mexico—there was a problem. Eight million human beings, rooted in soil of their own, covered by a veneer

Contr.

of civilization, and professing the Christian religion! This was a problem the magnitude of which O'Sullivan recognized. Racial homogeneity of the Anglo-American stock had seemed to him an element of strength in his doctrine. It had permitted him to differentiate expansionism of the American sort from that of the Old World, where the process had always involved domination by one state over aliens of another. But O'Sullivan did not despair of Mexico's future. Someday, a century hence perhaps, her people would, by patterning themselves on the model of the United States, have advanced sufficiently to come rapping for admission at the door of the Union with a good chance of being admitted. However, a few months after the penning of that hopeful augury came the outbreak of the Mexican War, which sent Manifest Destiny on a new tack.[17]

A doctrine is significant in politics in proportion to the degree of its acceptance. Acceptance in the case of Manifest Destiny is an unknown quantity. It has never even been estimated. The attraction of such a concept to a national public is not easy to measure, since ordinary gauges of measurement are not usable. No vote was ever taken on it. Votes cast in the presidential elections of 1844 and 1848 are of little use, for they were directed to bundles of issues rather than to one. The votes cast on issues of expansionism in Congress are, likewise, unrevealing, since they were directed to issues that were short of continentalism. If a measurement is to

[17] The augury is in the *Democratic Review*, XVII (October 1845), 243–8. In a lead editorial in the *New York Morning News*, on October 13, 1845, O'Sullivan wrote:

> The records of the past, teeming as they are with instructive lessons, fail to convey an adequate idea of what will be the history of this Republic. We are not merely to possess and occupy an unequalled extent of territory, or to extend our laws and institutions over a countless population, for the territory, though vast, will be compact, and what is of still greater value, the population will be homogeneous. This latter element of power and stability has heretofore been wanting to all great empires. Those which have passed away, were all, without exception, composed of dissimilar and hostile materials, and the same may be said of the great European monarchies of the present day. The glittering diadem of England must fade, the colossus of Russia must crumble, but who can foresee the decline of American freedom.

be made of the response of the American public to the vision of continentalism, a special gauge must be devised.

Such a gauge must have as part of its mechanism a roster of journals that preached Manifest Destiny. The purpose of the roster is to locate centers of concentration of such journals. These centers are likely to be centers of believers in the doctrine. Readers of a journal do not always approve of its doctrines, to be sure. But it is a safe assumption that where continentalism was expounded by editors numerous, persistent, and eloquent, its believers were numerous also. In party affiliation, journals of Manifest Destiny views were Democratic. Organs of the Polk administration were strongly represented among them. On the North Atlantic seaboard all the important dailies which were nominally independent in politics but Democratically inclined were exponents of Manifest Destiny, and vociferous in their advocacy of it. Only a portion, however, of the Democratic press in any section adhered to such doctrines, and a part bitterly opposed them. In Whig journals, continentalism was opposed, even denounced, by virtually all. This reflected a well-marked position of the party.

Supplemental to the press gauge is the congressional gauge. This consists of speeches delivered by Manifest Destiny politicians in Congress and on the hustings. By their temper and number the speeches reveal the regions in which the doctrine was popular. By combining what was said by politicians with what was printed by editors in the sections it is possible to estimate, with a rough approximation to truth, the location, the numerical strength, and the devotion of the disciples of the doctrine in the nation.

The Northeastern and Northwestern sections of the nation were, in particular, areas of concentration of journals that advocated Manifest Destiny. New York City had the greatest concentration of them in the nation. Here the leading philosopher of the faith, John L. O'Sullivan, presided over two of its organs, the *New York Morning News* and the *Democratic Review*. Here operated also the great penny newspapers—the *New York Herald,* with James Gordon Bennett as editor, and the New York *Sun,* edited by Moses Y.

Beach. These two papers each made claim to the distinction of having the greatest circulation among all dailies in the United States. The *Sun* had an offspring, the *True Sun*, which preached Manifest Destiny. Another crusader was the editor of the *Daily Plebeian*, Levi D. Slamm. He was a crusader by turn in many causes, Locofocoism, labor-unionism, Dorrism, and expansionism. In no cause was he more vehement than in expansionism. But he was deficient in business sense, and his papers failed. In 1845 the New York *Daily Globe* was set up for him to edit in the interests of Robert J. Walker, the ultra-expansionist among politicians.[18] The *New York Evening Post* was partial to Manifest Destiny, but its editor, William Cullen Bryant, was an independent as a Democrat and opposed the extension of slavery. The New York *Journal of Commerce* was in an independent class; it was moderately expansionist, especially in regard to California and New Mexico. The *Brooklyn Eagle* was of like outlook. These were outstanding journals of the metropolitan area and all were teachers of the faith in some degree.

In Massachusetts, in staid Boston, the *Bay State Democrat*, the organ of the historian and politician George Bancroft, was devoted to Manifest Destiny. So was the *Boston Times*, which took over the *Bay State Democrat*. In Connecticut the Hartford *Times* and in New Hampshire the *New Hampshire Patriot and State Gazette* were highly expansionist.

In upper New York the Albany *Argus* and the *Atlas* were believers. In Ohio the *Ohio Statesman*, edited by the redoubtable Samuel Medary, of Columbus, was conspicuous in championing the cause. The *Cincinnati Daily Enquirer* was of the same views. In Indiana the *Indiana State Sentinel* was a preacher. In Illinois the *Chicago Democrat*, Wentworth's organ, and at Springfield the

[18] When the New York *Globe* folded in 1846, Slamm was humanely taken care of by appointment to the Navy. He was made purser on a war vessel by George Bancroft, who knew a good Democrat when he saw one. Slamm got the job despite a warning that a "man who is not able to take care of his own family and property is not fit to be entrusted with the property of others." He remained happily in service as a purser until his death in 1862. James Lee to James K. Polk, June 10, 1845, George Bancroft Papers, Massachusetts Historical Society.

widely read *Illinois State Register,* were vociferous crusaders. Illinoisans were the western cousins of New Yorkers in enthusiasm for the cause. Illinois was the most expansionist, probably, of the Middle Western states. States bordering the South in the West repeated this pattern of allegiance by loyal Democratic editors to expansionism. But throughout the North and West there were Democratic editors of weak faith with qualms about the setting up of slavery in the new acquisitions, especially in Texas, and who, in the Mexican War years, became supporters of the Wilmot proviso.

Distinct differences existed between New York papers and those of the Middle West. The New York ones were purer in doctrine, more ready to wait as long as might be necessary for states which were good prospects to enter the Union. They were moderate on the Oregon question; they were willing to settle that issue by compromise at the line of 49°. Why fight for all of Oregon when all of British North America would ultimately enter the portals of the Union? [19] This may have been a response to pacifist voices in the commercial world. Slamm, however, one of the most ardent of the faith, would have no truck with compromise. On hearing a rumor in February 1846 of a compromise at 49°, he declared in a tone of authority that the administration had too much regard for the honor and wishes of the American people to yield to the arrogant pretensions of Great Britain. He believed it a "duty of our government to *seek* rather than *evade* a war with that power." [20]

Belligerence on the Oregon issue was normally a Western Democratic characteristic. The *Illinois State Register,* for instance, declared in May 1845: "Nothing would please the people of the entire West half so well as a war with England; and, for our part, we think enough has been done by Parliament, and said by Sir

[19] The *New York Morning News,* for example, on June 5, 1845, admitted that early offers by the United States of partition at the line of 49° had somewhat compromised the thesis of 54° 40′. This weakness in the *News* was associated by indignant Western editors with rumors of weakness in Buchanan. See also ibid., November 15, 1845. The West was chided for its belligerency in the *Democratic Review,* XVII (1845), 248. See also *New York Herald,* November 15, 1845, and New York *Sun,* March 2, 1846.

[20] New York *Globe,* February 18, 1846.

Robert [Peel] to justify Congress in declaring war against that country forthwith. . . . We are all for War! War!" [21] In Congress the Democratic spokesmen of the Middle West expressed the same relish for war. In the House, Andrew Kennedy, of Indiana, denied, in the Oregon debate early in 1846, that he was for war, but "Shall we pause in our career, or retrace our steps because the British lion has chosen to place himself in our path? Had our blood already become so pale that we should tremble at the roar of the King of beasts? We will not go out of our way to seek a conflict with him; but if he crosses our path, and refuses to move at a peaceful command, he will run his nose in the talons of the American eagle, and his blood will spout as from a harpooned whale." [22]

Notoriously bellicose were Michigan's congressional spokesmen on the Oregon issue. Lewis Cass, in the Senate, was, in particular, war-hawkish, or at least he seemed so to the East. And in the House, John S. Chipman, a few days after the Kennedy speech, drew attention to himself by declaring:

> He would pledge himself . . . Michigan alone would take Canada in ninety days: and if that would not do, they would give it up, and take it in ninety days again. The Government of the United States had only to give the frontier people leave to take Canada. If conflict should come between republican and monarchical systems he would be glad to see it in his day.[23]

Toward Mexico, Western exponents of Manifest Destiny were more combative, also, than Eastern. They were less inclined to wait while Mexico considered entering the temple of freedom; more inclined to drag her in, or, at least, some of her possessions.[24] Restless spirits were dreaming of sacking the Halls of the Montezumas before relations with Mexico were even at the point of clash. Still, those south of the National Road took a less hopeful view of the possibility of regenerating colored races. They viewed even free Negroes residing among them with distaste and suspicion. They

[21] *Illinois State Register,* May 9, 1845.
[22] *Cong. Globe,* 29 Cong., 1 Sess., 180 (January 10, 1846).
[23] Ibid., 207 (January 14, 1846).
[24] Detroit *Free Press,* August 29, 1845.

wrote into the codes of Ohio, Indiana, and Illinois the so called "Black Laws," limiting the rights of Negroes, including mulattoes, to establish residence and restricting their movements as residents.[25]

The South was the section least attracted to the full implications of the doctrine of Manifest Destiny. It certainly was not much interested in annexing all of Oregon or the frozen reaches of British North America. It was interested, at least its Democrats were, in Texas and the sparsely inhabited parts of Mexico west of Texas. It was deeply divided during the Mexican War, however, over the issue of absorbing the whole of Mexico. The South tended to be, as will appear, parochial in attitude toward Manifest Destiny and to be very color-conscious as well.

Some Southern papers, however, did have expansionist views. The Baltimore *Sun,* a penny sheet with a big circulation, was one of them. The Washington *Globe* of Francis P. Blair, and its successor, the *Daily Union,* edited by the veteran Thomas Ritchie, were others. But the *Sun* was primarily devoted to news gathering and to circulation, and the Washington dailies just named were administration organs.

Whigs objected to continent-wide expansion. Almost without exception they opposed immediate annexation of Texas, though Southern Whigs generally would have liked it in time. They opposed, also, an All-Oregon program. Among New England Whigs a peaceful acquisition of the harbor of San Francisco seemed desirable, but any aggressive pressures on Mexico seemed reprehensible. Whigs tended to approve Jefferson's concept of sister republics bordering the United States. Webster would have favored an independent status for Oregon. Henry Clay declared, in his famous "Raleigh" Letter, that if Canada won independence from England, she should, for the indefinite future, maintain only a sisterly relationship with the United States.[26] John Tyler, in one of his moods, declared, in his annual message to Congress in December 1843:

[25] The Mexican race seemed to Westerners "but little removed above the negro"; *Illinois State Register,* December 27, 1844. See also Edgar A. Holt: *Party Politics in Ohio, 1840–1850* (Columbus, 1931), passim.

[26] *Niles' Register,* LXVI (1844), 152–3.

> Under the influence of our free system of government new republics are destined to spring up at no distant day on the shores of the Pacific similar in policy and in feelings to those existing on this side of the Rocky Mountains and giving a wider and more extensive spread to the principles of civil and religious liberty.[27]

Whigs, as a party, were fearful of spreading out too widely. They adhered to the philosophy of concentration of national authority in a limited area, as contrasted with the Democratic philosophy of dispersion of authority over wide spaces. Webster best expressed this mood in advice he gave his followers in 1844, in which he repeated the admonition of an ancient Spartan to his people on the issue of expansion: "You have a Sparta, embellish it!"[28]

Outside politics some few intellectuals among Americans were attracted to Manifest Destiny as a widener of horizons of opportunity. Ralph Waldo Emerson was one of these, as revealed in his essay "The Young American" and in his journals. William Cullen Bryant was another, though objecting, because of his opposition to slavery, to annexing Texas or much of Mexico. He did, however, reluctantly and belatedly, throw his influence, in the election of 1844, to Polk. Walt Whitman, as editor of the *Brooklyn Eagle*, was an enthusiast for expansion. But his enthusiasm declined as a result of the conflict over the Wilmot proviso, and he resigned from the paper in 1847. George Bancroft, the historian, was consistently an expansionist. Alexander H. Everett, editor for a time of the *North American Review*, was notable as a preacher of Manifest Destiny. So was Charles J. Ingersoll, littérateur and politician from Pennsylvania and, also, Lieutenant Matthew F. Maury, oceanographer and writer on naval problems, who expressed such views under a transparent pseudonym. These names will appear again in the course of this narrative.

In every section of the Union, and at every level of intelligence, believers in the doctrine of Manifest Destiny were thus found. They differed widely in their definitions of the scope of the doc-

[27] James D. Richardson (comp.): *Messages and Papers of the Presidents* (11 vols., Washington, 1905), IV, 258.

[28] *Writings and Speeches of Daniel Webster* (18 vols., Boston, 1903), XVI, 423.

trine and in their enthusiasm for its separate parts. Those who were confirmed continentalists were still few in number in the early 1840's, though more numerous than they had been in the War Hawk days of 1812. Though still deemed sadly wrongheaded and unreliable prophets of the future, they were no longer considered a lunatic fringe.

The date at which the doctrine emerged as a force to be reckoned with in politics is important to ascertain. It serves as a means of identification. It can be ascertained only approximately, for many facets were present in this complex phenomenon and some of them came into prominence sooner than others. Some editorial voices proclaiming the full doctrine were heard already during the campaign of 1844. They were voices crying in the wilderness.[29] The date when the full chorus proclaimed the doctrine came after the election, as late even as the closing months of the Tyler administration. It came after the annexation of Texas had emerged as a good prospect in politics.

A good prospect in politics is a major stimulant to effort. It is especially so after a long period of frustration. The campaign for the annexation of Texas had been marked by frustration ever since the Texans had made their wishes for union evident in the Jackson administration. They had been turned away again and again. The issue had become dormant until Tyler reawakened it in 1843. He had drawn up a treaty of annexation with the Texans in 1844. Whether he had done this to save the province from falling into British hands, or to create an issue for purposes of re-election, was then, and still is, a debated matter. The issue was likely to create discord between sections, and between parties. Ratification of a Texas treaty would require a two-thirds Senate majority. In the hope of obtaining it Tyler and his Secretary of State, Calhoun, resorted to the "foreign devil" game, so the opposition charged. In the documents accompanying the treaty they maintained that Great Britain was plotting to reduce Texas to the status of a satellite,

[29] Detroit *Free Press,* September 9, 1844; *Illinois State Register,* December 27, 1844; *Cong. Globe,* 28 Cong., 2 Sess., App. 105 (January 10, 1845).

that she planned to abolitionize the Republic, that she aimed thus to destroy the slave structure of Southern society, and that the only means of defeating her plot was to annex Texas forthwith.[30]

The treaty, so defended, had encountered hostility in the Senate. It had been opposed by Northern Whigs on slavery grounds; by Southern, on grounds, among others, of the competition of Texan soils with the worn-out cotton and sugar soils of the South. The authors of the treaty were disliked, not only by Whigs but also by Van Burenites among the Democrats. Benton *ipso facto* opposed anything bearing the Tyler or Calhoun imprint. Early in the debate he blasted the treaty and the documentary defenses of it in a blistering three-day speech. He pointed out that a boundary dispute with Mexico involving a 2,000-mile stretch lay implicit in the treaty in the form of a Texan claim to territory up to the Rio Grande. Large parts of four Mexican provinces adjacent to Texas, including Santa Fe, the capital city of New Mexico, were brought in question by the Texan claim, and would, if the treaty were ratified, be transferred to the United States. The Tyler government, in forwarding the treaty, made no attempt, he said, to justify the boundary. It proposed merely to negotiate a new treaty with Mexico after a ratification. Would such a procedure be tried, Benton thundered, if the administration were annexing a revolted Canadian province? The answer was: "No! Sooner would they nip the forked lightning with their naked fingers." If such a procedure with Britain was inconceivable, why with Mexico? "Because Great Britain is powerful and Mexico is weak."

The alleged British plot was analyzed by Benton. It was, he said, "a pretext," a cover for the purposes of Tyler and Calhoun, a rumor of "imaginary designs," a "raw-head and bloody-bones," a "cry of wolf where there was no wolf." Four solemn disavowals had been made by Lord Aberdeen, the British Secretary of Foreign Affairs, of any design to interfere with slavery in Texas, or of any intent to convert Texas into a dependency, or of any plan "to acquire any dominant influence in Texas, or to have any kind of

30 Frederick Merk: "Safety Valve Thesis and Texan Annexation," *M.V.H.R.*, XLIX (1962–3), No. 3.

connexion with her except the fair and open trade and commerce which she has with all other nations." Dispatches of Edward Everett from London were read into the record to substantiate these disavowals. The charge of "plot," Benton thought, was discrediting to our government, insulting to England, and damaging to the United States in that it turned upon us the accusing eyes of the civilized world. The speech was read throughout the nation. Its impact was not diminished by the fact that Benton had a constituency overwhelmingly desirous of annexing Texas, that he was, or claimed to be, the earliest advocate in the nation of a legitimately acquired Texas, and that he was, when occasion required, himself capable of twisting the lion's tail a bit.[31]

The fight had spread beyond the closed doors of the Senate. A copy of the treaty and of its accompanying documents was leaked to the press by a senator of the Van Buren school. The Senate debates were, thereupon, ordered to be made public. Letters from Van Buren and Clay were published declaring their opposition to immediate annexation. The editor of the Washington *Globe,* Francis P. Blair, declared the treaty had been framed and documented with a view to being defeated and to uniting the Southern Democracy in a Calhoun secession movement.[32] The national convention of the Democrats met. It ignored both Tyler and Van Buren, and nominated Polk for the presidency. The Senate administered a heavy defeat to the treaty. The issue was thrown into the presidential campaign of 1844.

In the campaign the Democratic party and its candidate pledged themselves to immediate annexation of Texas. They won, but only by a bare plurality in the election. Annexationists considered the election a mandate, however, for action at once. In the lame-duck

[31] *Cong. Globe,* 28 Cong., 1 Sess., App. 474 ff. (May 16, 18, 20, 1844). Another speech was made by Benton on June 12, 1844. It is consolidated here, for reasons of brevity, with the first (ibid., 570). Clay believed there was "not the smallest foundation for the charge that Great Britain has a design to establish a colony in Texas"; Mrs. Chapman Coleman (ed.): *Life of John J. Crittenden* (Philadelphia, 1871), 209. The charge of a plot by Great Britain was deemed a fraud by the Tennessee Whig Spencer Jarnagan. A charge of that sort struck a chord that "always vibrates to the touch"; *National Whig,* May 21, 1847.

[32] Washington *Globe,* May 27, 1844.

session of Congress, which convened in December 1844, they brought a joint resolution of annexation before both houses. A counter measure was offered by Benton in December, proposing diplomatic negotiations, prior to annexation, between the United States, Texas, and Mexico, for a friendly adjustment of the boundary. The basis of the adjustment was to be a line running parallel to the Nueces in the desert prairie just west of the river, which Benton privately declared was Jackson's idea of the true boundary. The line was to continue along the highlands dividing the headwaters of the Rio Grande and the Mississippi to the 42nd parallel. If Mexico refused to negotiate on such a basis, then her consent could be dispensed with.[33]

After the election the factions among the Democrats had stronger incentives to agree on a Texas settlement than before. Tyler had been disposed of. So, in a sense, had Van Buren, and even Calhoun. Texas, after all, was desirable as an addition to the Union. In the course of the election Benton had received warning of the eagerness of his constituents for Texas. His fraternizing with Whigs, to the extent of supplying them ammunition to use against Tyler and Calhoun, was dangerous. In January 1845 he expressed in the Senate his approval of a set of resolutions which his state legislature had adopted, favoring annexation, with the understanding that the boundary would be left to "future" negotiation with Mexico.[34] Early in February he became still more tractable. In place of his precise December plan he offered a proposal authorizing the President (he had Polk in mind) to arrange with Texas for annexation.[35]

The Senate was the scene of the final battle. Lines were drawn there upon an annexation resolution adopted by the House late in January. The House resolution provided that the territory "properly included within and rightfully belonging to . . . Texas" may be erected into a state and admitted thus to the United States.[36] A Senate majority to pass it was not in sight, in the opinion of Walker.

[33] *Cong. Globe,* 28 Cong., 2 Sess., 19 (December 11, 1844).
[34] Ibid., 154 (January 20, 1845).
[35] Ibid., 244 (February 5, 1845).
[36] Ibid., 129, 193 (January 13, 25, 1845).

Therefore, when the debate ended, he moved an amendment to widen the resolution's base. The amendment provided that the President could select, for annexation purposes, either the House resolution or a new Texas negotiation. Walker hoped by means of the amendment to attract Benton's swing vote. An anti-Texan Whig moved that Benton's December resolution, which was favorable to Mexico, be adopted as a substitute for the Walker proposal. In making that motion he casually expressed the hope that Benton would not kill his own child. Benton's immediate answer was: "I'll kill it stone dead." He voted for the Walker proposal, which was adopted, as was presently the amended joint resolution, by a margin of 27 to 25.[37] The House readily approved the Walker modification and the resulting resolution went to the President.

The intention of Congress was that the incoming President would be the one to make a choice between the alternatives. By virtually everyone the outgoing President was thought disqualified, as a matter of courtesy, from acting. But Tyler was eager to act. He had been persuaded by Calhoun that the need for action was so compelling as to forbid delay for even as much as a few hours. He acted, choosing the initial House preference—immediate annexation. On the night of March 3 he sent directives to the American chargé in Texas to arrange immediate annexation. This was the situation when Polk assumed office the next day.

Polk was less impressed than Tyler had been with the need for instant action. He believed, moreover, he still had the right to the final word. He wanted advice from the Cabinet as to what the word should be. As the Cabinet was not yet formed, Polk sent a notice to Texas enjoining proceedings under the Tyler directive. On March 10 he met his Cabinet and they acted on the issue. They advised approval of Tyler's proceedings. Accordingly, a new directive, confirming Tyler's, was sent, offering immediate annexation to the Texan government. Andrew J. Donelson, a nephew of Andrew Jackson, was the American chargé. He found that the President of Texas and Sam Houston, the former President, were in favor of a new negotiation with the American government. They

[37] Ibid., 359–62 (February 27, 1845).

believed more favorable admission terms were obtainable. Further delay was the result. But sentiment in Texas was overwhelmingly in favor of immediate annexation; Donelson was an adroit diplomat, and Andrew Jackson exerted his great influence with Houston for immediate action. The result was that the Texan Congress and a Texan Convention were successively summoned. The Texan Congress voted unanimously for immediate annexation, and the Convention (on July 4) voted overwhelmingly for it, there being only one dissenting voice. A popular referendum confirmed these decisions, and all that remained was approval, by Washington, of the Texan constitution when Congress convened in December.

It was then, when frustrations were passing, that Douglas proclaimed he would blot out the lines on the map which marked the national boundaries, and make the area of liberty as broad as the continent itself. Then O'Sullivan wrote: "Yes, more, more, more! . . . till our national destiny is fulfilled and . . . the whole boundless continent is ours." [38] And Bennett wrote in the *New York Herald*, to the horror of the London *Times:*

> The patriotic impulses of the United States have been awakened to fresh and greatly augmented vigor and enthusiasm of action. . . . The minds of men have been awakened to a clear conviction of the destiny of this great nation of freemen. No longer bounded by those limits which nature had in the eye of those of little faith [in] the last generation, assigned to the dominion of republicanism on this continent, the pioneers of Anglo-Saxon civilization and Anglo-Saxon free institutions, now seek distant territories, stretching even to the shores of the Pacific; and the arms of the republic, it is clear to all men of sober discernment, must soon embrace the whole hemisphere, from the icy wilderness of the North to the most prolific regions of the smiling and prolific South.[39]

Texas was a perfect example of how Manifest Destiny would work, a pattern to be copied by the remainder of the continent. Prior to American occupation it had been a raw wilderness, rich

[38] *New York Morning News,* February 7, 1845. The title of the editorial was "More! More! More!" The fullest development of the theme of the Texan pattern is *Democratic Review,* XVII (July–August 1845), 5–10; (October 1845), 243–8.

[39] *New York Herald,* September 25, 1845; London *Times,* October 21, 1845.

in resources, but unused, or misused. American settlers had converted it into a smiling society of homes. Its people, by compact, had formed a state and had applied to the Union for admission. They had persisted, despite rebuffs, in applying, and at last had succeeded. Here was a plan, favored by God, for North America.

Several days after the adoption of the joint resolution of annexation, the New York *Sun* felt it must put to rest a bogy which had been frightening Whigs. The bogy was that expansionism would produce an unwieldy Union, a Union likely to collapse of its own weight, as Rome had done, in the process of empire building. Such a view, said the *Sun,* was un-American—circulated by the British party in America. It had no basis whatsoever. What had the provinces of Rome, with their hundred tongues, ruled by military force, in common with the sovereign and self-governing states of the American Union, all of one thought, language, and blood, and linked together by cordial fraternal ties in one happy family? No parallel to such moral greatness existed in history. "The energies of a people really free, governed by Christian institutions, have in them something of divine omnipotence." The Union was not too extensive. It had already doubled its original territory, and with it the number of the original states, but it had doubled its strength, also, in the process. The natural boundaries of the republic were the Atlantic and the Pacific, and the Arctic Ocean on the north and the Isthmus of Darien on the south. "Who shall say there is not room at the family altar for another sister like Texas, and in the fullness of time for many daughters from the shores of the Pacific." [40]

One of the daughters from the shores of the Pacific, expected at the altar soon, was Oregon. This was a region O'Sullivan had declared the United States had a perfect title to, a title that would be improved, however, by occupation. It was being so improved. American pioneers were flowing into the Willamette Valley, a restless crest on an advancing wave of population. Oregon society was maturing. Already in 1843 American settlers at Champoeg had adopted a compact of government. They, and their country-

[40] New York *Sun,* March 7, 1845.

men in the East, hoped the compact would be a prelude to admission to the Union. The Baltimore *Sun* was confident it would be. Oregonians "are sure to come home at last." [41] The *Sun* gave no thought to settlers of British origin, some of whom hoped that either an independent republic of the Pacific or a union with Great Britain would emerge from a compact—at least for the region north of the Columbia. The London *Times* and the *New York Herald* observed a "family resemblance" between what was happening in Oregon and what had happened in Texas. The *Times* bemoaned it; the *Herald* exulted over it. The pattern, according to the *Times,* was repeating itself in California. Its sameness was monotonous, but it was the sameness of a deep and determined policy. It was a law of "American progress." It would go on indefinitely unless "something," which the *Times* did not like to name, occurred to interrupt its progress.[42] The *New York Herald* believed Oregon would move not only as Texas had, but much more quickly; it was connected with all the political movements in the United States, and any administration which attempted to impede its course would be quickly deposed.[43]

In California, the inner valley was already virtually in American possession. Its coastal cities contained many Yankee merchants of affluence and growing influence. Letters from them and from other settlers describing the province as God's paradise were appearing in American newspapers in growing numbers. Editors, commenting on the letters, advised readers to "go West." The *New York Herald* cited the added attraction of California heiresses, who were beautiful and virtuous.[44] Early in 1845 a revolt of native Californians against a Mexican governor—one of a series—succeeded. The news was in the American press by the summer. To editors of journals preaching Manifest Destiny, it carried an obvious moral, which they pointed out for the less alert: inde-

[41] Baltimore *Sun,* June 4, 1845. On August 21, 1845, the editor recommended that the Oregon issue be left to "settlement." He thought that "the independence of today would, *à la Texas,* resolve itself into the annexation of tomorrow."

[42] London *Times,* October 1, December 15, 1845.

[43] *New York Herald,* October 1, 1845.

[44] Ibid., September 30, 1845. The *New York Herald* was filled with letters from and about California. "Ho! for California" was the word.

pendence for California, as soon as its American population had reached the right size, and after that—the Texas pattern.[45]

New Mexico seemed to have a similar future. Santa Fe, its capital, was an old center of American trade. Its population was believed to look with favor on the United States. The look was returned with longing by expansionist editors. Even Texas, while yet a babe among nations, had taken notice of the charms of New Mexico. Its curious Santa Fe expedition of 1841, a half-military, half-commercial venture launched by President Lamar, was to have swung the province into the Texan orbit. But the expedition was mismanaged, and landed its luckless participants in Mexican jails. When the Mexican Congress, after the American joint resolution annexing Texas had passed, ordered non-intercourse with the United States, the Albany *Atlas* commented: "There will be one result . . . her commercial intercourse with this country will cease, but the exportation of provinces to the United States, provided the Texas sample suits us in price and quality, will soon supply the place of its staples." [46] Some American editors thought that Yucatán also was qualified for admission to the Union,[47] and, indeed, the whole of Mexico.

The two Canadas were thought to be predisposed to a union with the United States. They had recently shown a rebellious mood to Great Britain. Sidney Breese, of Illinois, had assured the Senate early in 1844 that they favored republicanism.[48] In the same year, Levi Woodbury, soon to be a justice of the United States Supreme Court, speaking in the Senate, predicted that they would eventually be annexed peacefully.[49] The *Bay State Democrat,* of Boston, considered Canadian possessions less a chaplet of roses on the brow of Queen Victoria than a crown of thorns.[50]

[45] *New York Morning News,* December 16, 1845.

[46] Albany *Atlas* (weekly, *hereafter abbreviated* w.), April 24, 1845.

[47] New York *Sun,* March 11, 1846; *New York Herald,* September 17, 1845; *New York Morning News,* July 2, 1846.

[48] *Cong. Globe,* 28 Cong., 1 Sess., 330 (February 27, 1844). A brief account of American designs on Canada in the late 1830's is Ephraim D. Adams: *Power of Ideals in American History* (New Haven, 1913), 74–9.

[49] Ibid., 28 Cong., 1 Sess., App. 767 (June 4, 1844).

[50] *Bay State Democrat,* February 22, 1844; also Detroit *Free Press,* January 18, 1845.

Some expansionist editors predicted, after the annexation of Texas, that Canadians would shortly "become ashamed of their state of slavery, and, casting off the yoke of England, set up for themselves." Others felt that they still needed southerly breezes to warm them to republicanism.[51] But O'Sullivan raised the right question in the summer of 1845, when news came of action by Texas on the annexation resolution. He raised the question of priority. "Texas, we repeat, is secure; and so now, as the Razor Strop Man says, 'Who's the next customer?' Shall it be California or Canada?"[52]

Among the statesmen who lent glamour to Manifest Destiny in the mid-1840's was the hero of the Democrats, Andrew Jackson. He was in declining health but was still actively guiding events from the Hermitage at Nashville and did so until his death on June 8, 1845. He sent repeated letters in the years preceding his death to friends urging the annexation of Texas and the occupation of Oregon, and these were usually promptly transmitted to the press. Jackson urged annexation to insure the national safety and interest and to checkmate the machinations of the British. The death of the Old Hero was followed by a welling up of emotion among the Democrats and a renewed determination to carry out his wishes. As important as his personality in stimulating Manifest Destiny were the ideals of democracy he stood for, the new authority of the masses—especially of the urban masses—in national politics, and the improved techniques of mass propaganda, which had become the property of both parties after his rise to the presidency.

Of major importance in the growth of Manifest Destiny were technological changes, including those that transformed transportation and communication. The steam engine had come into its own in river, ocean, and land travel. From distant territories to the center of government travel time by water had been sensationally reduced. On land railroads had proved themselves practical. But even more remarkable than the actual achievements of these

[51] *New York Morning News,* July 14, 1845; *New York Herald,* November 30, 1845.

[52] *New York Morning News,* July 7, 1845.

agencies in contracting space was the stimulus given to the expansion of thought. In the mid-1840's projects to build transcontinental railroads to the Pacific by northern, central, and southern routes were on the lips of all. Asa Whitney's project of a line from Lake Michigan to the mouth of the Columbia or to Puget Sound was but one of such plans under public discussion. No doubt was entertained that all these plans would be realized. Railroads would, in the near future, bind the Pacific, the Mississippi Valley, and the Great Lakes in one iron clasp. They would bring congressmen from the Northwest coast to Washington in less time than it had taken those who had come from the Ohio a few years before. The success of Morse's magnetic telegraph fired the public imagination. It drew from President Tyler the awed exclamation: "What hath God wrought!" The immediate expansionist reply was: proof of the feasibility of Manifest Destiny. Electricity and steam had annihilated space and time as limitations on God's will. "The magnetic telegraph," the exuberant O'Sullivan wrote in the summer of 1845, "will enable the editors of the 'San Francisco Union,' the 'Astoria Evening Post,' or the 'Nootka Morning News' to set up in type the first half of the President's Inaugural before the echoes of the latter half shall have died away beneath the lofty porch of the Capitol, as spoken from his lips."[53]

Another force in the growth of Manifest Destiny was a vague, uneasy sense, in some quarters, of an insufficiency of good land. It was a new note in the national life. The old note had been confidence that the Republic's territorial resources were boundless. Jefferson had expressed it in his Inaugural Address. He had assured the nation (bounded still by the Mississippi) that it possessed "a chosen country, with room enough for our descendants to the thousandth and thousandth generation."[54] He was perhaps giving reassurance, merely, as to his purposes in the presidency. More likely he was voicing a national mood. But by 1845 western settlement was at the great bend of the Missouri. Beyond lay serried rows of Indian reservations, and farther west, semi-aridity. The

[53] *Democratic Review,* XVII (July–August 1845), 9.
[54] Richardson (comp.): *Messages and Papers,* I, 323.

plains and the intermountain plateaus were conceived of by many as the "Great American Desert." Travel across them to Santa Fe and to the Oregon Country had not entirely dispelled this illusion. Proposals to import Bactrian camels for travel there had appeared in the press. In the 1850's the Army experimented with several varieties of camels in western Texas. The prairies of the Middle West seemed—to Southerners at least—not very promising. They would not even give sustenance to trees. Yet a vast surplus of arable land would be needed if a refuge was to be kept open for the oppressed of the world.[55] The answer to the need was obvious. It was given by O'Sullivan: "Yes, more, more, more! . . . till our national destiny is fulfilled and . . . the whole boundless continent is ours." [56]

A boundless continent was expected to be attractive to the commercial and manufacturing classes. It would give them new markets. On this ground they were counted on to lend support to expansionist programs. In 1837 Jackson counseled the Texan representative, who was seeking admission of his people to the Union, to induce his government to claim California and especially the harbor of San Francisco, for it was Jackson's belief that this would make Texas palatable to New England and New York merchants.[57] Webster longed for San Francisco. He considered it worth twenty times all of Texas. In 1844 the Cushing treaty opened five new Chinese treaty ports to American commerce, and thus made the Pacific harbors more valuable to the business classes. In the final debates on the annexation of Texas, expansionists plied the commercial world with statistics showing the extent and value of the prospective trade with Texas.

Economic distress was another factor in the upsurge of Manifest Destiny. A succession of crises—in 1837, 1839, 1841—had crippled business and had been followed by four years of national pros-

[55] On December 28, 1844, the Baltimore *Sun* wrote: "As a commercial nation, we must lay our hand upon the Pacific Coast of this continent, else the time is not far distant when we shall, notwithstanding our 'broad acres,' find ourselves 'cabin'd, cribb'd, confined.' "

[56] *New York Morning News*, February 7, 1845.

[57] Frederick Merk: "The Oregon Question in the Webster-Ashburton Negotiations," *M. V. H. R.*, XLIII (1956–7), 398.

tration. The economy in nearly all its phases had fallen to depths not plumbed again until the mid-1890's. Cotton sank in price to an all-time low in 1844. The price of corn and hogs—the measure of the well-being of the Middle West—was, in 1843, at the disastrous level it had dropped to in 1822, and the upturn was slow to come. The depression was registered in the flight of defeated farmers to Oregon and California and in restless dreaming about the Halls of the Montezumas.[58] Voters in the election of 1844 attributed what had happened to a Whig administration and withheld crucial votes from Clay. Polk won votes he might otherwise not have had. Travail, nation-wide, was a characteristic of the era of the early 1840's. So was a nation-wide agitation for reform—reform of every kind, political, social, and spiritual. This was the era of the "roaring forties." Manifest Destiny was one of the reforms—perhaps the most important.

Youth was necessary for effective reform. It was needed to shake off the shackles of the past, to get the nation going again, to move to new frontiers. Youth had vision, generous idealism, the high enthusiasm demanded by the times. The hands of graybeards and of Hunkers were tied by expediency, by patronage of office, by corruption and crass materialism. The Hunkers, in any case, were associates of stockjobbers and money-changers and Whigs who should be driven out of the temple.

The *Boston Times,* near the end of 1844, observed:

> The spirit of Young America . . . will not be satisfied with what has been attained, but plumes its young wings for a higher and more glorious flight. The hopes of America, the hopes of Humanity must rest on this spirit. . . . The steam is up, the young overpowering spirit of the Country will press onward. It would be as easy to stay the swelling of the ocean with a grain of sand upon its shore, as to stop the advancement of this truly democratic and omnipotent spirit of the age.[59]

The *United States Journal* in Washington observed in the spring of 1845:

[58] *New York Morning News,* August 28, 1845.
[59] *Boston Times,* December 11, 1844.

> There is a new spirit abroad in the land, young, restless, vigorous and omnipotent. It manifested itself in infancy at the Baltimore Convention. It was felt in boyhood in the triumphant election of James K. Polk; and in manhood it will be still more strongly felt in the future administration of public affairs in this country. . . . It sprang from the warm sympathies and high hopes of youthful life, and will dare to take antiquity by the beard, and tear the cloak from hoary-headed hypocrisy. Too young to be corrupt . . . it is Young America, awakened to a sense of her own intellectual greatness by her soaring spirit. It stands in strength, the voice of the majority. . . . It demands the immediate annexation of Texas at any and every hazard. It will plant its right foot upon the northern verge of Oregon, and its left upon the Atlantic crag, and waving the stars and the stripes in the face of the once proud Mistress of the Ocean, bid her, if she dare, "Cry havoc, and let slip the dogs of war." [60]

Young America, in answer to the voice, appeared in Congress. It likewise manned the press. It came to Congress—more particularly from the Middle West—proclaiming that Texas and 54° 40′ were first installments merely of continentalism. Its spokesmen included such statesmen as Wentworth, aged 30; Douglas, 32; Edward Hannegan, 38; William Allen, 42; Sidney Breese, 45; Andrew Kennedy, 35. In the press its representatives were hardly more bent with years. In 1845, John L. O'Sullivan was 32; Levi D. Slamm, 33; William M. Swain, 36; James Gordon Bennett, 50; Samuel Medary, 44. Thomas Ritchie was 67. He was described by approving Democrats as "venerable"; by Whigs, as senile. Walt Whitman restored the average to the right level; he was 26.

One youth Young America called to office was James K. Polk. He was slightly overage. When he entered the White House, he

[60] *United States Journal* (semi-weekly, *hereafter abbreviated* s.w.), May 3, 1845. The *Journal* was edited by Theophilus Fisk, a champion of various causes. He was successively a left-wing Jacksonian, a hard-money man, an anti-clerical, a Calhounist, defender of slavery, ultra-expansionist, and Polkist. He never prospered in journalism, and ended his days as a writer of religious tracts. "Young America" was a term used interchangeably with "Young Democracy." The history of the term is sketched in James T. Adams (ed.): *Dictionary of American History* (6 vols., New York, 1940), V, 509. Fisk got some editorial ribbing from Whigs for his exuberant image of a young, flag-waving giant bestriding the continent from northern Oregon to the Atlantic crag. Whigs were dismayed at the quantity of broadcloth needed for the pantaloons of the young man. *Louisville Journal* (w.), May 14, 1845; *United States Journal* (s.w.), June 6, 1845.

was 49. He was the youngest President, until then, to appear there. He had been, in the campaign, confidently introduced to voters as "Young Hickory." On his election his jubilant followers emphasized the "Young" in the title as much as the "Hickory." He was advised to follow Old Hickory in his program: to take a strong position on foreign issues, to arouse "a degree of excitement amongst the popular masses similar to that which had supported and sustained General Jackson in his first term," and to reorganize the party to make it a Polk Democracy, as the General had made it a Jackson Democracy. He was told that Van Buren's type of leadership, which had cast a spell of timidity over the preceding eight years, would no longer do. As for the Hunkers, they were curtly advised to jump aboard.[61]

Youth was responsible, doubtless, for such characteristics of Manifest Destiny as its grandeur and scope, and for the moral exaltation with which it was set forth. But another force may also account for these results—the geography of the western country itself. A geographic explanation of Manifest Destiny was attractively offered by the Albany *Argus:*

> It is frequently asked why are those western people so peculiarly colossal in their notions of things and the prospects of our nation. Does not this inspiration spring from their extraordinary country? Their mighty rivers, their vast sea-like lakes, their noble and boundless prairies, and their magnificent forests afford objects which fill the mind to its utmost capacity and dilate the heart with greatness. To live in such a splendid country . . . expands a man's views of everything in this world. . . . Here everything is to be done—schools are to be established, governments instituted. . . . These things fill their lives with great enterprises, perilous risks and dazzling rewards.[62]

But a doctrine needs more than a set of favorable conditions to propel it into orbit. It needs means of dissemination to keep it in the air, and in this respect the doctrine of Manifest Destiny was well served. It was disseminated by the agencies of mass propaganda, of which the press was the most important. The press in the

[61] *New York Herald,* September 16, November 8, 1845.
[62] Albany *Argus,* July 26, 1845.

era of the mid-1840's reached a degree of effectiveness never known before. This was partly an outcome of improvements in communications, but principally of the development of the high-speed printing press. This press, in turn, was the creation of a number of inventors and firms, but especially of Richard M. Hoe, of the famous New York manufacturing firm of Hoe and Company. His machine, a revolving-cylinder press, was tested at the plant of the Philadelphia *Public Ledger* in 1846, and proved successful. It had a running capacity of 8,000 papers an hour. The next year a yet speedier double-cylinder press was in operation; it was capable of throwing off 10,000 papers an hour. Such presses transformed the printing plants of the great Eastern dailies and engendered astonishment and envy in newspapermen of the rural press.[63]

Accompanying this development came advances in the methods of news gathering. Telegraph lines were extended. Gaps in the lines were bridged by the use of railroads, packet steamships, pony express, and carrier pigeon. Organization to facilitate the gathering and dissemination of news was effected. Journalism, in these respects, came of age. The leaders of these enterprises were the giants of the penny press—Bennett, Beach, and Benjamin H. Day, of New York City; William M. Swain, of the Philadelphia *Public Ledger;* and Arunah S. Abell, of the Baltimore *Sun.* These men were interested in reaching the city masses and in drawing the profits of mass operation.

The penny press employed sensationalism to achieve these ends—especially the papers of Bennett and Day. For general news, nothing was more sensational or exhilarating than the soul-stirring doctrine of Manifest Destiny. For local news, Bennett and Day exploited police-court stories and stories of human interest and society scandal. Tastes in New York City were earthy, much more so than in Boston or Philadelphia or Baltimore. Whig papers commented sourly on the unpleasant contrast, in the New York papers, between heaven-scented editorials on such themes as Manifest Destiny and the smelly local items presented alongside. Edi-

[63] New Orleans *Picayune,* July 30, 1847; Baltimore *Sun,* September 9, 1847; *New Hampshire Patriot,* April 6, 1848.

tors of the Bennett type and those of the Whig type, such as Horace Greeley, were at opposite poles of journalism. Bennett supported causes that paid, was inclined to be flippant, irresponsible, chauvinistic; Greeley was high-toned, deeply interested in the uplift of mankind, in schemes for social reorganization, in the anti-slavery and peace causes. Yet Greeley was obliged to increase the price of the *Daily Tribune* to two cents in the year after its founding in 1841.

In politics the penny press was independent. By roaming over areas of interest to the masses, it increased its income from circulation and advertising so that it did not need the uncertain revenues paid to party organs in the form of printing patronage. It was the chief purveyor of Manifest Destiny to the nation. More persistently than even the organs of the Polk administration it spread the doctrine. And its influence extended deep into the interior, where its exciting and well-written editorials were copied widely by journals of lesser rank. Manifest Destiny was a product, thus, of many forces, and the vigor with which it was disseminated was a product of others almost as numerous and powerful.

But a single force is credited in some writings with having generated Manifest Destiny—nationalism in an invigorated form, dating from the early 1840's.[64] This view has been suggested rather than carefully developed or defended. It is out of accord with the temper of the era. The era was that of Tyler and Polk, which exhibited little nationalism, at least in terms of any definition Clay would have approved. It defeated efforts to resurrect a United States Bank. It insisted, instead, on an Independent Treasury. It accepted the burgeoning of state banking, and it approved the Walker tariff of 1846. It rejected the principle of federal aid for internal improvements. It left internal improvements to the states and to private enterprise. In the field of constitutional interpretation it upheld the Taney court, which had moments of nationalism but was not the Marshall court. If the test of nationalism be public

[64] Weinberg: *Manifest Destiny,* 101, 108 ff.; Adams: *Power of Ideals,* 66 ff.; John D. P. Fuller: *Movement for the Acquisition of All Mexico* (Baltimore, 1936), 38; Jesse S. Reeves: *American Diplomacy under Tyler and Polk* (Baltimore, 1907), 58.

sentiment, the era was marked by sectionalism—sectionalism emerging from such issues of expansionism as Texas, 54° 40′, and the Mexican War.

A nationalist explanation fits ill, also, into the ideas of Manifest Destiny held by the theorist O'Sullivan. In the *Democratic Review* of September 1844, O'Sullivan wrote an article entitled "True Theory and Philosophy of our System of Government." It was a simplification of Calhoun's "South Carolina Exposition" and of the "Fort Hill Letter," and was one of the most cogent brief defenses of states' rights and state interposition ever written. Its conclusion was:

> Each new State or people who may be associated with us, to the extent of their common interests and feelings, and to that extent only, would increase the strength and extend the beneficence of our institutions. The differences in national sentiment and interest, and the peculiarities in national genius, which are inevitable in so large a confederacy, would then cease to present formidable difficulties, for they are left to their own free development under the single restriction of not interfering with the equal rights of their neighbors, or coming into collision with others. How magnificent in conception! How beneficent in practice is this system, which associates nations in one great family compact, without destroying the social identity, or improperly constraining the individual genius of any; and cements into elements of strength and civilization those very sources of difference which have heretofore destroyed the peace of mankind! [65]

The harmonies flowing from a blending of states' rights and Manifest Destiny were described rapturously by other writers of the day, including all the editors of the Democratically-inclined penny press. A successor of O'Sullivan on the *Democratic Review* wrote that the constitutional principle under which authority over general matters is delegated to the nation, and authority over all others is reserved to the states, is more than human wisdom—it is "an emanation from Providence." [66]

Polk, in his Inaugural Address, gave formal approval to the con-

[65] *Democratic Review,* XV (September 1844), 219–32, 320.

[66] Ibid., XXI (October, 1847), 285. See also *Kendall's Expositor,* IV, Nos. 10 and 11 (May 21, 1844).

tribution of states' rights to expansionism. The Union, he pointed out, is a growing confederacy of "independent" states. The states have increased in number from thirteen to twenty-eight. Two have been admitted to the Union within the past week. New communities and states—especially Texas—are seeking to come under its aegis. In an earlier day some held the opinion that our system could not operate successfully over an extended territory. Serious objections were made even to such extensions as the Louisiana Purchase. The objections have been shown not to have been well grounded. As our boundaries have expanded and our population has grown, our system has acquired additional strength. Indeed, it would probably be in greater danger of being overthrown if our present population were confined to the narrow bounds of the original thirteen states. Our system may be safely extended to the utmost bounds of our present limits. Indeed, as these are extended, the bonds of union, far from being weakened, will become stronger.

Our population, Polk continued, has increased from three to twenty millions. Multitudes from the Old World are flocking to our shores to participate in our blessings. In this republican land of freedom all distinctions of birth and rank have been abolished. All citizens, native or adopted, are considered equal. Church and state are separate, freedom of religion is guaranteed, freedom of trade is maintained, peace is assured among the American states. If the Confederacy expands it will bring these blessings to other areas and to other millions. On such errands it should be clothed, the President made clear, in the garments of states' rights.[67]

But a special variety of nationalism—resentment in the nation over interference by Europe in the affairs of Texas—is credited in some accounts with having generated Manifest Destiny. British interference, particularly, is alleged, and its aim is said to have been to induce Texas to abolish slavery, to preserve a nominal independence, but actually to take the status of a satellite of England. Intriguing of this sort was a repeated expansionist charge in

[67] Richardson (comp.): *Messages and Papers,* IV, 375. The two new states referred to by the President were Florida and Iowa. For Tyler on the states' rights theme see ibid., IV, 335–6; for George Bancroft, a campaign speech reported in *New Hampshire Patriot,* June 13, 1844.

the campaign for immediate annexation of Texas, and the thesis that Manifest Destiny was a product of it has plausibility.

Yet a resentment, nation-wide, over alleged intriguing of this kind would have had to be apparent well before the summer of 1845, when Texas was voting to enter the Union, if the thesis has real validity. Nothing approaching that state of feeling appeared in the press or in Congress. Charges of British meddling with slavery in Texas were prominent in 1844, in the Senate fight over the ratification of the Tyler-Calhoun treaty. They were denounced at once by Benton and other Van Burenites as a fraud, as a cry of wolf where there was no wolf. They seemed no less a political trick to Whigs. The overwhelming rejection of the treaty by the Senate suggests no nation-wide acceptance of the charges.

In American politics the game of unmasking the foreign devil was no novelty. It was as old as the formation of national parties. It included efforts by each party to implicate the other in the plots of European states to harass the United States. In the era of Tyler and Polk, Whigs were dubbed the "pro-British party" by most Democrats. They were called, for variety, "blue-light Federalists," which meant a continuation of the treasonable relations their ancestors had maintained with the British before and during the War of 1812. Whigs and independents were accustomed to discount such charges.

The period of the Texas crisis was the foreground of the presidential election of 1844. It was filled with the extravagances of party campaigning, of the venom among Democrats, of factional infighting, and of bitterness produced in the sections by a clash over slavery. That a national spirit so strong and unified as to generate Manifest Destiny could have emerged from such a composite of disharmonies is inconceivable. The forces that produced Manifest Destiny were domestic for the most part. They were ample in number to account for Manifest Destiny, and among them one was undoubtedly powerful—the strong taste of expansionists for the doctrine of states' rights.

Chapter III

Polk

ON MARCH 4, 1845, Polk entered the White House. He had a choice of two programs for implementing "Manifest Destiny." One of them was Northeastern in spirit, as set forth by O'Sullivan —leisurely in time schedule, unaggressive in temper, allowing for the niceties of international conduct. The other was Northwestern, as envisaged by the war hawks—immediate, realistic, aggressive. He was himself a realist, unimaginative, averse to soft romanticism of any sort, with sights on earth, not in the stars. What interested him was land won for man's purposes, not those of Providence.

His Cabinet was of like temper. Its principal figure was James Buchanan, Secretary of State. Buchanan was an expansionist, but not a consistent one. His only very deep conviction was that he was properly in line for the succession to the presidency. At least this came to be the judgment of his chief. A skilled technician, he drew up smooth diplomatic notes and instructions. But he often did it with tongue in cheek, and with sights narrowed by the blinkers of expediency. As a statesman he was irresolute. His vacillation reached such proportions that it became the talk of the Cabinet. His chief, by contrast, was as resolute as any who ever occupied the office, and soon became aware that his Secretary could be bent to the will of a more determined man. The Secretary of the Navy was George Bancroft. He believed that democracy and republicanism are the will of God, and that the task of disseminating them had been assigned especially to the United States. Charged with the duty of maintaining the national interests in the Pacific, he was expected to devise tactics in respect to Oregon and California especially. He was content to leave policy there in the hands of the President. He was a scholar in his tastes, a man to whom administrative service was uncongenial, and, after the Oregon issue was settled and the future of California put in favorable train by the outbreak of the Mexican War, he obtained appointment as minister to the Court of St. James, where documents for his researches in American history were to be found. The Secretary of War was William L. Marcy, of New York. He reflected the expansionism of his state, and his orders to the Army prior to, and during, the Mexican War were revelations of administration strategy. Robert J. Walker was Secretary of the Treasury. He was one of the most extreme of the expansionists of his day and one of the most resourceful. He influenced the course of policy inside and outside the office, as he had, in the preceding administration, from his Senate seat. Over all the Cabinet brooded the spirit of Old Hickory, which was, on issues of expansionism, as realistic and as Western as Young Hickory's.

One of the issues awaiting Polk as he crossed the threshold of the White House was the annexation of Texas. On that issue Tyler had made an unmannerly decision the night before. Polk did not feel bound by it and was willing to make a new one, if needed. But he desired the Cabinet's advice. On March 10 the Cabinet advised acceptance of Tyler's actions, and a directive was accordingly sent the United States chargé in Texas to proceed with annexation. Texas was induced to agree to annexation, and only approval of her constitutional compact by the Congress of the United States remained for December.

In the December message to Congress, Polk recommended favorable action with a fervor hardly necessary any longer. He congratulated the nation on the acquisition of an immense new territory, all the more impressive because it had been won, not by the sword, but by the homage two peoples paid to the great principle of federative union. It was a triumph unparalleled in the history of the world. It signified that American jurisdiction had now been "peacefully" extended to the "Del Norte." The note of peace in that closing sentence clanked somewhat as it struck the words "Del Norte." Del Norte meant an unqualified declaration, which Congress had not made in the joint resolution of annexation, that the boundary of the United States was now the Rio Grande.[1]

To the north, another territorial issue awaited Polk—the Oregon issue, the twin in the 1844 campaign, of the Texas issue. On it the President was committed. He had pronounced for "All Oregon" in a pre-convention letter. His party was committed by a similar plank in the platform. The President held a true course, so it seemed, in his Inaugural. Then a few months later, in a negotiation in Washington inherited from Tyler, he put about. He proposed to the British a compromise at the line of 49°. The offer was unceremoniously rejected. It was not even taken by the British minister for reference to his government. It was withdrawn and the negotiation closed. The British government at once disavowed the action of its minister. It directed him to seek a resubmission of the offer. He obeyed but failed to move Polk. Polk carried the issue instead to Congress. He recommended to Congress in December 1845 that notice be served on the British government of abrogation of the agreement of joint occupation of Oregon which had kept the peace in the disputed country for a quarter century. He asked Congress to extend the laws of the United States over American citizens in Oregon, and to give consideration, also, to making donations of land, valid for the future, to patriotic pioneers who were preparing to migrate or who had already migrated there. He virtually promised such donations as soon as the issue with the British had been settled. A debate on these recommendations opened at once in Congress and ran to April of the following year.[2]

Two concepts, contradictory in tendency, were imbedded in Polk's message. One was of a leisurely occupation, bringing civilization to the Oregon wilderness gradually, and trusting that the

[1] Richardson (comp.): *Messages and Papers,* IV, 387.
[2] Frederick Merk: "Presidential Fevers," *M.V.H.R.*, XLVII (1960–1), 3 ff.

pioneers who had gone, or would go, there, would want to "come home" in good time. This was the concept the President had described exultingly in the Texas part of his message. The other was Western; its time schedule was shorter; it envisaged giving early notice to the British and precipitating a showdown as soon thereafter as permissible. Each concept had been in debate for years in Congress and in the party press. The first had been defended by Whigs and by Democrats, Eastern and Southern, who wished to see the controversy resolved peacefully. The second had been defended principally by Western Democrats, more intent on acquiring territory than on preserving peace. Calhoun had given the first a classic formulation in 1843 in a Senate speech opposing a Western proposal that would have established exclusive American jurisdiction over all of Oregon. His speech had been an exposition of the best means of acquiring all of that territory:

> There is only one means by which it can be done; but that, fortunately, is the most powerful of all—*time. Time* is acting for us; and, if we shall have the wisdom to trust its operation, it will assert and maintain our right with resistless force, without costing a cent of money, or a drop of blood. There is often, in the affairs of government, more efficiency and wisdom in nonaction than in action. All we want to effect our object in this case, is "a wise and masterly inactivity." Our population is rolling toward the shores of the Pacific with an impetus greater than what we realize.[3]

The opposing, Western view was set forth in 1846 with a new vehemence and even scorn for Calhoun. It was expressed in a House speech, delivered by an impatient young American, Charles W. Cathcart, of Indiana, early in February, in which a waiting policy was denounced. "We are told to remain quiet, and that Oregon will be conquered in our bed-chambers. Sir, do gentlemen forget that the bed-chambers of our own citizens are now in Oregon unprotected?" [4] Other Westerners denounced a waiting policy as actually self-defeating. A local clash might occur in Ore-

[3] *Cong. Globe,* 27 Cong., 3 Sess., App. 139 (January 24, 1843).
[4] Ibid., 29 Cong., 1 Sess., 323 (February 6, 1846).

gon between American and British pioneers, and this would set off the very war Calhounists and Whigs so cravenly feared.

A local clash in Oregon was certainly possible. Americans were settled in force on the south side of the Columbia River, in the valley of the Willamette. They were in far greater numbers than the British. The British were, for the most part, north of the Columbia, in and about the stockaded posts of the Hudson's Bay Company. Volatile spirits among the Americans were threatening to cross the river to eject the Company, even to set fire to its establishments. The Americans had brought rifles with them to Oregon. But stocks of gunpowder they did not have. The Company had gunpowder but sold it to outsiders with a sparing hand. Three British warships lay, in 1845–6, in Oregon waters, sent at the request of the Company: a sloop, anchored at Fort Vancouver, on the Columbia; a frigate, stationed at Puget Sound; and an armed steamer, kept at Vancouver Island. This was a show of strength new to Oregon and was an irritant to the Americans in the Willamette.

On December 5, 1845, an instruction, heavily marked "Secret," was sent from Washington to the Pacific squadron, located off Mazatlán on the west coast of Mexico. The sender was Bancroft; the addressee, Commodore John D. Sloat. Sloat was reassured regarding American relations with Mexico: they were less strained than they had been, and war was less likely. Sloat was ordered to move his squadron nearer Oregon and California. He was to keep watch on the British there, and to keep in touch with the American consul at Monterey in California so that the consul would always know his whereabouts. He was to carry out an instruction, earlier tentatively given him, to dispatch a vessel to the Columbia and Juan de Fuca Strait. He was to send, by that vessel, for distribution to the American settlers in the Willamette valley, 500 copies of the President's recently delivered message to Congress. Also:

> If you have any rifles or other small arms on board your ships which can be spared for the purpose, you may permit them to be

exchanged with the people of that region for wheat, flour or other stores, taking all possible care that they fall into the hands of no one who is unfriendly to the United States. These orders you will keep secret.[5]

Instructions of such a character would hardly have been framed by Bancroft alone. They were far too explosive in potentiality for that. They came from the President and the Cabinet. As such, they throw a flash of light on the attitude and policies of Polk. They reveal a deep suspicion of British activity in Oregon; a determination to counteract the overwhelming naval superiority of the British by increasing the superiority of the land forces of the American settlers; a willingness, also, to risk creating a state of war without consulting Congress. Finally, they reveal, in combination with other evidence, a strategy of timing, a strategy of applying heat to foreign fronts in turn. Two foreign fronts were smoldering when Polk took office—the Mexican, in Texas, and the British, in Oregon. Polk was resolved that they should not come to blaze simultaneously. The Mexican front had been especially dangerous because of the congressional joint resolution of annexation. By summer it had seemed ready to explode. This was the period when a compromise Oregon settlement with the British was proposed, only to be curtly rejected. On the Mexican front, a lowering of heat soon occurred, and by late autumn an American minister was on his way to Mexico City. This was the period when, on the Oregon front, heat was turned on; when Polk, with negotiations disrupted, rejected proposals for arbitration, sent a grim message to Congress on December 2, and approved the secret order to Sloat. A qualification should be added, that, if a conscious policy of alternating pressures was acted on by Polk, it broke down in 1846, as a result of developments over which the President had lost control.

The Bancroft instruction to Sloat traveled via Vera Cruz, across Mexico, to Mazatlán. It reached Sloat toward the end of March.

[5] George Bancroft to Commodore John D. Sloat, December 5, 1845, Navy Department, Confidential Letters Sent, Vol. I, p. 163 (National Archives). The earlier instruction referred to, of October 17, 1845, appears in the same volume on page 161.

On April 1, he issued an order to Lieutenant Neil M. Howison to take the schooner *Shark* to the Columbia River settlements and to ascertain there the number of the American settlers, the number of the British, and the number of annual arrivals on both sides. He was to bring cheer to the Americans by giving them a sight of the flag, by distributing the 500 copies of the President's message, and also, for good measure, copies of the bellicose Washington *Union,* an organ of the Polk administration. He was to implement the order to supply rifles to the settlers. His instructions ended with the heavily underscored words *"These orders you will keep secret."* [6]

By July 1846 Howison was among the settlers. He found them in a state of excitement over the boundary issue. The fact that the issue had already been settled by diplomacy was not, of course, known to them. Indeed, it did not become known until November. The mission was harassed by local obstacles. The Willamette River was at a stage so low that it would not admit a vessel of the *Shark's* tonnage. The vessel had to be anchored a few cables' length from the British sloop at Fort Vancouver. Here its activities were under constant surveillance. Exchanges of rifles for wheat may nevertheless have been effected in an undercover trade, as part of overland travels. Wherever the Lieutenant went, he and his men were received with demonstrations of joy. He sought, so he later reported, to calm the excited settlers, enjoining his officers not to stir up feeling over the boundary question.

At Fort Vancouver, however, Hudson's Bay Company officials, though polite as always, had doubts about the peacefulness of his intentions. They wrote home that he and his men stirred up the settlers by imprudent "communications" and seriously disturbed the tranquillity of the settlements. A disturbance that occurred during Howison's temporary absence was attributed to his visit. A large party of Americans crossed the river, prepared to survey land near the Company's fort, and started building a cabin on a

[6] Sloat to Lieutenant Neil M. Howison, April 1, 1846; Navy Department, Pacific Squadron, Commodore J. D. Sloat's Cruise, October 16, 1844, to October 23, 1846 (National Archives).

tract that had been pre-empted in the Company's name. The leader of the trespassers was arrested by a representative of the provisional Oregon government at the Company's demand, and was kept jailed until he agreed to keep the peace. Howison subsequently approved this ending to a potentially dangerous clash.[7]

At the end of some months of observation Howison left the settlements to rejoin his squadron. He met disaster crossing the bar at the mouth of the Columbia. His vessel went down; he and his crew with difficulty saved their lives; all of the ship's records were lost. Whether the rifles, once part of the cargo, were also lost, or had been exchanged despite all difficulties for wheat and flour, is one of the tantalizing mysteries of Oregon history. Howison shed no light on it in the report he made early in 1847 to his commanding officer.[8]

In these same years American expansionists interested themselves in British territory nearer home than Oregon. They wanted Canada. The British grip on that province was weak, they believed, and might be broken. Young America was Hercules. If he should ever set forth with his war club, "the *lion*'s skin is the spoil of which his favorite garment is made." [9] Should a war be set off by the Oregon issue, one of its important theaters would assuredly be the Great Lakes. The War of 1812 had been fought there. Navy strategists of expansionist leanings therefore gave thought to this area in anticipation of war. One of them was "Harry Bluff, U.S. Navy." The man behind the pseudonym was Lieutenant Matthew F. Maury, Superintendent of the Department of Charts and Instruments at Washington. He was a frequent contributor on strategy, naval organization, and science to professional and lay periodicals.[10] By 1845 his pseudonym no longer screened his identity effectively. In the second quarter of that year he published a series of five articles, addressed "To the People of the Lake

[7] Frederick Merk: "Oregon Pioneers and the Boundary," *A.H.R.*, XXIX (1923–4), 687–9.

[8] *House Misc. Docs.*, 30 Cong., 1 Sess., No. 29 (Serial 523).

[9] Baltimore *American*, February 24, 1845.

[10] A useful, if incomplete, bibliography of Maury's writings is Ralph M. Brown: *Bibliography of Commander Matthew Fontaine Maury* (Blacksburg, Va., 1944).

Country and Mississippi Valley," in the *National Intelligencer.*[11] In them he urged, as preparation for war, an Illinois–Michigan canal connecting the waters of the Mississippi with those of the Great Lakes, a naval depot at Chicago, a navy yard at Mackinaw, and a repair dock with magazines for coal and implements of war at Buffalo or some other locality on Lake Erie. He believed such facilities would join the commercial and military strength of the Mississippi Valley and the Great Lakes so effectively for offense and defense that the British would cease to consider war a useful means of achieving their ends in Oregon. He offered his readers on May 20, in concluding the series, a map for handy reference:

> Look at the map: the eastern waters of Lake Huron reach within twenty or thirty miles of Lake Ontario; a straight line across here from one Lake to the other is the natural boundary of the United States. It was never intended that a great country like this should have its parts separated, as they are here, by the most military and grasping nation in the world. Here you see a long slip of foreign territory obtruding itself between two states of the Union, and reaching down for several degrees of latitude into the very heart of the country. By means of this portion of Upper Canada, Great Britain divides with us the great Lakes, the navigation of which *we* should control. The peninsula of Upper Canada separates Michigan from New York, takes from us the *Sole* command of the rivers St. Clair and Detroit, and puts it in the power of Great Britain to stop our merchantmen whenever she pleases on the great highway between the upper and lower Lakes. France, nor England, nor any other nation, of the old world, would permit such dangerous proximity, such thrusting of foreign territory beyond the safe and natural limits of national boundaries. Nor should we, the greatest of the new, permit such a thing longer than it can be honorably avoided. Should ever war again arise between the two countries, no exertions on our part should be spared for the conquest of this part of Upper Canada. And if the success of arms should place it in our power to dictate terms, the dismemberment of the British provinces of at least that territory that is south of a line from the headwaters of Lake Simcoe to Ontario should be the *sine qua non* of peace.
>
> The boundaries here pointed out are strongly marked by Nature. Ontario on the east, Erie on the south, Michigan State and

[11] Six articles were intended, but only five actually appeared. They were in the *National Intelligencer* of March 14, 21, April 2, 15, May 20, 1845. Italics are in the original.

> Lake Huron on the west—this important peninsula is a convenient size for a State, and if war comes it must be "annexed." We would then have the great body of the Lakes, with their connecting links, wholly within our own territory, and we should then be perfectly impregnable there for all time to come.
>
> In a military point of view, and simply as it regards national defense, the importance of Texas sinks into utter insignificance in comparison with this tongue of a British province. With the ship-canal from the Mississippi, through which to marshal upon the Lakes in war, the military strength and prowess of the West, there is nothing to prevent us from conquering and annexing the "State of Toronto." The people in it would be glad to join the Union.[12]

These articles, especially the concluding one, delighted Western expansionists. Here was the voice, even if the vision was not quite continental, of Manifest Destiny. Especially pleased were the Illinoisans, who had long been aware of the importance of federal funds for constructing works of defense such as the Illinois–Michigan canal. The articles were enthusiastically cited by Stephen A. Douglas in an address at Springfield on June 10, 1845. Douglas was then preparing a program for Illinois to be submitted to the great Memphis Convention of July, which had been summoned to consider Western problems of internal improvements, defense, and others. With the address Douglas offered a set of resolutions to be approved and sent to Memphis. The address and resolutions directed attention to the critical state of our foreign relations, the danger of our being forced, in protection of our territorial rights, into war with "one of the most powerful nations on the globe," and the duty, therefore, of the government to place the country in an impregnable defensive position especially on the Great Lakes. The best method of doing this was to open a passage from the Mississippi by way of an Illinois–Michigan canal to the Lakes, to establish a navy yard at Chicago, and to act on the other proposals of the excellent articles of "Harry Bluff," who was identified as Lieutenant Maury and warmly thanked. Douglas was confident that if the works referred to were built, and war came, the American fleet would be left in exclusive control of all the up-

[12] Ibid., May 20, 1845.

per Lakes; any "joint occupancy" of the Lakes system would forever cease; and Upper Canada would become part of the Republic. Finally, Douglas gave assurance that he was not disposed to indulge in dreams of foreign conquest, "if indeed that of Canada could be considered foreign." The extension of the area of freedom would come "as natural consequences from causes over which we have no control, and which he had no disposition to arrest." He was urging the resolutions as a defensive, not an aggressive measure.[13]

The resolutions were enthusiastically approved and presently laid before the Memphis Convention. They were, in part, adopted and included in a memorial sent to Congress. But in Congress they got short shrift. That crucial "defense" project in particular, the Illinois–Michigan canal, was considered by states'-rights men just another of those Western internal-improvement schemes.[14]

In the meantime the articles of "Harry Bluff" fell under the eye of the British press, which was accustomed to rely on the *National Intelligencer* for American items. They were not favorably received. The London *Spectator* commented on them sourly in an editorial entitled "Encroaching Policy of the United States." The editor first told the story of Texas—emigration, revolution, and annexation. Then he declared the same process was repeating itself in California. He continued:

> The lust of the United States Government and people to appropriate the territory of their neighbours is not confined to the Southern frontier. Passing over the popular cry, encouraged by the President, that the whole of Oregon must be theirs, as palliated by the absence of any final decision in that case of disputed possession, the language in which Lieutenant Maury, a Government employé, is allowed, if not encouraged to write about Canada, has nothing equivocal in it.[15]

British readers were asked especially to take notice of Maury's arresting thesis that, on the first favorable occasion, the United

[13] Ibid., June 28, 1845.

[14] For an account of the Memphis Convention and its significance, see St. George L. Sioussat: "Memphis as Gateway to the West," *Tennessee Historical Magazine*, III (1917), 77–114.

[15] *The Spectator*, August 2, 1845.

States must seize the strip of "foreign territory obtruding itself between two states of the Union" and "reaching into the very heart of the country." Surprise was expressed that citizens of a democracy should be employing the very arguments of European despots of old, in justification of forcible seizure of territory thought necessary to their defence "regardless of the views and wishes of the occupants." This, and the agitation of American expansionists generally, was noticed by the British government, and doubtless contributed to the decision, when the Oregon crisis became acute, to station quietly a force of British regulars in the western country where it would be available if needed.[16] One charge of the *Spectator* was probably baseless, that encouragement was given to Maury by his government to write as he did. Encouragement was not needed. It was in the air and in the heavens in the form of Manifest Destiny.

But encouragement was given in the right quarters to meet an undesirable situation in California. Government in California, at the provincial and at the national level, was chaotic. A civil governor, named in Mexico City, maintained headquarters in the southern part of the province. A military authority, the *comandante general,* was stationed in the northern part—the frontier portion of the province. Between those two, relations were usually at dagger's point. The central authority in Mexico City was distant. Parts of California were as far away from the capital, almost, as from Washington. Roads were over mountains. Sea communication was infrequent; Mexico was without a marine. The province was virtually self-governing. Disorder was chronic. Four revolutions occurred in the province in the twelve years prior to 1846. To the outside world, California seemed a derelict on the Pacific. By the knowing, it was considered likely to be towed soon into an American port.

In 1844 a consul was named by the State Department to represent American interests in California. He was Thomas O. Larkin,

[16] Charles P. Stacey: *Canada and the British Army* (London, 1936), 20–1. The Sir Robert Peel Papers in the British Museum show the Cabinet much occupied in this period with problems of the defenses of Canada.

a prosperous merchant at Monterey and one of a number of American traders of influence living in the coastal towns. He desired, as did his compatriots, an ultimate transfer of the province to the United States. He was distrustful of British and French consuls in other California localities, whom he considered harborers of aggressive designs on the part of their governments.[17]

On October 17, 1845, Buchanan sent Larkin an important dispatch containing the good news that the President had entrusted to him the duties of a confidential agent of the State Department in addition to his duties as consul, with a corresponding increase in his emoluments. The promotion was to be kept quiet, so as not to arouse jealousy on the part of the British and French consuls. The duties of the new post were to discover and defeat any attempts by foreign governments to take over the country. The President could not view with indifference, Buchanan pointed out, the transfer of California to Great Britain or to any other European power. Colonization of the North American continent by foreign monarchies would, and must be, resisted by the United States. It could result in nothing but evil to the colonists, to the United States, and, in the end, to the foreign monarchies themselves. Rumors of participation by a Hudson's Bay Company agent in San Francisco in an uprising of the preceding year against a governor of the province, which Larkin had reported to Washington, and rumors that the British had subsequently reversed their position and were actually financing a return of Mexican troops to California—these gave the State Department great concern. The government and people of California should be warned on all proper occasions of the dangers of such interferences, so as "to inspire them with a jealousy of European dominion, and to arouse in their bosoms that love of liberty and independence so natural to the American Continent."

As for the United States, its government "has no ambitious aspirations to gratify and no desire to extend our federal system

[17] A graphic picture of society and government in California in this era is to be found in the correspondence of Larkin. George P. Hammond (ed.): *The Larkin Papers* (7 vols. to date, Berkeley, 1951–).

over more territory than we already possess, unless by the free and spontaneous wish of the independent people of adjoining territories. The exercise of compulsion or improper influence to accomplish such a result, would be repugnant both to the policy and principles of this Government."

> Whilst the President will make no effort . . . to induce California to become one of the free and independent States of this Union, yet if the people should desire to unite their destiny with ours, they would be received as brethren, whenever this can be done without affording Mexico just cause of complaint. Their true policy for the present in regard to this question, is to let events take their course, unless an attempt should be made to transfer them without their consent either to Great Britain or France. This they ought to resist by all the means in their power, as ruinous to their best interests and destructive of their freedom and independence.[18]

This instruction was highly confidential. Arrangements for transmitting it were, therefore, very secret. A trusted courier, Lieutenant Archibald H. Gillespie, of the Marines, was chosen to carry it. He was directed to head across Mexico from Vera Cruz to Mazatlán. He was to go in civilian dress. He was provided by Bancroft with identification papers obtained from a Boston firm (Bryant, Sturgis & Company) representing him to be their business agent proceeding to Monterey to look after their commercial affairs.[19] Since he might nevertheless be examined, he was directed to commit the dispatch to memory before reaching Vera Cruz and then destroy it, which he did. His subsequent reproduction of it, on reaching Monterey, was a faithful rendition of the original in Washington, and remains a tribute to the Marines. All these precautions indicated the importance the administration attached to Larkin's task, and its delicacy also.

Full provision was made in the instruction for the contingency that the Whigs in Congress might at any time demand to know what the administration was up to in California. The instruction contained its own built-in defenses. Among them were materials

[18] Ibid., IV, 44–7. The instruction is found, also, in John B. Moore (ed.): *Works of James Buchanan* (12 vols., Philadelphia, 1908–11), VI, 275–8.

[19] Bancroft to Samuel Hooper, October 17, 1845, George Bancroft Papers, M.H.S. Hooper was a junior partner of Bryant, Sturgis & Company.

Larkin had provided Buchanan in his most recent report—charges of Hudson's Bay Company interference in the affairs of California and rumors of British and French designs there. Buchanan took care to repeat these in directions to counteract them.

Bancroft showed the same interest as did Buchanan in cultivating the good will of Californians. He arranged to have a duplicate of the Larkin dispatch go by sea to Sloat at Mazatlán, and directed the Commodore, at the same time, to "do everything that is proper to conciliate towards our Country the most friendly regard of the people of California." Moreover, he gave Californians a suggestion as to means by which freedom could be attained. He sent Sloat, by some conveyance not yet identified, copies of the Texas Constitution translated into Spanish, for distribution at Monterey and at San Francisco. Thus, in the season when Oregonians were being sent the President's December message and the rifles to hearten them, Californians were being offered the heady wine of the Texas compact as incentive to seek freedom.

Commander John B. Montgomery, of the sloop of war *Portsmouth,* was detailed to distribute this literature to Californians. He was told:

> When on that coast you will communicate frequently with our consul at Monterrey and will ascertain as exactly as you can the nature of the designs of the English and French in that region, the temper of the inhabitants—their disposition toward the U. States and their relations toward the central Government of Mexico. You will do every thing that is proper to conciliate towards our country the most friendly regard of the people of California.
>
> When at Monterrey and San Francisco you will distribute the accompanying constitutions of the State of Texas printed in Spanish.[20]

Rumors of designs of the English and French, especially of the English, loomed large in all these measures. One rumor especially persistent in the press and in Polk circles was that bonds of the Mexican Republic, in large quantity, were about to be transferred,

[20] Sloat to Commander John B. Montgomery, April 1, 1846, Letters from Officers Commanding Squadrons, Naval Records Group 45. Pacific Squadron Letters, II, 108, National Archives. The Montgomery copy is printed in Fred B. Rogers: *Montgomery and the Portsmouth* (San Francisco, 1958), 19–20. The Bancroft instructions are cited on page 66, footnote 5.

by the investors in England who owned them, to the government of England, and that in them the province of California was collateral security. Another rumor was that purchase of California by England was imminent. Another was that seizure of the province by the British Navy was planned.[21]

In March 1845, an article appeared in an irresponsible Paris journal, *La Presse,* describing a British plot to purchase the province for the sum of 25,000,000 piastres; also, a charge that in 1837 an offer had been made of 85,000,000 piastres just for the harbor of San Francisco. The article reflected Anglo-French strains of the moment, strains arising from British objections to French expansionism in Tahiti and elsewhere. The article reappeared promptly in translation in the London *Times.* A day later the British Prime Minister, Sir Robert Peel, was questioned about it in Parliament. His reply, prepared for him by the Foreign Office, was that the report was utterly without foundation so far as the government then in office was concerned. Immediately afterwards Lord Palmerston, speaking for the preceding administration—not in agreement with Peel often—declared that neither in 1837 nor in any year of his tenure in the Foreign Office, had a sum of £5,000,000 or any sum whatsoever been offered for San Francisco.[22]

Newspaper gossip and rumor of this sort was met with wide disbelief in Whig circles in the United States. It was regarded as merely more of the anti-British expansionist propaganda so heavily discharged in the battles over the annexation of Texas. The truth of the rumors was not put to final test until the twentieth century, when the British archives for the 1840's were opened to

[21] Mexican government bonds held by investors in England were covered by a consolidation agreement made by their London agent and the Mexican minister in the years 1837–9. Holders were given an option of exchanging a portion of deferred principal for vacant lands in several Mexican departments, including California. Few, if any, of the bondholders ever exercised this option. *Littell's Living Age,* VIII (1846), 211–16; George L. Rives: *United States and Mexico, 1821–48* (2 vols., New York, 1913), 45–52, 94–100. Some American journals (even expansionist ones) scoffed at talk of mortgage rights of England in California. The *Illinois State Register,* on July 10, 1846, thought: "The pretended mortgages of England [on California] are a humbug."

[22] *Hansard's Debates,* LXXVIII, 430–2 (March 7, 1845); also Lord Aberdeen to Sir Robert Peel, March 7, 1845, Peel Papers, British Museum.

scholarly research. Early in this century Ephraim D. Adams examined the Foreign Office and Admiralty records with the rumors specifically in mind. He found that Richard Pakenham, British minister to Mexico, and James Forbes, British vice-consul in San Francisco, both suspicious of American designs on California, had favored British acquisition of the province and had pressed the idea on London, but had found no encouragement for it at all. Professor Adams reached the conclusion that a charge of British designs on California was totally without foundation.[23] Yet expansionists in America, and especially those who were preparing the Larkin and Sloat dispatches, had no doubt, or at least confessed none, that the British had sinister designs on the province.

In the summer of 1845 an exploring expedition was sent to the trans-Rocky Mountain country by the American government. It was commanded by Captain John C. Frémont, of the Topographical Corps, who had already twice led exploring parties through parts of this wilderness. The expedition was to examine the area where the Arkansas, Rio Grande and Colorado rivers take their rise, and particularly the region around the Great Salt Lake. This was indubitably Mexican country, but American trappers had long ignored this fact, and a supposedly scientific expedition could venture, perhaps, to do so also. The expedition, according to Frémont's later account, was to find, among other things, a route for a railroad to the Pacific, terminating either in California or in the Oregon Country. The party comprised sixty-two men, some already familiar with the region to be explored—mountain men, Canadian *voyageurs,* Indians, and, also, scientific personnel. For a scientific expedition, this was a powerful force. It may have been made so with a view to contingencies arising out of a war with England or with Mexico.

The expedition made its point of departure the outfitting base of frontier Missouri. It reached the Great Basin by autumn, entered the inner valley of California just ahead of the Sierra Nevada snows, at the end of December, and arrived at the American set-

[23] Ephraim D. Adams: *British Interests in Texas, 1838–46* (Baltimore, 1910), ch. 11.

tlements, at Sutter's Fort, by the middle of January 1846. Frémont was soon after at Monterey applying for permission to winter in California for refitting, and to engage, in the meantime, in examining the Salinas Valley behind Monterey for a possible railroad route. His application was neither explicitly granted nor was it denied. It was forwarded to higher authority. Frémont proceeded to examine the Salinas, and frictions resulted. Early in March he received a reply to his application. It was a rejection, and was followed by an abrupt order to leave the Department.

Frémont considered the order insulting. Instead of obeying it, he threw up a fortification and raised the American flag. A battle impended with a force of several hundred native Californians who had been sent to dislodge him. It was averted by Frémont's withdrawal, first to the inner valley, then up the Sacramento to the edges of the Oregon Country. There, word came that a courier of the American government was trying to reach him. The courier was none other than Gillespie, who had delivered his dispatch to Larkin and was taking messages to Frémont, who was still presumably in California. A meeting was effected south of Oregon and the messages were delivered. The Larkin dispatch was among them, repeated to Frémont for his information, and, also, a packet of private letters from Senator Benton, Frémont's father-in-law. The Benton letters were never subsequently given to the public. They had been written in a kind of family cipher, Frémont later declared.

Frémont made a number of errors in interpreting the Larkin dispatch. An initial error was his supposition that the dispatch had been intended for him, despite the fact that it had been addressed to Larkin. In later years Frémont insisted to Josiah Royce, the Harvard philosopher, who was interviewing him for a history of this phase of California's experience, that Larkin was not the kind of person the administration could have intended for a role of such significance, in a transaction so important. Directions to Larkin to keep an eye on British activity in California, Frémont took to mean that a British seizure of California was imminent and that the only way to avert it was for Americans to effect a seizure themselves. Directions to quietly encourage a native Californian separation movement were taken by Frémont to mean that an uprising by Americans in the inner valley would meet with favor in Washington. Whatever the alleged letters in cipher from Benton may have been, they probably were misread in the same way. If any directions altering those in the Larkin dispatch had been in those letters, they would have had no authority. Benton was only a senator and not even in the good graces of the President. He had been a strong Van Buren supporter in the party's pre-convention fight in 1844; he had declared his disgust with the outcome of the convention and had sulked in his tent afterward. Any suggestion that the Cabinet was aware of alterations allegedly made by Benton in the orders to Larkin, was dismissed by Josiah Royce with the trenchant observation that for a cabinet to command at the same time two policies as contradictory as the dispatch and the interpretation placed on it by Frémont, would have been "the foulest and silliest of treacheries." If any doubts occurred to Frémont about his interpretations—so self-exalting—of the dispatch, he dismissed them with the reflection that an unsuccessful uprising could readily be disavowed by his government.

Supported by such reflections, Frémont reversed his course and returned to Sutter's Fort. There he found rumors in abundance. Indians in the valley, he was told, were being incited by the Mexican *comandante general* to burn the homes and wheat fields of the American settlers. The settlers themselves were to be ordered out of the country, or were to be driven out, or massacred by the Indians. Such rumors were heavily discounted by the conservative elements among the settlers. By Frémont, and the volatile elements, they were given full credence. The explorer's defiance of the authorities in returning to California emboldened a party of settlers to stage an uprising. They seized a band of horses of the *comandante general* which he had ordered gathered in preparation for a brush with the governor of California; sent the attending vaqueros home with insulting messages; occupied a town (Sonoma) in which war supplies were stored; and proclaimed the "Bear Flag Republic." Frémont contented himself, at first, with giving them moral support. Then he obtained, by requisition, war materials from a United States war vessel stationed in San Francisco Bay, declaring that they were needed for the scientific work of his expedition. Finally, he cast aside all pretense of neutrality, joined the insurgents, and led them in the conquest of northern California. His conquest included no part of the more heavily populated southern region. Southern California was left to be conquered by regular United States forces, which reached California following the outbreak of the Mexican War.[24]

An episode in Frémont's subsequent career sheds light on his role in the Bear Flag Revolution. In the Civil War he was the general in charge of the Missouri Department. A Republican of strong anti-slavery views, he had been the party's presidential candidate in 1856. He was impatient with President Lincoln's cautious policy in regard to emancipation. He sought to force the President's hand by a local emancipation order of his own. He refused to withdraw the order when directed to do so; it had to be canceled for him. He was sent to another front, where he did not distinguish himself. Vain, rash, obsessed with ambition to play a role in affairs greater than that assigned him, he constituted a factor of peculiar importance in such a program as Manifest Destiny—the personality factor.

The Bear Flag Revolution resembled the "patriot" uprising in East Florida led by General Mathews in 1812, and that of James Long in Texas in 1819. Its fate, left to itself, might have been as inglorious. A force of a few hundred pioneers, led by an American army captain, could have plunged California into civil war; it

[24] Frémont's role in the Bear Flag Revolution has elicited a voluminous literature. A penetrating pioneer work is Josiah Royce: *California,* in Horace E. Scudder (ed.): *American Commonwealths* (Boston, 1886). It drew forth, by way of reply, Frémont's *Memoirs of My Life* (Chicago, 1887). A discerning and dispassionate newer work is Werner H. Marti: *Messenger of Destiny* (San Francisco, 1960), ch. 2. The best biography of Frémont is Cardinal Goodwin: *John Charles Frémont* (Stanford, 1930). Two biographies by Allan Nevins have appeared, one before, the other after, Goodwin's. Both defend Frémont's California adventure uncritically. They follow Frémont in foisting upon the shoulders of Benton responsibility for the attack on California, though Benton's policy was based on friendly relations with Mexico even during the Mexican War. Benton's attitude toward Mexico is well set forth in a speech he delivered on May 13, 1847, at St. Louis: *Indiana State Sentinel,* June 2, 1847.

could hardly have conquered a populated province. It merely roused the loyalist southern Californians to a fighting pitch, and rendered more costly the work of the armed forces of the United States in reducing them to submission later.

Three methods of acquiring California, exclusive of purchase, were open to the Polk government. One was the O'Sullivan method of Manifest Destiny—waiting passively until California had resolved to apply for admission. A second was the Buchanan and Bancroft method—enticing her by means spelled out in the Larkin dispatch and the visible bait of the translated Texas constitution. The third was to drag her in. That was not desirable politically. It would be compulsion of a neighboring people, which Buchanan himself had described in his dispatch as "repugnant both to the policy and principle of this Government." Compulsion, nevertheless, was used by the blundering Frémont. Deterioration of method often occurs in the course of implementing programs of expansion. A concept is set forth in terms of loftiest principle. To be applicable it must be brought down to earth. It takes on then the practicalities of a Buchanan dispatch or a Bancroft instruction. Finally it sinks to the level of handling by a subordinate and is completely remade by a self-important individual of the Frémont type.

The winds of Manifest Destiny struck Mexico elsewhere than in California and found her unprotected by shelters of the kind British power had built in the North. As soon as Polk took office they struck her in full force. Her minister in Washington, after Congress had adopted the joint resolution annexing Texas, withdrew in protest. A severance of diplomatic relations followed. Mexico's President threatened to go to war if annexation took place. But her Congress alone possessed the power to declare war. Her troops were ordered to the Rio Grande after Texas had agreed to annexation. War was eagerly anticipated in the expansionist press of the United States. As early as July 1845, the outcome of such a war was foreseen in the Hartford *Times*. The outcome would be acquisition by the United States of beautiful California.

> If our country is called to a conquest of Mexico, by an unprovoked commencement of hostilities on her part, we shall believe the call is

> from heaven; that we are called to redeem from unhallowed hands a *land,* above all others, favored of heaven, and to hold it for the use of a people who know how to obey heaven's behests.[25]

Heaven's behests to redeem fair lands by war seemed not altogether manifest to most of Puritan Connecticut. But it seemed decidedly so to New York City expansionists, and for days in early September 1845 the *New York Herald* featured articles under such headlines as "The War," or "The Seat of War," just as if the cannon were already in full deployment.[26]

In Washington, Polk was nervous about a possible merging of two crises—the British and the Mexican. He asked Buchanan, on vacation in Pennsylvania, to return to his desk. But Buchanan was untroubled. He was aware that the war talk in Mexico City was for local consumption, and that the sending of troops to the Rio Grande was as much to rid a revolution-prone capital of them as it was to frighten the Texans. He had learned this from trusted agents in Mexico City. He was not eager, clearly, to return to Washington in stifling August, or to interrupt a needed vacation. Though he did return presently, a calm letter he had written Polk proved correct. War talk subsided. Even expansionists in the New York press became quieter. Late in August reports, received from American agents in Mexico City, showed that the government desired restoration of diplomatic relations and would even receive an accredited minister. By the middle of September Polk was dealing with problems of restoring relations with Mexico.[27]

The terms of restoring relations were spelled out to the Cabinet. Upper California and New Mexico were to be obtained for a certain sum of money as part of an adjustment of the Texan boundary. A good boundary, the President thought, would be the Rio Grande to El Paso, in latitude 32°, and thence west to the Pacific. For such a boundary the amount of money paid would be of secondary importance. A sum of fifteen or twenty million dollars was

[25] Hartford *Times,* July 24, 1845; Detroit *Free Press,* August 29, 1845.
[26] *New York Herald,* September 2, 3, 4, 1845.
[27] Polk to James Buchanan, August 7, 1845, in Moore (ed.): *Works of Buchanan,* VI, 223; Bancroft to Buchanan, August 7, 1845, ibid., 224; Buchanan to Polk, August 11, 1845, Polk Papers, Vol. 73, 6893, Library of Congress.

mentioned, but the President was willing to go to forty millions. These proposals were unanimously approved by the Cabinet.[28]

The coupling of Texas and California was an old favorite in American expansionist circles. It has been proposed to the Texas agent in Washington in 1837 by Andrew Jackson, as already noted, as a means of sweetening annexation for the mercantile and whaling interests of the Northeast. It had been in Sam Houston's mind in May 1844, when Texas, spurned by the United States, seemed to him destined to expand in the not distant future over California and even over the Oregon Country.[29] It was in the mind of many a Southern extremist who conceived of secession by the South in the event of a failure to annex Texas, and the formation of a new confederacy which would include Texas and California.

In far-off Europe the news of the annexation of Texas led to predictions that wherever Texas went California would go. Commentators were not agreed that joining the pair would be proper. In monarchical Europe they thought it would be highly improper. But in Ireland, among a people who admired American freedom as much as they detested British tyranny, it was given a hearty blessing. The *Dublin Freeman*, for instance, offered this kindly sentiment in the summer of 1845:

> But the annexation of the [Texan] territory . . . is not the sole significance of the event that has just taken place. Texas has hitherto suggested the notion of a country lying on the Gulf of Mexico; but we are forcibly reminded that the ill-defined limits of that region must extend to the Pacific, and must now make the people of the United States much nearer neighbors of the Californias than they could have claimed to be by right of Oregon. The government of the United States have passed their arm down to the waist of the continent, and, now that they have got it there, they certainly will not hesitate to pass it round. Again: when settlers from the United States swarm upon the borders of California (as, of necessity, they soon will), can it be doubted but the people of California—consisting, as they do, of the inhabitants of a

[28] Milo M. Quaife (ed.): *Diary of James K. Polk* (4 vols., Chicago, 1910), I, 33–5.

[29] Amelia W. Williams and Eugene C. Barker (eds.): *Writings of Sam Houston, 1813–1863* (8 vols., Austin, 1938–43), IV, 320–5; also *Southern Quarterly Review,* VIII (1845), 191–243.

few trading villages, separated by vast wildernesses from the distracted state to which they pay a nominal allegiance—will find abundant inducements to fall into the body of that vast confederacy, whose happy constitution confers all the protection and all the pride of imperial greatness, without derogating a particle from local independence? We regard the annexation of Texas, therefore, as a step that at once opens to the Americans the horizon of California. Such prospects must, for obvious reasons, confer upon the Oregon question great additional importance in the eyes of the Americans; and we can well believe, with our New York correspondent, that people would now reject with disdain the boundary, which in early negotiations, they themselves proposed as a compromise of their claims: the 49th degree of latitude.

This friendly Irish encouragement seemed to American expansionists well worth wide reading and the article was at once reprinted in the organ of the administration in Washington, the *Union.*[30]

By November 1845 a new minister to Mexico had been chosen and his instructions drawn up. He was John Slidell, an expansionist of decidedly Southern views, though a New Yorker by birth and upbringing. In 1845 he was a lawyer and politician in New Orleans, and a representative of Louisiana in Congress. As an expansionist he was much interested in Cuba—so much, indeed, that he was predisposed to filibustering there. He was to become during the Civil War, an active agent of the Confederacy in Paris.[31]

Slidell's instructions dealt at length with damage claims lodged by American citizens against Mexico. These had originated, for the most part, in the repeated revolutions in Mexico. Much padded, they had been passed upon by a mixed commission that had been set up in 1840. Out of $8,513,000 presented, the commission had given awards, in principal and accumulated interest, of $2,016,-139. Other claims, submitted too late for adjudication by the commission, totaled $3,336,000. The awards made by the commission were to have been paid in installments, but only a small part of

[30] Washington *Union,* August 25, 1845. An admirable account of Texan expansionism is William C. Binkley: *Expansionist Movement in Texas, 1836–1850* (Berkeley, 1925).

[31] Louis M. Sears: *John Slidell* (Durham, N. C., 1925).

them had been paid when, in 1844, bankruptcy overtook the Mexican treasury.

In the Slidell instructions the Texas boundary question—the one Benton had discussed in the Senate in 1844 with such fiery eloquence—was closely associated with the claims. Polk's thesis was that the boundary was the Rio Grande. In the Slidell instructions this thesis was not maintained with confidence for the country north of El Paso. But south of El Paso, there could not be, the instructions declared, "any very serious doubt." Since Mexico clearly could not pay damages in money, the American government would assume the burden of paying them, in exchange for a Mexican recognition of the river as the boundary throughout its length. If Mexico would transfer the western half of New Mexico to the United States, in addition to agreeing that the eastern half belonged to the United States, not only would all the damage claims be assumed but five million dollars would be added. By such a transfer Mexico would rid herself of a remote and detached province and of the expense of defending its inhabitants against attack by wild Indians. For Upper California the United States would not hesitate to pay as much as twenty-five millions. Selling it would be of great advantage to Mexico. It was virtually independent anyway, and the prospect of a restoration of the authority of Mexico there was more than doubtful. To the United States, California was of vital importance. The American government could never permit it to pass to any European state. To impress these ideas on the mind of Slidell and to make him more keenly aware of the dangers of European intervention in California to which that province was exposed, he was given a copy of the Larkin dispatch. Finally he was informed that, on principle, the United States would reject without hesitation any Mexican proposal for mediation by a European power in the disputes between Mexico and the United States, or any European guarantee of an eventual settlement.[32]

The departure of Slidell on this mission was intended to be very secret. The Senate was not even asked to approve him as "en-

[32] The instructions appear in Moore (ed.): *Works of Buchanan,* VI, 294–306. They embody, in addition to the terms, much of the dogma of Manifest Destiny.

voy extraordinary and minister plenipotentiary," though in his credentials he was named as such. Polk was fearful of unfriendly meddling by the British if the mission became known. He probably also feared a repetition of the leaking by the Senate of confidential documents which had marked the Texas treaty debate in the session of 1844. But secrets were hard to keep bottled up in Polk's day. Even the Cabinet was a leaky vessel. Rumors of the mission and half-informed guesses as to its instructions were soon circulating in Washington and in the press.[33] In the end the President himself announced in his message to Congress of December 2 that Slidell had been sent.

Slidell's arrival in Mexico came at an inopportune time. The government of Herrera, which was disposed to come to terms with the United States, was tottering to its fall. Powerful groups, vocal in Mexico City, were unreconciled to a loss of Texas and bitterly opposed to a recognition of its annexation to the United States. A general, Mariano Paredes, who had been ordered to the Rio Grande in the summer, and had refused to go, had remained at the capital and was overshadowing it with his army. An influential archbishop of the Catholic Church was equally opposed to accepting the loss of Texas. The Mexicans were an emotional and a stubborn people. They refused to face the hard facts of life: that Texas had won her independence in 1836, that she had maintained it for nine years, and had a right, recognized in all manuals of law, to dispose of her destiny as she liked. Mexicans remembered that the Texan revolution had been the work of recent immigrants from the United States, that the forces of Houston at San Jacinto had been recruited partly from volunteers who had crossed the Sabine from the United States in reliance on weak enforcement of American neutrality obligations, and that such distinguished American statesmen as John Quincy Adams and hosts of Whigs and Northern abolitionists were openly charging that the entire process of migration, revolution, and annexation had been an unholy conspiracy. Mexicans, moreover, entertained the fond hope

[33] *New York Herald,* November 13, December 2, 1845; Quaife (ed.): *Diary of Polk,* I, 34, 35, 93.

that the United States would become embroiled, through its grasping Pacific Northwest policy, in a war with England, which might bring them rescue. The government, accordingly, refused to recognize Slidell. It made objection to his credentials, challenging them on the ground that it had agreed to receive only a commissioner empowered to settle Mexican grievances, and, also, that Slidell's appointment as minister plenipotentiary had never been confirmed by the United States Senate. Slidell finally withdrew from the Mexican capital in discouragement and waited outside the city for the impending revolution. The revolution did occur, bringing Paredes to power. But Paredes was even less inclined than Herrera to receive an American minister.

When Polk received word of these rebuffs he resorted, in January 1846, to tactics of pressure. He ordered a squadron of the Navy to Vera Cruz, which earlier, in a gesture of conciliation, he had withdrawn from there. He ordered the Army under Zachary Taylor, held until then at Corpus Christi, to advance across the disputed territory. This was a belligerent order, and was implemented in the same spirit. When Taylor arrived at the mouth of the Rio Grande, he emplaced his cannon so as to command the public square of the Mexican port of Matamoros on the south side. He sent naval units to blockade the city, so that food could not get to the Mexican army which was stationed there. An explosive situation was generated, out of which an incident soon developed. A Mexican force crossed the river well above its mouth. It discovered a reconnoitering party of sixty American dragoons and surrounded it. The dragoons undertook to fight their way out. They were, however, taken prisoner, with casualties of three killed and a number wounded.[34]

News of this affair reached Washington late in the afternoon on Saturday, May 9. Earlier on that day Polk had informed his Cabinet that he thought a war message ought to be sent to Congress on the succeeding Tuesday. He believed the Mexicans would commit an act of aggression at Matamoros, though he had not yet heard of any. He was aware of public excitement over the coming war.

[34] *House Exec. Docs.*, 30 Cong., 1 Sess. (Serial 520), No. 60, pp. 288–92.

He believed a failure to recommend war would be a failure of duty. A poll of the Cabinet was taken. All, except Bancroft, agreed that by Tuesday a recommendation of war should be sent. Even Bancroft came around to it, though confessing he would have felt better if a hostile act on the border had occurred. The President began composing a message.

At five in the afternoon news came of the hostile act. The Cabinet was hastily reconvened. Without demur, now, it endorsed an immediate war message. The President devoted the evening and the next day to writing it, with regrets that he must use the Sabbath that way. On Monday the message went to Congress. In it the claims and the boundary issue were reviewed. The President declared he had not entertained for a moment the thought that claims should be "postponed or separated from the settlement of the boundary question." The cup of forbearance had been exhausted, before any clash on the border had occurred. Now Mexico "has passed the boundary of the United States, has invaded our territory and shed American blood upon American soil." War exists, and "notwithstanding all our efforts to avoid it, exists by the act of Mexico herself." [35]

[35] Richardson (comp.): *Messages and Papers,* IV, 437 ff.

Chapter IV

War and the Opposition

IN CONGRESS the message was heard with mixed feelings. It was cheered by expansionists and by all who had ears close to the ground. It evoked dismay in the opposition, among both Whigs and Democrats. Its thesis that an American boundary had been crossed, that American territory had been invaded, that American blood had been shed on American soil, became a battleground itself. A dissident Whig, John J. Crittenden, pointed out at once that when the resolution to annex Texas had come before Congress, few persons had considered the Rio Grande the boundary. Another Kentucky Whig, Garrett Davis, declared forthrightly that all the area between the Nueces and the Rio Grande was Mexican soil. Others declared it was at least debatable soil, and that Polk, in ordering an American army into it, and taking possession of it, had been the aggressor.[1]

A war bill came before the House along with the President's message. Prepared during the Sabbath by the Committee on Military Affairs, it was destined to become a fighting issue in both houses. As initially submitted, it was politically inoffensive. It was merely a bill "to authorize the President of the United States, under certain contingencies therein named, to accept the services of

[1] *Cong. Globe,* 29 Cong., 1 Sess., 792–5 (May 11, 1846).

volunteers, and for other purposes." But a Democratic member of the Committee soon added a preamble, which was held to be necessary to give formal congressional recognition to a state of war. It read, in final form: "Whereas, by the act of the Republic of Mexico, a state of war exists between the United States and that Republic." To dissident Whigs and Democrats this seemed designed to confront the opposition with the harsh dilemma of endorsing the President's thesis as to the origin of the war or of voting to reject a supply bill, thus opening themselves to the charge of preventing rescue of imperiled American troops.[2]

A virtual gag on debate was imposed, especially in the House. A war-minded majority, "haughty and dominating," as described by Garrett Davis, insisted that the bill be approved the day it was presented.[3] The President had submitted voluminous documents with his message. They amounted, as ultimately printed in the congressional set, to 144 pages.[4] In manuscript form, they reposed ponderously on the Speaker's desk during the debate. Selections from them were read by the clerk of the House, but examination of them in the course of debate was virtually impossible. Whigs begged for a day to examine them, but were denied.

In other ways debate was muzzled. Whigs, on rising to the floor, became invisible to the Speaker. To get the floor, a parliamentary trick had to be employed by Garrett Davis. He asked to be heard on a point of personal privilege, which was that he wished to be excused from voting and to state his reasons for such a request. The request could not be denied. On obtaining the floor he took longer than expected to state his reasons. One of his reasons was the preamble. It was "so bold a falsehood" as to defile, at the outset, the whole bill. It had been added to the bill to force the Whigs against their will to build a shelter over the administration. Other reasons were the denial of a chance to study the documents and the denial of an opportunity to state what was in them. An important reason was the likelihood that General Taylor, strengthened

[2] Ibid., 791–4.
[3] Ibid., 794.
[4] *House Exec. Docs.*, 30 Cong., 1 Sess. (Serial 520), No. 60, pp. 4–148.

by militia from Texas and adjacent states, was in no imminent peril, and that even if he were, his fate would be settled before Washington could get help to him. Yet another reason was a willingness of the Whigs to vote men and supplies instantly if the majority would only agree to remove that preamble from the bill. More reasons would have flowed forth except that Stephen Douglas interrupted with a point of order, namely, that all those reasons were an attack on the preamble rather than an elucidation of a request to be excused. Davis was ordered to desist, which he did, but only after he had withdrawn his request (having had his say) to be excused from voting. Another member of the opposition, a moderate Democrat from Virginia, Thomas H. Bayly, also requested to be excused and to give reasons. His reasons resembled those of Davis. Also, like Davis, having given them, he withdrew his request and sat down.[5]

To forestall more requests, a vote on the bill was hastily taken. It showed an overwhelming majority for the bill, 174 ayes, 14 nays. The 14 nays were profiles in courage, which abstentions from voting highlighted. The abstentions were numerous—35, of which 25 were Northern, 10 Southern. Apportioning them in party terms, 22 were Democrats; 13 were Whigs.[6]

In the Senate a day was given to the House bill. Part of the preceding day had been given to the President's message. Minority senators objected to the thesis of the message and to its restatement in the House bill. They protested the precipitance of the proceedings and the denial of any real opportunity to study the documents before voting. Especially eloquent in stating this were three Whigs—John M. Clayton, of Delaware (later to be Secretary of State), Crittenden, and John M. Berrien, of Georgia. Clayton thought the President, by his orders to Taylor, had committed acts of war without consulting Congress. Moreover, the implementation of his orders—the pointing of cannon at Matamoros and the blocking off of the river—were as much aggression, he thought, as pointing a pistol at another's breast. The Crittenden view was that

[5] *Cong. Globe,* 29 Cong., 1 Sess., 794–5 (May 11, 1846).
[6] Ibid., 795.

the American government ought to foster republicanism in the New World through continuing friendly relations with sister republics to the south, and especially with our nearest neighbor, which in her troubles should have been dealt with in especial compassion and generosity.[7] All the Whig speakers urged striking out from the House bill the false and offensive preamble. Among Democrats, Calhoun especially was impressive. Not normally emotional, he declared he would find it more impossible to vote that preamble than to plunge a dagger into his own heart. With characteristic penetration of mind he went beyond the question of who had been the aggressor (he made clear he thought it had been Polk) to the more basic issue—whether a local rencontre, a mere skirmish between parts of armies on the Rio Grande, constituted war. War, he insisted, required a declaration by Congress in both republics, and he would not make war on Mexico by making war on our Constitution.[8]

The vote in the Senate on the war bill was as one-sided as it had been in the House. It was 40 ayes, 2 nays. The valorous nays were Clayton, of Delaware, and John Davis, of Massachusetts. The vote concealed, as it had in the House, as much as it disclosed. Benton voted aye, though he had told the President the day before that he disagreed with the war message and with the order given Taylor to advance to the Rio Grande.[9] John A. Dix, of New York, voted aye, and wrote Van Buren four days later that the war was "a violation of every just consideration of national dignity, duty, and policy."[10] Crittenden and William Upham, a Vermont Whig, voted "aye, except the preamble." Calhoun, Berrien, and George Evans, of Maine, declined to vote. Calhoun declared a few days after the vote that not 10 per cent of Congress would have agreed to the war bill if time had been given to examine the documents.[11]

[7] Ibid., 788.
[8] Ibid., 796.
[9] Quaife (ed.): *Diary of Polk,* I, 390.
[10] John A. Dix to Martin Van Buren, May 16, 1846, Martin Van Buren Papers, Library of Congress.
[11] Calhoun to Henry W. Conner, May 15, 1846, Henry W. Conner Papers, Charleston Library Society. Calhoun's opinion was that if a single day had been

Eleven senators were absent, including Webster, who was out of town. The absentees were almost equally divided between Whigs and Democrats.

Expediency figured in the vote more than usual. It did so in both houses, especially among Whigs. Garrett Davis, for example, having excoriated the bill, voted aye on it. In the Senate, Crittenden, having insisted that the war would constitute aggression by the United States, voted his equivocal aye. Berrien and Evans, of like views, registered only eloquent silence in the vote. Thomas Corwin, the Ohio Whig, gave an aye vote, yet ten months later, in a speech that startled the nation, pronounced the war "flagrant" and "desolating," "a usurpation of authority," a senseless quest for more room, a quest he would, if he were a Mexican, respond to with the words: "Have you not room in your own country to bury your dead men? If you come into mine, we will greet you with bloody hands and welcome you to hospitable graves." Corwin predicted that the war would precipitate a sectional clash over slavery. It would plunge the sister states of the Union into the bottomless gulf of civil conflict. Yet he did vote aye on May 12.[12]

How are these personal inconsistencies to be reconciled? How is the sum of them, so pregnant with consequence for this war, and so full of meaning for all war, to be explained? Questions of this sort permit conjectural answers only. Voting is a product of balances of pressures, and never are the pressures more complex than in times of crisis. Yet some of the emotional pressures in the voting of May 11–12 were almost primitive in their simplicity.

A welling up of emotion, a rallying round the flag, a demand for

---

allowed for deliberation and if a single Democrat of standing had come to his side, war would have been averted. Calhoun to Wilson Lumpkin, December 13, 1846, John C. Calhoun Papers, Duke University.

[12] *Cong. Globe,* 29 Cong., 2 Sess., App. 211 ff. (February 11, 1847). The course the Whigs took was afterwards used by Polk and other Democrats to prove unanimity of concurrence by Congress in the justice of the war. Richardson (comp.): *Messages and Papers,* IV, 534; *Cong. Globe,* 30 Cong., 1 Sess., App. 211 ff. (Douglas, February 1, 1848). Lincoln rebuked the President for this "misrepresentation" in one of his early speeches in Congress; ibid., 30 Cong., 1 Sess., 154 (January 12, 1848).

quick revenge, is the response of men to news of an attack on the homeland. When the attack is unprovoked (and the President had assured the nation this one was), when it is launched by Mexicans, and when it results in the shedding of American blood, frenzy is likely to be the result. A government without ulterior purposes and genuinely loath to go to war asks Congress and the public to remain calm until the circumstances of the attack can be ascertained from the documents. A minority in Congress, if self-confident and courageous and given time, can hold up voting long enough to permit information to be gathered. The framers of the Constitution, in entrusting the war-making power to Congress, assumed that majorities would meet their responsibility and that alert minorities would have an even greater incentive to do so.

Such assumptions proved a house of cards in the voting of May 11–12. An assault on an American force by a Mexican force had occurred, assuredly. But whether on American soil, and whether unprovoked—both highly controversial issues—were not inquired into, nor could they be in a day. An administration which had set the stage for the attack, would not be too much interested in an inquiry. It was content to have an uninformed vote, even a stampeded vote. It spurred on public opinion and Congress by the war message. As for the minority, it failed to perform its constitutional function.

Why did the minority fail; why was it so ineffective? The answer lies partly in its past. It was primarily Whig. The Whigs were descendants of Federalists who, by resistance to the War of 1812, had destroyed themselves. In an era of almost pathological partisanship the Whigs were aware of the penalties visited on a losing side. Victims already of an image drawn of them by Democrats in ordinary public discussion, as "blue-light Federalists," "British allies," "traitors to the flag," they hesitated to become, in addition, "Mexicans," "allies of Mexico," "givers of aid and comfort to the enemy," which they did become despite all their endeavors. Their leader, Henry Clay, in retirement at his home in Kentucky, sadly ascribed his party's failure to resist more effectively the country's entrance into an iniquitous war, to a fear of repeating that traumatic experience of the past.[13] What he said in public, other leaders of the party were saying in private. These men were prisoners of their history.

They were prisoners, also, of fear of what would happen to the party if its action impeded reinforcement of Taylor and a disaster should befall. Such a disaster would never be lived down. Assurances were given to the House by Garrett Davis, and to the Senate by Crittenden, that old "Rough and Ready," aided by the militia he had called from Texas and Louisiana, would more than take care of himself. But the slightest risk to the party had to be avoided. From dissident Democrats little aid could, in this case, be expected. They were as frightened as the Whigs; they were also prisoners of their history. Each group, without any hope of stemming the tide, thought only of saving itself.

Calhoun and his friends were especially prisoners of their past. They had called forth the jinni of expansionism by encouraging Tyler to reopen the Texas question and to submit to the Senate a treaty from which a boundary issue would emerge. In 1844 the jinni had enveloped the Democrats. It had grown, with the annexation of Texas, to uncontrollable proportions—to Manifest Destiny proportions. To recapture it or to seek to control it in a moment of crisis was, from the viewpoint of party harmony, dangerous. Calhoun did say in the course of the debate that he was contemptuous of popularity and the clamors of a majority, that he "did not care the snap of his finger for it." But others, exposed more than he to majorities, were more prudent, and even he was courageous only to the extent of not voting.

The Whigs, having voted for the war, became committed to the further support of it. Denouncing the war unceasingly as iniquitous and unconstitutional, they regularly voted supplies and men for it. They were caught in the trap of first impulse. Even John Quincy Adams voted supplies, while recognizing the inconsistency of doing so. Toward the end of 1847 he wrote Albert Gallatin: "The most remarkable circumstance of these transactions is, that the War thus

[13] Address at Lexington, Kentucky, November 13, 1847, in *Niles' Register*, LXXIII (1847–8), 197 ff.

[unconstitutionally] made has been sanctioned by an overwhelming majority of both Houses of Congress, and is now sustained by similar majorities, professing to disapprove its existence and pronouncing it unnecessary and unjust." [14] Abraham Lincoln, who entered Congress in 1847, regularly voted supplies. In the Senate, Corwin undertook to persuade Webster and Crittenden to join him in voting to withhold supplies, but failed, and then, himself, approved them. The intellectual defense for thus voting was set forth by Robert C. Winthrop in the House and by Crittenden in the Senate. Congress, they pointed out, cannot abandon armies it has called into the field. Soldiers at the front cannot question orders on moral grounds. To do so would be subversive of all discipline. A war, right or wrong, which Congress has voted, must be upheld.[15]

A dour Ohio anti-slavery Whig, Joshua R. Giddings—Lincoln's roommate in Washington—challenged the worth of this reasoning. He cited the great British Whigs, Charles James Fox, Isaac Barré, and the Duke of Grafton. They had announced in Parliament, in 1776, their refusal to vote supplies for an unjust and oppressive war against America. Such pressure, Giddings believed, should be applied by American Whigs to Polk to force him out of Mexico. But Winthrop frowned on so revolutionary a method of achieving results, and thought British precedent inapplicable in any case, since in England the defeat of a supply measure brought down an administration and forced the creation of a new one, whereas, in the United States, it would merely paralyze an administration, which would still hang on.[16]

The Whigs were content in general to denounce the war and the manner of making it, while lauding its generals, especially the glory-covered Whig ones, and extolling the gallantry of the front-line troops. This was good politics for the short run, and it paid handsome dividends. In the congressional elections of 1846 it en-

[14] Adams to Albert Gallatin, December 26, 1847, Adams Papers, M.H.S.

[15] *Cong. Globe,* 29 Cong., 2 Sess., 143 ff. (January 8, 1847); 30 Cong., 1 Sess., 364 (February 16, 1848).

[16] Ibid., 29 Cong., 2 Sess., 35–6 (December 15, 1846); 29 Cong., 2 Sess., App. 278 (February 2, 1847); 30 Cong., 1 Sess., 364–5 (February 16, 1848).

abled the party to exchange its minority position in the House (77–142) for a majority position of 115–104. The party was victorious on the Atlantic seaboard, north and south, retained an overwhelming strength in New England, gained a little in the Middle West, and stayed even in the interior South.[17] Its victory was attributed by disheartened members of the Polk Cabinet to the low-tariff Walker Act, recently passed. Buchanan, a protectionist, explained it so to Polk, even though the act had not yet gone into operation. The Whigs regarded their victory as meaning that the war had lost its appeal, especially on the Atlantic seaboard.[18]

The Whigs were encouraged now to resort, on a wider scale, to tactics of split personality. They thought ahead to the election of 1848. They calculated that a war hero with a clean political record would be an ideal candidate. Taylor was surely a war hero. He had to his credit a succession of astounding victories against overwhelming odds, and was the idol of the nation. He was clean in politics. He had never voted in a presidential election. He was a slaveholder, but so was Clay. A few anti-slavery fanatics might bolt the party rather than vote for a slaveholder, but moderate Whigs had voted for Clay again and again. The masses were likely to be drawn to a general, brilliantly successful in the field, especially the element enjoying the sensation of winning in a presidential contest. A very practical Whig, Thurlow Weed, of New York, was one of the earliest to catch the vision of a man on horseback leading the faithful, as in 1840, to victory.[19] A moderate from the border states, Crittenden, who had given up hope that Clay could ever be elected, was similarly discerning. Whig eagerness to enlist Taylor as a leader grew as his laurels accumulated.

[17] *Whig Almanac* (1848), 3.

[18] Quaife (ed.): *Diary of Polk,* II, 217–18. An estimate of the *National Intelligencer* (tri-weekly, *hereafter abbreviated* t.w.), of October 20, 1846, was that two-thirds of the press of the country was denouncing the war as having its origin in no adequate cause, "as having been prompted on our side chiefly, if not solely, by personal ambition, by motives of territorial acquisition and aggrandizement, for party ends."

[19] Taylor was suggested as a Whig candidate as early as June 18, 1846, by Weed in the Albany *Evening Journal.* A revealing account of the promotion of the General's candidacy is in Harriet A. Weed (ed.): *Autobiography of Thurlow Weed* (Boston, 1883), I, 571–83.

In Congress resolutions of thanks to Taylor, presented somewhat naïvely by war-minded Democrats, were gladly supported, therefore, by Whigs. The first resolution, presented by a freshman Democrat, William H. Brockenbrough of Florida, two weeks after the declaration of war was unanimously passed in the House, and without even a recorded vote in the Senate.[20] A second resolution, also presented by a Democrat, appeared in the House in 1847, in the lame-duck session. A Democrat offered an amendment, designed to improve it, to the effect that the war in which the hero was engaged had been forced on the United States by Mexico. It was passed by a partisan vote in that form. It was replaced in the Senate by a decently neutral resolution, offered by Webster, and was agreed to thus in both houses.[21]

After the House had passed under Whig control, another resolution was offered, under Whig auspices. It was improved by a Whig amendment so as to read that thanks were owed for distinguished services rendered "in a war unnecessarily and unconstitutionally begun by the President of the United States." In that form it passed the House by a vote of 82 to 81, but got no further. It was superseded by another which simply tendered thanks, offered by Alexander H. Stephens, an anti-war Whig from the South, and was approved almost unanimously.[22] Only "one member voted in the negative," Joshua R. Giddings, as the *Journal* of the House tersely recorded.[23]

The resolution went to the Senate, where a newly arrived member from New Hampshire, John P. Hale, made it the subject of a fiery exchange of views with Crittenden. Hale was a heretic Democrat, violent in his opposition to the extension of slavery and to the war, which he considered related to each other as cause and effect, in the same manner as did radical Northern Whigs. He had already been read out of his party, because of such heresies, by his state organization. He was disposed to vote nay, not merely on resolu-

[20] *Cong. Globe,* 29 Cong., 1 Sess., 880, 1064.
[21] Ibid., 29 Cong., 2 Sess., 295–6, 315–19.
[22] Ibid., 30 Cong., 1 Sess., 95, 304. Of the Whigs who censured the war in this vote, 14 had approved the declaration of war.
[23] *House Journal,* 30 Cong., 1 Sess. (Serial 513), 364–5.

tions of thanks but also on supply bills in the form of appropriations and loans. Crittenden rebuked him, in the course of the debate on the resolution of thanks, for taking so extreme a stand. For purposes of argument Crittenden joined the issues of thanks and voting supplies. The reply made by Hale to the rebuke was: "I have not sufficient skill in splitting hairs to enable me, without uneasiness, to denounce the war as a war of robbery, as unconstitutional and unjust, as begun by the President, and at the same time thank the agents who have been engaged in carrying out this unjust and unconstitutional war." [24]

Here were the dilemmas, the dishonesties, the timidities of the Mexican War rising to the surface uncompromisingly in a debate over resolutions of thanks. A war voted almost unanimously by Congress, fought in the field by generals known to be Whigs and to whom thanks were overwhelmingly voted, yet disapproved widely in the nation by Whigs and anti-slavery Democrats! What gave seriousness to these peculiarities was that disapproval of the war was coming to be increasingly sectional—concentrated in the Northeast and in the Northwest. The Senate, after the debate, voted the thanks unanimously, except, as the *Senate Journal* recorded, "Mr. Hale voted in the negative." [25]

Single negative votes under such circumstances were meaningful. They were signals of revolt and of the manner of revolt. One warned of a rising among Whigs, the other among Democrats. One was Northwestern, the other Northeastern. The tone of the two was important. It was summons to a crusade.

The trumpets for the crusade were radical newspapers such as the *Independent Democrat,* of Concord, New Hampshire (Hale's organ); the *Republican,* of Boston, soon to be edited by Henry Wilson; the Cleveland *True Democrat,* Whig in antecedents, edited by Edward S. Hamlin; and the *Western Citizen,* of Chicago, edited by Zebina Eastman. The temper of these journals and dozens like them was uncompromising, emotional, and extravagant. The editors upheld liberty in the language of license. To them Zachary

[24] *Cong. Globe,* 30 Cong., 1 Sess., 364 (February 16, 1848).
[25] *Senate Journal,* 30 Cong., 1 Sess. (Serial 502), 177–9.

Taylor signified a large-scale slaveowner, a military chieftain, untutored, pressing an unrighteous cause, a man on horseback whom Whig politicians, interested only in winning an election, were proposing to elevate to the chief magistracy of the nation. Taylor, as a planter, was known to be a purchaser of slaves. He must, therefore, be a seller of them as well. In December 1846 the editor of the *Independent Democrat*, the secretary of state in New Hampshire, indignant at the trend of the times, wrote: "Gen. Taylor is not merely a Whig; he is one of the greatest slaveholders in the United States. He raises babies for the market and makes merchandize of his fellow men! He has a hundred mothers, with or without their babes for sale in the shambles. He furnishes creole virgins for the 'hells' of New-Orleans, and riots on the ruins of souls for whom the Man of Sorrows died." [26]

Repugnance to Taylor was expressed in Boston in like terms. It was featured in the columns of the Boston *Republican* and in a broadside it scattered to the public during the campaign. It appeared in a Boston pamphlet published by Charles Stearns during the campaign, the title of which carried its message: *Gen. Taylor, The Cuba Blood-Hound Importer, the Extensive Slave Holder.*[27] Intellectuals in Boston of the type of Charles F. Adams, Charles Sumner, and John G. Palfrey, carried on the fight without resorting to such means. They fought in the spirit of William Ellery Channing, who, in 1837, had resisted the annexation of Texas as an aggression against Mexico and as an extension of slavery. In New York, Lewis Tappan; in Ohio, Salmon P. Chase; in Illinois, Owen Lovejoy; led in repudiating the tactics of expediency.[28]

These men and their followers embodied the awakening moral sense of the North. They were the answer of conscience to Young

[26] Concord *Independent Democrat*, December 17, 1846; also, April 29, 1847.

[27] Charles Stearns: *Facts in the Life of General Taylor, The Cuba Blood-Hound Importer, the Extensive Slave Holder* (Boston, 1848). "Blood-Hound Importer" referred to Taylor's activities in hunting down Indians during the Seminole War.

[28] The Whig game of politics distressed Calhoun. He complained frequently in his correspondence of the failure of the Whigs to co-operate with him in resisting the war policies of the administration. J. Franklin Jameson (ed.): *Correspondence of John C. Calhoun*, in American Historical Association: *Annual Report for the Year 1899*, Vol. II (Washington, 1900).

Democracy, the answer by one young element of the North to another. National greatness, the reformers held, lies in no forced extension of the national institutions, in no overwhelming of neighboring republics, in no postponing of the great issue of the extension of slavery. It lies in purifying, ennobling, refining the national institutions, in helping neighboring republics, especially distracted Mexico, and in halting at once the spread of the contagion of slavery.

Early in 1848 a unification of the scattered anti-slavery forces was under way. In the summer of 1848 a convention was held at Buffalo, the halfway point between New England and the West, the center of greater New England. There a banner was designed on which was inscribed the moral purpose of the crusade: "Free Soil, Free Speech, Free Labor, and Free Men." Standard-bearers were chosen—Martin Van Buren, a redeemed Democrat, an opponent of the annexation of Texas, and Charles Francis Adams, a converted Whig, who, as the son of John Quincy Adams, embodied the anti-slavery faith. The party of Free-Soilers was born, which, in the election of 1848, was to attract five times the vote of the Liberty party of 1844, was to defeat Young Democracy's candidate, Lewis Cass, and was, in the not distant future, to destroy the Whig party by applying to the ties of expediency that held it together, the corrosive solvent of conscience.

Polk, in the meantime, unable to read the future, was concerned about the present. He was concerned chiefly about the challenge an adverse congressional election had flung at him. His reply to it was made in his annual message in December 1846. Two-thirds of the message was given to reviewing the origins of the war, with emphasis on the boundary issue but with attention also to the damage claims. The boundary was re-examined historically, beginning with arguments derived from the Louisiana Purchase and ending with those set up by the Texan Congress. The boundary in 1846, the President maintained, was unquestionably the Rio Grande, and the Mexican army, in crossing it, had invaded American territory and shed American blood on American soil. The American government had shown, Polk insisted, forbearance toward Mexico. Forbearance, however, had merely emboldened her to open aggressive war. Charges that he was the real aggressor, which the Whig opposition broadcast, he deplored. A more effectual means, he thought, of encouraging the enemy, of adhering to their cause, of giving them "aid and comfort," could not be conceived. He did not use the word "treason" in all this. What he did was merely to use quotation marks. Even yet, he said, he was eager for peace. He called to witness his dealings with Santa Anna. The latter, he pointed out, had been in exile in Cuba before the war. He seemed to represent the forces of liberalism in Mexico, of opposition to European interference in Mexican affairs, of objection to the creation of a foreign monarchy. He had shown a wish to cross over to Mexico to restore peace with the United States, and to include in the peace a territorial settlement. No possibility of barring his return had existed in any case. The Navy, which was blockading Mexico, had, therefore, been instructed not to prevent his return. The return had occurred; the reactionary Paredes had been overthrown; favorable results were hoped for. Not confided to Congress were earlier aspects of this case—that communication had already been established with Santa Anna through an agent of his in Washington, in February 1846, and that actual assurance had been given Santa Anna, after the war opened, of permission to slip into Mexico through the blockading squadron, the understanding being that an insurrection would follow and, if successful, a peace containing a territorial cession.[29]

The President also included in the message, separated by some pages from this narrative, and presumably not part of it, a history of a recommendation he had made to Congress in the summer of 1846, that several million dollars be provided him by Congress to be used as a down payment on a treaty he hoped to obtain from Mexico.[30] The recommendation had been made the day after he received assurance from Santa Anna that a negotiation would be opened if he could get across to Mexico. This naturally was not

[29] Richardson (comp.): *Messages and Papers,* IV, 471 ff.

[30] Ibid., 456. The background of this recommendation in cabinet discussion is in Quaife (ed.): *Diary of Polk,* I, 305–17.

discussed in the message. The appropriation bill—the so-called "Two Million bill,"—had encountered obstacles in Congress in the form of the Wilmot proviso, and of suspicions that the money was to be used to bribe Santa Anna. The bill had failed of enactment, a failure, the President said, he regretted.

A few weeks later another message was sent Congress. It contained an important recommendation, that a new rank be created in the Army. The rank was later specified as "lieutenant general." The President showed reticence in explaining the need for the new rank. It was needed, the President said in a brief paragraph, to facilitate a more efficient organization of the Army. The Army was composed of regulars and volunteers, and the new rank would render possible a unified command of all the military forces in the field.[31]

The messages were greeted by an explosion of wrath on the part of Whigs in Congress and in the press. The explosion re-echoed for the remainder of the war. It was especially violent against the President's thesis concerning the Texas boundary. That thesis got a canvassing now such as it had never had before. The *Congressional Globe* and the party press boiled over with it. The Rio Grande, the Whigs insisted, had at no time in Spanish or Mexican history been the boundary of Texas. Nor had it been made so by Santa Anna on his capture by the Texans after the Battle of San Jacinto. Whatever had been the meaning of the vague agreement then signed, the agreement had been invalid, as made by a prisoner of war and as repudiated at once by the Mexican Congress, the only treaty-making authority in the Republic. The mere claim to the riverbank by Texas established no boundary, and Texan military power had never sustained it. Both banks of the river had been controlled by the Mexicans and the northeast bank had been regularly farmed by Mexicans until they had fled on Taylor's approach.[32]

[31] Ibid., 508.

[32] Examples of the replies to the President appear in *Cong. Globe,* 29 Cong., 2 Sess., App. 47 ff. (Joshua R. Giddings); 106 ff. (Garrett Davis); 282 ff. (Luther Severance); 354 ff. (Milton Brown). One criticism of the President was that he had taken upon himself to determine that Texas did "rightfully and properly ex-

A Whig who had been a neighbor of the President in Tennessee, Meredith P. Gentry, set forth these views with special force. His speech in the House was a cold legal and historical analysis which tore the President's thesis to shreds. It then set fire to the shreds. Gentry considered this part of the President's message "an artful perversion of the truth—a disingenuous statement of facts—to make the people 'believe a lie.'" It was absurd, and productive only of a feeling of contempt for one who could "imbody such stuff in a grave state paper." Gentry widened his charge of misrepresentation. He held that a like disingenuousness had characterized the President's handling of the Oregon crisis. A deadly array of evidence was marshaled to drive that charge home. He expressed utter disgust for the tactic of ascribing treason to the Whig opposition. This was a "foul imputation" for purposes of intimidation. It would have, as one Whig after another defiantly declared, an effect the opposite of the one intended.[33]

Other speakers forbore to use the short, ugly word Gentry had used in describing the message. They used longer words. Garrett Davis said he did not "charge Mr. Polk with promulgating falsehoods in this message; but I do say, that more numerous and palpable misstatements of fact, intentional or unintentional, have never characterized any previous Presidential message." He thought the maneuver of allowing Santa Anna to slip through the American blockade "degrading." Aware that before the war the President had been discussing this project with Santa Anna's agent, he asked: "Does history furnish an example of more abhorrent perfidy? Was any government through its Chief Magistrate ever more vilely prostituted?" [34] For the picture of Santa Anna as a Mexican liberal, Whig ones were substituted—betrayer of the Mexican Constitution of 1824, butcher of Texan prisoners, "monster of iniquity and corruption." The Whigs made the charge again and again that the

---

tend to the Rio Grande, when Congress in using those terms in the Joint Resolution had deliberately refrained from saying so." Baltimore *American,* October 23, 1847.

[33] *Cong. Globe,* 29 Cong., 2 Sess., App. 56 ff. (December 16, 1846).

[34] Ibid., App. 104 ff. (December 22, 1846); also 336 ff. (Solomon Foot).

money asked in the "Two Million bill" was meant to bribe this creature into agreeing to a peace of cession.

The purpose the President had in recommending a new military rank, about which he had been so reticent, became known. It became almost as known as if he had broadcast his diary, in which he had been discussing it in detail. The chief purpose was to overtop Whig generals, especially Taylor, who had become so popular. The brow on which laurels yet to come would rest should be a Democrat's. Perhaps on the same brow would alight the Democratic nomination for the presidency in 1848. Polk had clearly in mind the soldier to be so signally honored. He was none other than the Senator from Missouri, Thomas Hart Benton. Benton had been a frustrated lieutenant colonel in the War of 1812. He had long served, also, as chairman of the Senate Committee on Military Affairs, a post which had given him deep knowledge of fighting matters. Whigs learned by the underground that he was the President's choice. They deemed a plan to create, for an erstwhile lieutenant colonel and subsequent politician, the rank of lieutenant general—a rank temporarily set up for the great George Washington in 1798, under very special circumstances—little short of preposterous. One North Carolina Whig, George E. Badger, blurted out the common view: "It is but the first step for perpetuating, by passing into other hands, the powers of the Chief Magistracy." [35] The proposal was resisted even by members of the Cabinet, especially, on the quiet, by Buchanan, whose thoughts also were on a crown alighting on a brow in 1848.[36] The project never had a chance of success in Congress and it endeared the President to no one.

The net effect of continued debate on such topics was to create in the minds of the Whigs in Congress and in the press a picture of a President uncandid to the nation, devious in his language, and underhanded in his methods. It was to set before the nation as a

[35] Ibid., 29 Cong., 2 Sess., 186 (January 15, 1847).

[36] Quaife (ed.): *Diary of Polk*, index, entries "Benton" and "Buchanan." Benton and Polk had become reconciled.

major political issue the character of its chief magistrate. A summation of these discussions was given before the House of Representatives by a Whig, Alexander H. Stephens, shortly after the war: "Why, if a man were ambitious of acquiring a reputation for duplicity and equivocation, he could not select a better example in all history than to follow in the footsteps of our President. He did not know any better or more fitting appellation in after times, than Polk the mendacious!" [37]

This judgment was agreed to by historians of Whig persuasion. It long shaped accounts of the entire administration. Early in the twentieth century, however, a distinguished Texan historian, George P. Garrison, who had been given the privilege of examining the Polk diary, wrote a judgment less severe. He described the expansionist President in terms of mental traits. He believed Polk's mind a place of easy lodgment for dogmas supporting his expansionist ambitions. Polk, he thought, was convinced of the righteousness of his purposes and of his means of attaining them, and undeserving the title "mendacious."

> Such men as he rarely catch an historical perspective or see the whole truth that lies in any group of facts; and they are often involved in painful struggles by their own unconscious inconsistencies. No paralyzing scrupulosity or forecast of possible danger holds them back; and woe to the land if they be misguided, for they do things.

This penetrating appraisal reflected a new reliance by historians on psychology as a tool of interpretation. It reflected, also, in a concluding sentence, a robust new nationalism—that of Theodore Roosevelt, during whose presidency Garrison wrote: "But there are few in this day even of those who condemn the methods of Polk, that would be willing to see his work undone." [38] The work not to be undone was the acquisition of territory by conquest.

[37] *Cong. Globe,* 30 Cong., 1 Sess., 912 (July 10, 1848).

[38] George P. Garrison: *Westward Extension,* in Albert B. Hart (ed.): *The American Nation,* XVII (New York, 1906), 207.

Chapter V

"*All* M*exico*"

ACQUISITION OF territory by conquest was a question the Cabinet had considered the day the war was formally declared. It had been broached by Buchanan. He proposed issuing a declaration to foreign governments that the war was not for conquest or for any dismemberment of Mexico, that its purpose was simply self-defense. This proposal was a characteristic exhibit of his weakness. It was quashed immediately and completely by the President. Such a declaration, Polk said, would be improper and unnecessary. The war would not be fought for conquest, "yet it was clear that in making peace we would if practicable obtain California and such other portion of the Mexican territory as would be sufficient to indemnify our claimants on Mexico and to defray the expenses of the war." [1]

The idea that the war would not be fought for conquest was upheld in some Democratic papers. Even in the school of Manifest Destiny it was earnestly supported. The great teacher of this school, O'Sullivan, had always emphasized the view that no people or state ever entered the Union except of their own free choice. A people made application for entrance, and the application was carefully scrutinized before a ticket was issued. A forced entrance was unthinkable; it would be a violation of American freedom; it would undermine and overturn all principles of the American Constitution. It would reduce our government to the low moral level of Europe. Texas was the exemplification of the American method of

[1] Quaife (ed.): *Diary of Polk,* I, 396–7.

expansion. She had applied repeatedly for admission, and only after her people and her Congress had shown a wish to enter by virtually unanimous votes, had she been taken in. Poland was the horrid example of the European process of expansion—a destruction by partition of a nationality and a people by three greedy neighboring monarchs. Never, O'Sullivan had pointed out at the end of 1845, could a forced admission of a people take place under the American system:

> There are some things this nation will never do. It will never be the forcible subjugator of other countries; it will never despoil surrounding territories; it will never march through the blood of their unoffending inhabitants; it will never admit within its own Union those who do not freely desire the boon. The parallel of its territorial extensions will not be found in the history of the dismemberment of Poland or of the British conquests in India; and no patriots will ever rally upon their native hills to protect their own rights or their country's liberties from our rapacity.[2]

O'Sullivan, on learning of the armed clash between American and Mexican forces on the Rio Grande, was actually critical of the administration; indeed, he was almost Whiggish. He wondered what business Taylor had to be "under the walls of Matamoros, with his batteries commanding the town." The General, to be sure, was within the limits of Texas, "as claimed by that State," but whether an occupation so irritating to the Mexicans, and so likely to lead to collision, was necessary or wise, O'Sullivan doubted. He was critical, also, of war preparations on so massive a scale as Congress was authorizing. He deprecated them whether intended merely "to frighten our miserable little adversary," or to overwhelm her by conquest. He most earnestly objected to conquest.[3]

But he recovered soon from this startled, this unthinking, mood. Within a few days he had become more rational, after some nudging from the Washington *Union*, the organ of Polk, and, doubtless, from home readers, also. On May 18 he published an article in the *Morning News* lamenting that we should be forced, by

[2] *New York Morning News*, November 15, 20, 1845. Such views were echoed by expansionists in Congress. Polk, in announcing the annexation of Texas, gloried in its bloodlessness.

[3] *New York Morning News*, May 11, 13, 1846.

the gross wrongs and outrages we had suffered from Mexico, to waste so much life and treasure there. But this was not to be helped, and the question was how we would get the treasure back. O'Sullivan reminded his readers of his frequent editorials pointing out the inestimable value of California. The province contained a growing American community. It would naturally—as surely as water finds its level—have become American anyway. The cost of purchasing it from Mexico would have been twenty millions. Now we can get it more easily. It ought to be immediately occupied by American forces. Its retention would be readily achieved because the feelings of so many of its inhabitants are with us. In this way the pecuniary costs of the war will not be entirely wasted. "We therefore insist upon the *immediate acquisition of California.*" [4] Clearly, the charms of California were too much for a young man whose virtue had no other support than cold theory.

Other Manifest Destiny editors succumbed with even less struggle to the same attractions. Upper California, the New York *Sun* moralized, separated, as she is, from her Mexican consort, would come naturally to the United States in lieu of an indemnity in money. The Baltimore *Sun* thought her coming "a thing inevitable as destiny itself," apart from any war consideration. The *Indiana State Sentinel* exclaimed, with a sigh of relief, on May 13: "WAR AT LAST," and in the same breath gave pleasant news of California. The *Illinois State Register* thought the golden opportunity for California was come.[5] In general, the expansionist press now heard from heaven the authentic call to redeem California, which the Hartford *Times* had heard nearly a year before, but only in anticipation.

But the addition of California would mean a ragged demarcation line in the Far West. Between California and the United States would lie awkwardly the whole of New Mexico. This would create for the United States another of those angular and indefensible boundaries which Lieutenant Maury had complained of in the

[4] Ibid., May 18, 1846.

[5] New York *Sun,* June 2, 1846; Baltimore *Sun,* June 9, 1846; *Indiana State Sentinel* (s.w.), May 13, 1846; *Illinois State Register,* July 10, 1846.

Great Lakes region. If the ports of California were to be of use to the United States, an easy overland access to them was indispensable, as the Baltimore *American* conclusively demonstrated.[6] The concept of an isolated California soon faded out from the newspapers, therefore. The concept of a California accompanied by New Mexico took its place. By August 8, 1846, O'Sullivan was proposing, as a basis for a settlement, the northern part of the dominions of Mexico, "extending from the Rio Grande to the Pacific, mostly comprising the province of California, which is in the main unsettled, and with which the mass of the Mexican nation have but little intercourse or sympathy. This territory Mexico has but little interest in retaining, while we have a large one in acquiring it. If the inhabitants of the territory are willing to be transferred to us, it certainly is a very proper item for Mexico to propose to peace on the credit side of the account. The account being arranged on this basis, whether upon balancing it equitably, the balance shall be found to be on our side or the Mexican, is not of great consequence in comparison with the enjoyment of peace. Certainly all the money we could possibly be asked to pay for the territory, would not be equal what the war will cost if prosecuted to a favorable termination."[7]

But Whigs, and some Democrats refused to become interested in a seizure under whatever name. They charged that the penetration of the interior of Mexico by American armies was but a preliminary to a dismemberment, and that a war waged for the pretended purpose of "conquering peace" was already a war to conquer a helpless neighbor. This charge O'Sullivan took care strongly to rebut in the *Morning News:*

> But it by no means follows when we invade our enemy's country that we are bound or intend to keep it; nor have we seen even the slightest evidence of any intention on the part of the administration, to acquire by conquest and hold permanently by virtue of such conquest, a single foot of Mexican territory. Could we by any fair construction infer any such design on the part of the govern-

[6] Baltimore *American,* November 18, 1847, February 29, 1848; Philadelphia *Pennsylvanian,* December 27, 1847; *Indiana State Sentinel,* January 5, 1848.
[7] *New York Morning News,* August 8, 1846.

> ment, we would be among the first to lift our voice against it. Nothing upon earth, or above or below the earth, can be farther from the genius and principles of this Republic than the acquisition of territory by military conquest. The attempt would be as monstrous as it would be new in our history and short-lived, indeed, would be the power and influence of those who should undertake it. They would be looked upon as the worst of traitors, striking at the life of their country, and laying the foundation for its speedy and certain ruin.[8]

Denials by others that the United States had any intention of dismembering Mexico appeared, but they were not always as sweeping as those in the *New York Morning News.* The *Illinois State Register,* in discussing the subject, was satisfied to hold merely that invasion did not mean "as a matter of course" a permanent retention of territory. The administration might decide to receive California, and perhaps New Mexico, in lieu of indemnities due, or to become due, but this would not make the war one of conquest.[9]

Other expansionist journals showed reluctance to judge prematurely so crucial an issue. Mexican provinces might want of their own accord to come into the Union. The editor of the New York *Sun,* a few days after the declaration of war, affirming he had no thirst for conquest, declared: "If the Mexican people with one voice ask to come into the Union our boundary in that case may extend much further than the Rio Grande." [10] Walt Whitman took the same view. In June 1846 he called attention to reports that Yucatán, a discontented province of Mexico, had set up her own government. In an editorial entitled "More Stars for the Spangled Banner," he reported contentedly that "she won't need a long coaxing to join the United States." He thought Mexico would become, unless she brought the war with the United States summarily to a close, a severed and cut-up nation. Most of her provinces, instead of rushing to her rescue, would exult in her downfall.[11] The suggestion made prior to the war by exponents of Manifest Destiny

[8] Ibid., July 10, 1846.
[9] *Illinois State Register,* June 31, August 14, 1846.
[10] New York *Sun,* May 15, 1846.
[11] *Brooklyn Eagle,* June 25, 1846.

that some Mexican provinces were eager to enter the Union was sedulously kept alive, and it helps explain orders sent the Army and the Navy, after the fighting began, to conciliate the people of the invaded areas in every way and to condition them thus to a pleasant change of allegiance. The Baltimore *Sun,* commenting on July 2, 1846, on the exemplary behavior of Taylor's troops in Mexico, added: "And the consequence of this is to be foreseen already; a people will be prepared for a common union with us, in all probability, before we shall be prepared for them." [12]

Indemnity was an idea that early entered the minds of expansionist editors. It appeared there almost as promptly as it had in Polk's mind. It was carefully differentiated from any idea of conquest. O'Sullivan, on July 10, 1846, after denouncing any executive who would attempt a war of conquest as the "worst of traitors," went on to say:

> No terms [of peace] can however be contemplated which will not require from her [Mexico] indemnity, to some extent, at least, for the many wrongs which we have suffered at her hands. And if, in agreeing upon those terms, she finds it more for her interest to give us California than to satisfy our just demands in any other way, what objection can there be to the arrangement, or in what respect can it be properly called a military conquest? It will be a simple matter of contract and accommodation, by which we accept payment in land instead of money.[13]

Indemnity is an elastic term. It stretches as the need requires. In logic it has no limits. Its limits, in the mind of O'Sullivan, were at first California. To others, including the President, they seemed at the outset to be California plus New Mexico. Those limits were, however, predicated on the assumption of a short war. As the war stretched out, so did the limits. By the end of 1846 they had become the Sierra Madre Mountains and Lower California, and the concept was still expanding. James Russell Lowell, a Whig and a cynic, hardly differentiated at all between indemnity and Manifest Destiny. In the *Biglow Papers* he wrote that as our troops pene-

[12] Baltimore *Sun,* July 2, 1846.
[13] *New York Morning News,* July 10, 1846.

trated deeper and deeper into Mexico "our Destiny higher an' higher kep' mountin'." [14]

The rich silver mines of Mexico appeared frequently now in expansionist newspapers. Those of the New Mexico region, occupied by General Kearny, were described with enthusiasm in the Hartford *Times* in the autumn of 1846, and a hope was expressed that our government would not part with them.[15] An item was cited in the Baltimore *American,* from the *New York Herald,* which showed that Mexican exports of bullion, mostly to England, amounted to fourteen millions annually. If Mexico were annexed, that bullion would come to the United States.[16] The *Boston Times* gave space in its editorial columns early in 1848 to a letter, signed "Logic," describing the immense stretches of wilderness land in Mexico which the United States wanted for the use and benefit of mankind. "Mexico does not want it, and forbids it to our race. The people [outside Mexico] are bursting the bounds of human habitation. . . . But they must not come upon Mexican ground. . . . Will you bid God defend the right of that contemptible administration to bar men out of his blessed and fruit bearing earth?" [17] References were frequently made to a transit route across the Isthmus of Tehuantepec for a canal or a railroad to the Pacific.[18]

During all this discussion American armies were battering their way into the interior of Mexico. That of Taylor was moving from the north; that of Winfield Scott, from the seaboard. Scott had taken Vera Cruz after a thorough softening by naval bombardment. Both armies won brilliant victories against great odds. Not a single defeat of any consequence was suffered. The fighting qualities of American troops impressed a grudging Europe.

But fighting was costly in money and blood. Money had to come, in the later stages of the war, from a Whig House. Glory was not in itself an attraction to Polk, especially if Whig generals battened on

[14] James Russell Lowell: *The Biglow Papers* (Boston, 1885), 102.
[15] Hartford *Times,* October 3, 1846.
[16] Baltimore *American,* October 12, 1847; *New York Herald,* October 8, 1847.
[17] *Boston Times,* January 28, 1848.
[18] *De Bow's Review,* III (June 1847), 496–502.

it. Polk had never wanted a long war. He wanted, according to Benton, a little war, just enough to require a peace.[19] His eagerness for peace was shown in the spring of 1847 when he named a commissioner to proceed to Scott's army and to make a treaty with Santa Anna at the earliest favorable moment. The commissioner was Nicholas P. Trist, Chief Clerk of the State Department, whom Buchanan had recommended. He was a friend of Andrew Jackson's nephew, Donelson, was considered to have good judgment, and had a speaking knowledge of Spanish. He was empowered to sign a treaty with Santa Anna forthwith. He was to obtain in the treaty the two Californias, Upper and Lower, as well as New Mexico and a right of transit across the Isthmus of Tehuantepec. For such a treaty he was authorized to offer as much as $30,000,000, though, of course, he was to get it for less if he could.[20] A treaty on such a basis would be beyond the gunfire of Whigs. It would surely not be a treaty of conquest. Even malevolent Whigs could not criticize it except as a forced sale to the United States of a territory which Mexico had found it a burden to hold.

An essential to the success of the mission, Polk believed, was secrecy. The operation would be sabotaged by Whigs in advance, if they became aware of it, by denouncing publicly whatever terms, even of purchase, Trist was authorized to propose. The mission was to be announced only when its success had been achieved. Greater than usual precautions went, therefore, to keeping it a secret in the official family.[21] The precautions were in vain. The *New York Herald* and other journals almost at once had the news, enabling the *National Intelligencer* to make it a leading item in its columns.[22] The fat was in the fire.

In Mexico, Scott continued to pound his way toward the Mexican capital, with Trist now in his impedimenta. He and Trist quarreled bitterly as they pursued Santa Anna. Santa Anna ex-

[19] Thomas H. Benton: *Thirty Years' View* (New York, 1856), II, 679–80.

[20] Quaife (ed.): *Diary of Polk,* II, 471–8. The instructions appear in Moore (ed.): *Works of Buchanan,* VII, 271–9.

[21] Quaife (ed.): *Diary of Polk,* II, 478–85.

[22] *New York Herald,* April 20, 1847; Boston *Post,* April 19, 1847; *National Intelligencer* (t.w.), April 22, 1847.

hibited his lack of principle again. He had, under a gentleman's agreement, been admitted to Mexico. He no sooner arrived there than he ignored the agreement. In dealings with Trist he exhibited the same amorality. He would pretend a desire for negotiation, after reverses, obtain a cease-fire to engage in peace talks, accept bribes, drag out discussions interminably, while all the time re-forming his lines; then he would go on with the fighting. This interfered so seriously with Scott that he threatened to resign his command unless Trist's powers were canceled. But the march to Mexico City went on inexorably, and, by the middle of September, Scott was in the Halls of the Montezumas.

The military situation had now become hopeless for Mexico. Her chief port and her capital were in enemy hands. Upper California and New Mexico were gone. Her armies were broken, those of the foe flushed with victory. Her treasury was empty. By every rule of war she should have surrendered to her conqueror. But the Mexicans were impractical people. They were mulish in their stubbornness, as noted by Polk in discouragement. They could not be made to realize that they had been beaten. They negotiated, Polk complained, as though they had been victorious. They offered to recognize the loss of Texas but insisted on defining Texas as extending only to the Nueces. They proposed to make the region between the Nueces and the Rio Grande a buffer state. They refused to cede either Lower California or Upper California or New Mexico. All they would consent to cede, even for a money payment, was a fraction of Upper California. They declined to consider the cession of a right of transit across the Isthmus of Tehuantepec. They demanded even that the United States pay Mexico damages for depredations committed on private property by American troops. "Such were the unreasonable terms," Polk expostulated, proposed by them.[23] The mission failed.

A hardening of temper was Polk's response to the breakdown of the negotiation. He contemplated, when the news reached him in October 1847, more indemnity, more land, less payment for land, if any. Cancellation of Trist's powers was ordered. He was directed

[23] Richardson (comp.): *Messages and Papers,* IV, 539.

to return home. Orders were sent Scott to levy for the support of his troops on the conquered country. Customs were taken over for that purpose.[24] Looting became more common.

A final solution of the Mexican problem—the absorption of All Mexico—was considered by the Cabinet. It was embraced by the expansionist press. This might be achieved by a phased or by a single operation. In the phased operation, California and New Mexico would come first. They were the northern, the sparsely inhabited parts. They could enter the Union without the formality of a cession. The southern, or heavily populated portion, could wait. It could be left in the Army's possession as an occupied province. The occupation would continue until an accord on indemnities was reached. For such a procedure a strong case could be made. California and New Mexico would be put on the road to freedom and prosperity at once. The problem of southern Mexico could be deferred. The future would decide whether its native population could be made fit to enter the Union. The future seemed to expansionists a good time to decide race questions.

The outcome of a prolonged occupation seemed to reflective persons obvious. A large force of occupying troops would have to be used to preserve order in Mexico. Costs would be heavy. They would have to be borne by the Mexican treasury, leaving little revenue to apply to cancellation of indemnities. Cancellation would recede far into the future. In that time Americans and Europeans would settle in Mexico. They would take root and would prefer in the end not to be disturbed. Also, according to the Philadelphia *Public Ledger,* "the most intelligent and moral of the Mexican people will accommodate themselves to American, as far better than Mexican rule, and will insist . . . upon continuing American. Thus will annexation be forced upon us as the inevitable result of a long military occupation whether we want it or not." But a further thought occurred to the *Public Ledger*. If occupation inevitably ends in annexation, what is the good of waiting? Question and answer were given on November 12, 1847. "Then as those changes . . . must be the *end* of our military occupation, should

[24] Quaife (ed.): *Diary of Polk,* III, 186.

we not act more wisely by shortening the process, and making them in the *beginning?* In other words, is not conquest for the very purpose of annexation our best, our only wise course?" [25]

But the President, for present purposes, preferred a phased operation. In his annual message of December 7, 1847, he recommended that California and New Mexico be taken over as partial indemnity at once, that they have American laws extended over them, and that they be given American governments. This would be possible without the formality of a treaty. Other provinces occupied by the Army should remain under military control until the making of peace. This would give the United States security against guerrilla attacks, and the peacable and well-disposed Mexicans, security against their war lords. It would help Mexico herself on the road to freedom and prosperity. A premature withdrawal of American forces would have the opposite effect. The better elements in Mexico would be without protection to person or property. Wearied by successive revolutions, they would be inclined "to yield to foreign influences and to cast themselves into the arms of some European monarchy for protection from the anarchy and suffering which would ensue. This, for our own safety, and in pursuance of our established policy, we should be compelled to resist. We could never consent that Mexico should be thus converted into a monarchy governed by a foreign prince." [26]

[25] Philadelphia *Public Ledger,* November 12, 1847.

[26] Richardson (comp.): *Messages and Papers,* IV, 545–6. The Philadelphia *Pennsylvanian,* an expansionist sheet, showed an awareness on November 8, 1847, of the difference between occupation and conquest of Mexico, and also of the inevitable outcome of occupation.

> The public mind is apt, we perceive, to regard as synonymous the two distinct propositions of the occupation and the conquest of Mexico. The first, on the contrary, looks to a mere temporary, the last, to a permanent government of of the country. There are thousands who think that the occupation of the country would be the most judicious, and the most certain to produce a safe and solid peace. If, they say, this policy would require new levies of troops, etc., if the occupation were general, these troops could be subsisted upon the country; and if the result did not show that we had conquered the country as William the Conqueror did England after the battle of Hastings, it might show that we had imitated the policy of Napoleon, who in some of his brilliant campaigns, filled the coffers which he had formerly emptied. We should, by the occupation of Mexico, they allege, collect her revenues of all sorts, as well as from her mines as from her imports, and from the other taxes levied upon her

This statement of war aims was phrased with especial care. It had been two months on the President's mind. Its purpose was to assure critics that expansion over Mexico had never been a war aim of the Administration. In an early draft the President declared unequivocally that he had never contemplated annihilation of the nationality of Mexico, that he had always wished merely to vindicate the national honor and obtain indemnity for past wrongs and security for the future. Buchanan had preferred to add a warning that if Mexico persisted in her stubbornness, and rendered peace otherwise unattainable, then "we must fulfill that destiny which Providence may have in store for both countries." But the President considered this too indefinite. At a point in his message safely removed from war aims, he added the sentiment that, if all honorable means of peace with Mexico should have been exhausted to no avail, then we "must continue to occupy her country with our troops, taking the full measure of indemnity in our own hands, and must enforce the terms which our honor demands." [27] "Our honor" was somewhat indefinite too, but less ominous than "that destiny which Providence may have in store for both countries." Buchanan was obliged to pocket his pride, and his phrase, for

---

people. Our government of the country, although merely temporary, should be as mild and as liberal as any military government could be. It should be in strong contrast with the iron rule of military despotism which has so long oppressed and impoverished poor Mexico. It should be active in reducing burdens and in punishing disorders. It should respect the religion of the country. It should encourage the arts and the sciences, and introduce, if possible, those mighty improvements by which time and space are annihilated in our own land. It should disavow all purpose of hostility to the people. Such a government, argue the advocates of occupation, would effect a brilliant peace, glorious in all its aspects, and would leave Mexico more than half-prepared, for the great duty which destiny has marked out for her, and which she cannot evade.

[27] Richardson (comp.): *Messages and Papers,* IV, 544. An honorable peace must include, Polk believed, "indemnity for the past and security for the future." This immediately attracted Whig fire. The comment of Senator Clayton, of Delaware, was: "What that cant phrase means I do not exactly understand; but I have been told by an ingenious friend, that indemnity for the past means half of Mexico, and security for the future, the other half." *Cong. Globe,* 30 Cong., 1 Sess., App. 74 (January 11, 1848). The Baltimore *American* of February 21, 1848, could not resist a shot: "As for *indemnity,* no one knows how much the administration claims. The *security* it seeks . . . —as though the eagle should require security from the sparrowhawk—is left in equal uncertainty."

later use. He had come a long distance in his thinking since his proposal, at the outbreak of the war, to forswear the taking of any Mexican territory by conquest.

Even after the message was in final form and ready for delivery, the President was asked to allow the All Mexico idea to re-enter his program by a back door. The request was made by Walker. At a cabinet meeting he asked to be allowed, in his forthcoming annual report as Secretary of the Treasury, to canvass the fiscal advantages of a complete incorporation of Mexico into the Union. The proposal was objected to by Buchanan on tactical grounds—that a departmental advocacy of that sort would run counter to the milder Presidential advocacy in the message. That view was taken by others and by the President.[28]

But Buchanan was not averse to hoisting a balloon of his own. He persisted, after several weeks of reflection, in believing that any ordinary indemnity would be insufficient for a war aggressively begun by Mexico and senselessly prolonged. On December 17, 1847, he sent a letter to a public meeting in Philadelphia in which his war aims were put into such a framework:

> Heaven has smiled upon the just cause; and the character of our country has been illustrated [*sic*] by a rapid succession of brilliant and astonishing victories. The exploits of our army have elevated our National character, and shed a lustre upon our name throughout the civilized world. . . .
>
> The war has not been prosecuted for conquest. At every stage in its progress, we have been willing to conclude a just and honorable peace. Indeed, we can never wage a war for conquest in the popular sense of that term. Our free institutions forbid that we should subject nations to our arbitrary sway. If they come within our power, we must bestow upon them the same blessings of liberty and law, which we ourselves enjoy. Should they be annexed to the Union (as in the case of Texas), they must participate in the freest and best Government upon earth—on equal terms with ourselves.
>
> The Capital of Mexico is now the Head-Quarters of our conquering Army, and yet such is the genius of our free institutions, that, for the first time, its peaceful and well-disposed citizens enjoy security in their private rights, and the advantage of a just and firm Government. From all that can be learned, they appreciate our

[28] Quaife (ed.): *Diary of Polk,* III, 241–2.

protection at its proper value; and dread nothing so much as the withdrawal of our army. They know this would be the signal for renewed and fierce dissensions among their military leaders, in which the Mexican people would become the victims. In this wretched condition of affairs, justice to them and to ourselves may require that we should protect them in establishing, upon a permanent basis, a Republican Government, able and willing to conclude and maintain an equitable Treaty of Peace with the United States. After every effort to obtain such a treaty, should we finally fail in accomplishing the object, and should the military factions in Mexico still persist in waging upon us a fruitless war, then we must fulfil the destiny which Providence may have in store for both countries.[29]

Such sentiments were likely to be pleasing to the Democratic national convention soon to gather to elect a party standard-bearer. They gave the impression of a man proud of his country's present, and entertaining exhilarating ideas concerning its future. That image of himself the author of the letter doubtless wished to leave with the public. Cass was thinking of a like image in his public pronouncements. He declared at just this time in Congress that, though the extinction of Mexican nationality might be unfortunate, he believed in the sovereignty of the popular will. "To attempt to prevent the American people from taking possession of Mexico, if they demand it, would be as futile in effect as to undertake to stop the rushing of the cataract of Niagara." [30] Cass was already constructively thinking of problems a cession might raise, as will appear. In Pennsylvania, a rival of Buchanan for high office, Vice-President George M. Dallas, was ready to help destiny in a co-operative spirit.[31] So were Douglas, Dickinson, Breese, Hannegan, and William Allen. All had impeccable expansionist records on

[29] The letter appeared in the *Pennsylvanian* on December 20 and 25, 1847, and in the Washington *Union*, December 24, 1847. It has not been included in the Moore edition of the *Works of Buchanan*, and it is absent from the Buchanan Papers in the possession of the Pennsylvania Historical Society. Buchanan's aim had become, by November 9, 1847, the Sierra Madre line; Quaife (ed.): *Diary of Polk*, III, 216–18. Among the persons inciting Buchanan and Polk to go for All Mexico was George Bancroft, who wrote from London; Mark A. D. Howe: *Life and Letters of George Bancroft* (2 vols., New York, 1908), II, 23, 27–8.

[30] *Cong. Globe*, 30 Cong., 1 Sess., 79 (December 30, 1847).

[31] George M. Dallas to William S. Conely *et al.*, January 28, 1848, Washington *Union*, February 12, 1848.

Texas and 54° 40′ in Oregon. All were ready to let destiny shape their country's future and their own.

But the public evinced a persistent reluctance to absorb All Mexico. Absorption of eight millions of a mixed race, obliteration of a republic of foreign tongue, retention of a subjugated province for the indefinite future—these were prospects from which a democracy shrank. Such a future was too utterly contrary to the instincts of Americans and to earlier teachings, even of Manifest Destiny. There had been too little favorable public response to the advocacy of annexation, in the first half of 1847, by such Eastern penny journals as the New York *Sun* and Philadelphia *Public Ledger*. In Congress, Whigs and opposition Democrats were too obviously collaborating to defeat an All Mexico program. The congressional elections in November 1846 had been too unfavorable to the Democrats.

In deference to this reluctance to have All Mexico, expansionist editors and politicians of the North—of the Northwest especially—took the "if" tack. If Mexico should remain obdurate, if she just would not listen to reason, if she persisted in aggressive resistance to pacification, all her territory might have to be absorbed, as a last resort, in the interests of peace. Temporary problems might be created. The morsel might prove indigestible; it might produce discomforts. Still, in the end it would add immeasurably to the well-being and strength of both the absorbed and the absorber.[32]

Around the stark form of annexation, a cover, pleasing in design, was draped. It was regeneration. Its pattern in general resembled that employed for California earlier, but differed in detail. In the case of California a *region* had needed rescue from "unhallowed hands" and marriage to the rescuer. In the case of Mexico, a *people* was to be saved from cruel and selfish rulers, a

[32] Baltimore *American,* October 15, 1847. "But while a moderate morsel may be swallowed without difficulty, an immoderate one might choke to suffocation. That which would nourish when taken in quantities that could be digested and assimilated, might cause a surfeit and produce disease and death if excessive quantities should be forced into the system." The editor favored the Sierra Madre line. He was one of a few expansionist Whigs in the nation, but he wanted only the lightly populated parts of Mexico.

community was to be lifted, and was to have bestowed on it the blessings of American order and peace and freedom.

Humanitarians dedicated to advancing this program came principally from the North. They were the editors of the Northern expansionist journals. More specifically they were the editors of the Democratically inclined penny press of the Northeastern seaboard. These men, whether in Boston, New York, Philadelphia, or Baltimore, were the heart and mind and soul of the All Mexico crusade after the failure of the peace negotiation.

The *Boston Times,* which claimed a circulation larger than the combined circulation of three other major Boston papers, had this to say on October 22, 1847, under the caption "Subjugation and Occupation of Mexico":

> The "conquest" which carries peace into a land where the sword has always been the sole arbiter between factions equally base, which institutes the reign of law where license has existed for a generation; which provides for the education and elevation of the great mass of the people, who have, for a period of 300 years been the helots of an overbearing foreign race, and which causes religious liberty, and full freedom of mind to prevail where a priesthood has long been enabled to prevent all religion save that of its worship,—such a "conquest," stigmatize it as you please, must necessarily be a great blessing to the conquered. It is a work worthy of a great people, of a people who are about to regenerate the world by asserting the supremacy of humanity over the accidents of birth and fortune.[33]

The New York *Sun* was quite as idealistic. Its editor, Moses Y. Beach, a Yankee from Connecticut, believed that Providence had "willed the Mexican War to unite and exalt both nations." [34] On October 22, 1847, he wrote:

> The [Mexican] race is perfectly accustomed to being conquered, and the only new lesson we shall teach is that our victories will give liberty, safety, and prosperity to the vanquished, if they know enough to profit by the appearance of our stars. To *liberate* and *ennoble*—not to *enslave* and *debase*—is our mission. Well may the Mexican nation, whose great masses have never yet tasted liberty,

[33] *Boston Times,* October 22, 1847.
[34] New York *Sun,* November 20, 1847.

prattle over their lost phantom of nationality. . . . If they have not—in the profound darkness of their vassal existence—the intelligence and manhood to accept the ranks and rights of freeman at our hands, we must bear with their ignorance. But there is no excuse for the man educated under our institutions, who talks of our "wronging the Mexicans" when we offer them a position infinitely above any they have occupied, since their history began, and in which, for the first time, they may aim at the greatness and dignity of a truly republican and self-governing people.[35]

The *New York Herald* thought likewise. It was, however, less consistent. It seemed, indeed, almost flighty in its frequency and suddenness of change. It seemed to wish to titillate, rather than to educate or persuade, its readers. On October 8, 1847, it believed that Mexico, annexed, would be "gorgeously" happy. "Like the Sabine virgins, she will soon learn to love her ravisher." Eleven days later her editor disclaimed all wish to absorb Mexico. "When the bride is reluctant, the marriage is generally ill-starred and unhappy." Indeed, if Mexico should become convinced soon of the sad fruitlessness of her struggle, "we should gladly see restored to her, every foot of her territory except such as we should have acquired from her by honorable treaty." Nine days later the candid editor felt compelled to admit that he had once believed immediate annexation an evil. "But as we are forced to encounter it, we should grapple with this evil manfully, vigorously, and as becomes a great nation." On January 22, 1848, in response to rumors of British intermeddling in peace negotiations in Mexico, he warned against any withdrawing of American troops and ventured the opinion that "the annexation of Mexico is as important, and will be as beneficial to New York and New England . . . as the annexation of Louisiana was nearly half a century ago." On March 9, he considered the Trist treaty a "monster and an abomination."[36] These changes of pace stimulated reader interest, doubtless, and built circulation.

By contrast, the *Public Ledger* of Philadelphia was one of the most steady of advocates of All Mexico. On October 25, 1847, its youthful editor, William M. Swain, wrote:

[35] Ibid., October 22, 1847.
[36] *New York Herald*, October 8, 19, 28, 1847; January 22, 1848; March 9, 1848.

We are believers in the superintendence of a directing Providence, and when we contemplate the rise and amazing progress of the United States, the nature of our government, the character of our people, and the occurrence of unforeseen events, all tending to one great accomplishment, we are impressed with a conviction that the decree is made and in the process of execution, that this continent is to be but one nation, under one system of free institutions. This is said in no spirit of prophecy, but in the conclusion of reason, . . . and the natural tendency of the moral and physical elements at work. On this hemisphere principles have been developed calculated to revolutionize the old habits of thinking among men, to disprove the divine right of kings, to explode the reverenced maxims of tyranny, and to establish a rational political liberty for the human race. These principles have already, in some measure, regenerated the rights of man in Europe, but to its full accomplishment the example of a continent of freemen may be required whose power can awe the opposition of kingdoms, and whose moral influence will impress a deep sense of human rights upon the minds of all mankind. When the spectacle of a whole continent, reposing in peace and prosperity, where every one enjoys the same religious, civil and political rights, is beheld from beyond the Atlantic and Pacific, the principles of despotism, no matter how mild their form, must give way, and men will resume their rights and prerogatives. The progress of events points to a time when men will be astonished that their ancestors were ever so sunk in ignorance and delusion, as to have patiently submitted to wear the yoke of subjection that so long galled their necks, and still more, that they should have boasted of their humiliation, under the profession of loyalty to kings.[37]

Here, reincarnated, was the soul of O'Sullivan! To the inspired Philadelphian had been handed the torch by the first of Manifest Destiny philosophers, who, the year before, had deserted his editorships and was on the way to the field of direct action. Swain was not merely an idealist; he was eminently practical. Early in 1848 he pragmatically considered the question why we should conquer and annex Mexico. He wrote:

To remove a hostile neighbor in itself; to prevent it becoming a neighbor both hostile and dangerous in European hands; to enable us to command the Pacific and the Gulf of Mexico; . . . to develope for the benefit of ourselves and the world the ample re-

[37] Philadelphia *Public Ledger,* October 25, 1847.

sources of Mexico; to redeem the Mexican people from anarchy, tyranny, debasement; to redeem security, civilization, improvement; to keep Cuba from the hands of our cunning, indefatigable, unscrupulous rivals, the British; to facilitate the entire removal of those rivals from this continent; to open Mexico, as an extensive market to our manufactures, an extensive producer of that material [silver] through which we command the manufactures of Europe; to prevent monarchy from gaining any additional ground on the American continent, North or South, and thus to facilitate its entire removal.[38]

Helpfully concrete suggestions were made by the Philadelphian, also, for implementing an incorporation of Mexico. He wrote:

Then pursue the conquest; hold all the seaports and large cities; seize all the public property, all sources of revenue; introduce the common law and the English language as fast as possible; establish schools; protect the religion of the country, and tolerate all others; give to Mexico a local legislature, composed of three or four deputies from each State, to meet at Mexico; make General Scott Governor of the Whole, as General Harrison was made Governor of the Northwestern Territory; allow it three or four delegates in Congress; open it to emigration from the United States and Europe; let the local legislature, for the first three or four years, have power merely to inquire into and report subjects of legislation, its acts to be subject to ratification, first by the Governor, afterwards by the President and Congress; let a deputy-governor, commander of the garrison, be appointed for each State and let the State deputies, elected by the people, be subject to his approbation. Thus will Mexico have a mild and equitable and intelligent government to protect its people and promote its prosperity, and a good stiff authority to keep down its tyrants. Gen. Scott is the very fellow for the head of such a government. Our Yankee young fellows and the pretty senoritas will do the rest of the annexation, and Mexico will soon be Anglo-Saxonized, and prepared for the confederacy.[39]

The same combination of idealism and practicality appeared in the Baltimore *Sun,* whose editor, Arunah S. Abell, a transplanted New Englander, was willing by the autumn of 1847 to absorb Mexico in entirety, if she did not soon quit fighting and make peace. He wrote:

[38] Ibid., January 25, 1848.
[39] Ibid., December 11, 1847.

> The longer and more steadfastly we dwell upon these necessities, the more are we disposed to regard them as auspices for good, the harbingers of a new and a glorious era to the benighted and oppressed people of Mexico. In the contemplation of such a conquest as that which ours must be, if accomplished at all, even those who cannot approve the project, must be sensible to the moral grandeur of the achievement. Considered in its simplest aspect, it is really nothing more than the overthrow and systematic suppression of a gross and heartless military despotism on one hand, and the elevation of the people on the other. It is the rescue of the constitutional energies of republicanism from the degradation, selfishness, and prostitution of factious ambition, and the restoration of the same in all the renovated beauty and efficiency with which our experience can invest them, to the enraptured apprehension of the popular mind. . . . [The Mexican people are in a deplorable state.] Would it not be an act of benevolence, clothed too with an inexpressible moral sublimity, to revolutionize such a state of things, and restore the powers of government to the sovereignty of the people? [40]

Practical means of attaining these high ends were sketched a month later. First, the grip of the war lords on the country was to be broken:

> But this influence once destroyed, the intercourse, and the labor, and the fruits thereof, which must attend upon a season of peace, and even the cessation of hostilities, will beget in the popular mind a sentiment of equality with our people; the Mexican populace will be elevated to the enjoyment of privileges they know not of, and experience a sensible relief from the heartless incumbrance of a military despotism. The steamboat, the railroad, the telegraph, and above all the schoolhouse, with various minor instrumentalities of a refined and enlightened civilization, will do the rest; aye, in a few years, work wonders, and subjugated Mexico become, as it were, in her own right the glory of the northern Union.[41]

An appeal to American self-respect was made on behalf of All Mexico. Self-respect would be lost unless All Mexico were taken. Mexico had insolently forced war on the United States. The war had backfired. It had knocked the aggressor down and left her helpless. The costs of the war had been high in blood and treasure. Yet,

[40] Baltimore *Sun,* October 15, 1847.
[41] Ibid., November 19, 1847.

even so, peace had been magnanimously offered her twice, only to be spurned. Guerrilla fighting had been resorted to instead. If the armed forces of the United States were now to be withdrawn from any part of the unpacified land, the fighting would go on indefinitely. If an entire withdrawal without indemnity were ordered, American soldiers would have sacrificed themselves in vain, the heroic dead would be dishonored, and the nation would be the laughing stock of the world. The only dignified response to Mexican intransigence was to station the Army for an indefinite period in Mexico. This was a note heard over and over in the penny press and in administration organs in the autumn and winter of 1847. Always the plaintive question would introduce it: "What shall we do with Mexico?" Back, as if pre-recorded, would come the answer: "Keep hold of her, or you will be the laughing stock of the world!"

"We cannot," the *Public Ledger* observed on December 9, 1847, in reply to its own question, "let go without disgrace." Even if we wished to do so she would not consent to be shaken off. "Her fools can resist us no longer, and her wise are imploring our protection against the fools. We cannot *back out* entirely; we cannot take part and leave the rest. We have got the whole and *must* do something with it." [42]

The New York *Sun,* on December 18, 1847, asked the same question and the answer was: "Mexico has thrice refused peace, she has now no government either to reject or accept it. Our claim is indemnity for the past and security for the future. That indemnity lies nowhere but in Mexican soil—the treasury of Mexico was robbed of its last dollar by her great robber-tyrant [Santa Anna] as he deserted the capital, and her bond is as worthless as her faith; and security either for her fulfillment of a treaty or our possession of whatever we may be forced to take must depend upon our occupancy of her strongholds." [43]

The *Illinois State Register* pointed out: "Mexico has challenged the issues of battle, and suffered inglorious defeat; she is foiled at

[42] Philadelphia *Public Ledger,* December 9, 1847.
[43] New York *Sun,* December 18, 1847.

every point at her own game—and what then? She retires from our advance, leaving her people to our mercy, and scoffs at our overtures for peace. And these overtures include what? Simply the redress of our wrongs, the security of our own territory, the recovery of debts due to our citizens, and a just and equitable indemnity for the war. To conclude a peace short of the attainment of these objects would be on our part to become the laughing stock of the world." [44]

Retention of All Mexico was necessary, also, to fulfill an ancient aspiration of mankind. If Mexico came into American possession, an interoceanic canal could be built for the world's use across the waist of the hemisphere. Such a canal had been dreamed of ever since the truth became known that the Strait of Anian was a fable merely. Cortez had crossed the Isthmus of Tehuantepec in search of a passage. When he saw that none existed he had suggested a man-made one, and the idea had become a challenge to the Western world. At least four other routes had been suggested—at the Isthmus of Panama, at Darien, at the Lake of Nicaragua, and at the Atrato River. Each had been recommended in turn by explorers, engineers, and just ordinary writers, on the basis usually of some special advantage a particular route would confer on the writer's own government. Yet each had been found fraught with difficulties.

The Tehuantepec route was favored above all others in the United States during the Mexican War. By Polk it was deemed best. An alternative at the Isthmus of Panama had been acquired in the form of a transit privilege. It had been obtained from New Granada without authorization, or instruction, by an enterprising chargé d'affaires in December 1846. But its provisions had seemed to Polk to constitute an entangling alliance, and it had been kept under wraps. It was not ratified until the summer of 1848.[45] The Tehuantepec route was favored by the Cabinet. It would be nearer

[44] *Illinois State Register*, November 12, 1847. The same sentiment was feelingly presented by Buchanan in his public letter cited above.

[45] An account of the New Granada negotiation, with helpful citation of documents, is Hunter Miller (ed.): *Treaties and Other International Acts of the United States* (8 vols., Washington, 1931–48), V, 125–60.

the United States. A canal there would be a mere elongation, so to speak, of streams of the United States flowing into the Gulf of Mexico or directly into the Atlantic Ocean. It would deflect commerce moving between American ports and the Pacific less far to the south than any others. It would be easier to defend. It would, indeed, convert the Mexican gulf into a kind of American lake.

Its costs of construction would be moderate. Heavy excavation would be unnecessary on the side of the Gulf of Mexico. On that side a noble stream flows from the west to salt water—the Coatzacoalcos—deep enough to carry ocean-going vessels. The upper waters of the river might have to be cleared of obstacles, but that was all. On the Pacific side, water to feed a canal would be provided simply by deflecting the course of the Chicapa River. Harbors were to be found at either end. They were barred, to be sure, but the bars were not major obstacles. The one at the mouth of the Coatzacoalcos was pierced, so the argument ran, by a channel that was stable and deep enough to carry ocean-going vessels. Marking it out clearly was all that would be necessary. As for the bar on the Pacific side, that could be managed too. The total cost of all improvements would be not much more than twenty or twenty-five million dollars.

The benefits to be gained from such a canal were felt to be incalculable. One was the integration into the United States of its far-flung western territories. Oregon and California would be brought next door, virtually, to the Eastern seaboard. The commerce of the nation would take on new dimensions. The vast surpluses of the Mississippi Valley would go cheaply to all the markets of the Pacific. The commerce of the Eastern seaboard would acquire advantages no European state ever could overcome. Mariners would take manufactured goods from Eastern industry, foods from Eastern agriculture, and pick-ups from Oceania of sandalwood, *bêche-de-mer*, and other exotic products, and exchange them all in China for teas, silks, and chinaware. The doors of mysterious Japan would be opened; the traffic of the world would become an American monopoly. The whaling fleet of New England, the nursery of our seamen, would go to the catch, and return, spared the hazardous and interminable voyage round Cape Horn. The fleet's annual productiveness would be doubled. The pearl fisheries of the Gulf of California would become ours. Not least of these blessings would be the overthrow of the selfish monopolies the British held in all corners of the world.

Promises of equal wonders were held out, to be sure, by transcontinental-railroad promoters. Transcontinental railroads would solidify the Union, would be part of a railroad and sea connection with teeming China, and accomplish yet more. They would colonize the routes along which they would run, and redeem a wilderness from savagery. Three routes were suggested, in various orders of preference. One, at the north, was suggested by Asa Whitney. It would run from Lake Michigan to the mouth of the Columbia or to Puget Sound. Its construction would be by private enterprise, encouraged by a land grant from Congress. Already in 1845 Whitney was before Congress asking a grant for it. A central route was proposed, in 1846, by George Wilkes, a writer and politician of New York City and owner there of a scandal sheet. The line was to run between the Missouri River and the Pacific via South Pass. It would be constructed by the government—the first such suggestion—and would preserve the public domain from being the plaything of speculators. Frémont's notable third expedition had, for its purpose, to find the best route at the center. That route was favored by Benton. A southern route was favored by Colonel James Gadsden. It was to run from Charleston, South Carolina, to Memphis or New Orleans, thence to El Paso, and thence, via the Gila River, to the coast at Monterey. Calhoun favored that route.[46] Lieutenant Maury, who was in touch with Calhoun, favored it also. Maury not only favored a southern route but greatly preferred it to any interoceanic canal constructed across Tehuantepec. Rivalries were thus well established between alternative routes for a railroad, and, between the alternatives of an overland or of an interoceanic tie with California even before California was ready to be tied. These

[46] The beginnings of agitation for transcontinental railroads are sketched in Lewis H. Haney: *Congressional History of Railways in the United States* (Madison, 1908), Book III.

rivalries were to have results significant for the Union in the mid 1850's.

During the Mexican War railroad projects went into an eclipse. A railroad must climb the soaring masses of the Rockies and, also, those of the Cascades, or Sierra Nevadas. Its costs, therefore, would be greater than a canal's. Also, the time needed for completion would be greater. Asa Whitney, in 1851, in discouragement over the reception of his railroad project in Congress, took it to England for use in British North America. He described it at a meeting of the Royal Geographical Society at King's College, only to be told by a military expert in the audience that the time for completing it would be 220 years.[47]

In the meantime, early in the Mexican War, the Tehuantepec route came more clearly into public view. It was discussed with growing enthusiasm in the expansionist press. It was first considered in terms merely of a right of transit through territory presumably remaining Mexican. The right would be exercised by responsible American entrepreneurs. A right of transit across Tehuantepec had already been conferred on a Mexican citizen. It had been given by Santa Anna in 1842, to José de Garay, together with a lavish grant of land. A survey of the route had been made by an Italian engineer, Cayetana Moro, and an account of the project and survey had been published in book form in several editions in London and in Mexico City in the years 1844–6 in efforts to attract capital. The expectation of American expansionists was at first merely to redirect the right into the hands of Americans at the peace table.

A farsighted expansionist who early glimpsed these possibilities was the editor of the New York *Sun,* Moses Y. Beach. In the autumn of 1846 he believed that a quick peace with Mexico was possible. He, himself, would help to secure it, and with it, a transit right. Peace would be favored, he believed, by the better elements in Mexican society and, especially, by the hierarchy of the Roman Catholic Church. The military element, he thought he could

[47] William M. Burwell: *Memoir Explanatory of the Transunion and Tehuantepec Route* (Washington, 1851), 13.

reach through an influence he had with General Juan N. Almonte, once the Mexican minister in Washington. He had little knowledge of the Spanish language, but he had a comely and intelligent woman assistant, who spoke Spanish fluently and was, besides, a Roman Catholic. She could be taken along to Mexico City as interpreter. She was Jane McManus Storms, of an age approaching forty and experienced in the ways of the Mexican world. Daughter of a Troy, New York, politician, who had been a member of Congress (William T. McManus), she had married William F. Storms at an early age, but was separated from him. She and her father had been associated with Aaron Burr in New York in an unsuccessful attempt, in the early 1830's, to establish a German colony in Texas. At that time she had lived briefly in Texas. Her relationship with Aaron Burr had been resented by Madame Jumel Burr. She was the "woman in the case" in an uncontested suit for divorce in 1834. She was well known in New York journalistic circles as a Washington correspondent and editorial writer for the New York *Sun,* writing under the pen name "Montgomery." Apparently she was in the good graces of Buchanan.[48]

The plan of Beach was to get the war settled and then to take, as a broker's fee for his services, the right of transit across the Isthmus. He was aware, without doubt, of the Garay right but believed it could be transferred. He hoped to acquire, also, for good measure, a banking privilege in Mexico City. He probably did not expect to engage in canal building himself. He was no more an expert in that field than in diplomacy. He doubtless expected to interest capitalists in the franchise, when obtained, and let them do the grubby work of excavation. He would content himself with an entrepreneur's profit. In the autumn of 1846 he brought his idea to Buchanan, and received encouragement. The President, also, encouraged him. Polk had a weakness for casual contacts in diplomacy and thought a treaty worth considering might conceivably emerge from this enterprise.[49]

On November 21, 1846, Beach was given a commission as con-

[48] Edward S. Wallace: *Destiny and Glory* (New York, 1957), ch. 12.
[49] Quaife (ed.): *Diary of Polk,* II, 476–7.

fidential agent of the Executive. That was five months before Trist's mission was ordered. Beach was directed to proceed to Mexico City to explore peace possibilities with an understanding that he might turn any he found to good account. He was informed of the terms he must obtain as a minimum. He was warned to confide his official status to no one, except, possibly, to the American consul in Mexico City. If questioned he was to let it be known that he was going on private business. He was to receive compensation for his services at the rate of six dollars a day and, in addition, traveling expenses.[50]

His preparations for the mission were unconventional. He acquired letters in good number from Roman Catholic prelates on the Atlantic seaboard addressed to their opposites in Mexico City. He took along, as chaperon, either his wife or his daughter—the records are not clear as to which. He traveled via Cuba, picking up a British passport in Havana, together with further letters of introduction from Catholic prelates.[51] Armed thus, he and his entourage arrived in Vera Cruz in January 1847. He was arrested and held there for several days as a spy. His letters, however, were apparently effective, for he was permitted presently to go on to Mexico City.

In Mexico City he opened friendly relations at once with the Catholic clergy. He gained full value from his letters and from the charm and energy of his interpreter. He found the Catholic hierarchy in distress. Santa Anna's cohorts were extorting contributions from the Church for the support of the war. The dictator, an anti-clerical himself, was in the north with the army, fighting the invading forces of Taylor. An insurrection of clericals at the capital occurred. Beach rashly joined it. He may have done so in discouragement. He had found Almonte a member of the war faction, uninterested in peace. Worse yet, reports circulated, later found to be true, that the precious transit right had passed into the

[50] The commission given Beach appears in Moore (ed.): *Works of Buchanan,* VII, 119–20.

[51] The presence of the party in Havana in January 1847, is attested by a letter from there signed "Montgomery," describing the exceptional value of the Tehuantepec route, which appeared in the New York *Sun,* January 20, 1847.

hands of the hated British, and was out of reach. It had passed, together with its land grant, to Ewen C. Mackintosh, British consul at Mexico City, by articles signed in December 1846 and January 1847.[52] It was held by a London banking house, of which Mackintosh was the Mexican partner. Most disheartening and terrifying was that Santa Anna, in the midst of the clerical uprising, appeared unexpectedly on the scene, boasting he had defeated and driven Taylor back at the great battle of Buena Vista. The clerical uprising collapsed on the return of the soldiery.

Beach was obliged to take to his heels, leaving behind his hopes, and even his personal belongings, and carrying only a price on his head.[53] He and his party with difficulty, by using unfrequented roads and, doubtless, clerical help, managed to reach the seaboard, where Scott had, in the meantime, established himself. Leaving "Montgomery" at Vera Cruz, Beach returned to New York City, crestfallen and unrewarded, except to the extent of his six dollars a day and traveling expenses. On his arrival in New York he sent Buchanan a report in which he claimed that the insurrection, touched off by him in Mexico City, had held Santa Anna and five thousand troops long enough in the city to ensure the success of Scott's operations at Vera Cruz.[54] The most significant outcome of the misadventure was that, in the heart of the editor, was generated a desire for a Draconian solution of the Mexican problem.

The Polk government still hoped, however, that a peace treaty would include the transit right. In March and April 1847, in preparing for the Trist mission, it kept this objective prominently to the fore. In these months Vice-President George M. Dallas prepared for the press an article on Tehuantepec and its canal route. He was a relative and close associate of Walker, and doubtless knew what was transpiring on the subject in the inner circles of the Cabinet. His article saw the light of day in a not very conspicu-

[52] Mackintosh was a member of the London firm of Manning & Marshall, which had been active as agents in the readjustment of the Mexican debt. He was consul general in Mexico from 1842 to 1852.

[53] Justin H. Smith: *War with Mexico* (2 vols., New York, 1919), II, 11–14, 330–2.

[54] Moses Y. Beach to Buchanan, June 4, 1847, Department of State, Special Agents, Vol. XV, National Archives.

ous semi-literary Philadelphia journal, the *Spirit of the Times,* on April 19, 1847. Why that journal was chosen for so notable a piece is not clear. Perhaps the idea was to conceal from Whigs the intent of the administration to open a new negotiation, and to inform the public of the canal route without revealing that it was to be a condition of peace. The public would hardly suspect that such a journal would contain an inspired article. The piece, in any case, was at once taken over into the columns of the Washington *Union,* and thence into an engineering periodical, the *Journal* of the Franklin Institute, and into the *Bankers' Magazine* of New York, and into other journals.[55] The gist of the article was that in any peace settlement with Mexico an item not to be overlooked should be a right of way, irrevocably ceded, or a strip of land, across the Isthmus of Tehuantepec for a canal or railroad. A sketch of the background of the project was given. The value of a canal there for the United States and for the world was emphasized. The ease of construction and low cost were dwelled upon. Dallas knew that a right of way had been conferred on Garay, and he had before him, as he wrote, the published account of the Moro survey of the route. He relied heavily on that survey for the very optimistic judgments he rendered of the feasibility of the route and for his low estimate of twenty or twenty-five millions as the cost of construction. He obviously assumed that ownership by a Mexican of a right of way and of a land grant could be transferred to the United States and thence to an American citizen or citizens.

At the cabinet meeting described earlier in this narrative in connection with the Trist instructions, the transit right was discussed with special earnestness. It seemed worth paying for handsomely. No itemized list of prices was considered, but lump sums for concessions to be obtained were debated. A lump sum suggested by Buchanan as a maximum for New Mexico, the two Californias, and the transit right was $15,000,000 in cash, plus assumption by the United States of the damage claims of American citizens. A

[55] Philadelphia *Spirit of the Times,* April 19, 1847; Washington *Union,* April 26, 1847; Franklin Institute *Journal,* XLIV (July 1847), 15 ff.; *Bankers' Magazine,* II (October 1847), 224 ff.

higher figure was suggested by the President. He was willing to go as high as $30,000,000. So was Walker, whose thinking showed the influence of conversations with Dallas. Walker attached greater importance to the transit "across the Istmus [*sic*] of Tehuantepec than to the cession of New Mexico & the Californias, and if that object could be obtained he was willing to pay $30,000,000, but without it he was not." He thought the transit right should be made a *sine qua non* of a treaty. A figure of $25,000,000 as a maximum, if no transit right could be obtained, was finally agreed on, which apparently meant an evaluation of $5,000,000 for the transit right alone.[56] These were the terms Trist carried to the abortive negotiation with Santa Anna already described.

In the meantime the diplomat of the New York *Sun* who had fared so badly in his effort at peace in Mexico City, had been urging, since his return, a complete military occupation of Mexico. He had accelerated his output of editorials on the Mexican question. He had become the *avant coureur* of "occupation" in the press. For a time he was content to define occupation, in the normally accepted sense of the term, as of a temporary nature. He thought it ought to continue for only about five years. It should continue until Mexico had paid full indemnity to the United States for past injuries. The presence of American troops in Mexico would be a stimulus to her. It would release and channel her creative energies. It would end the disorders and oppressions of her war lords, encourage the development of her resources, and facilitate an early and easy payment of the indemnities. Upon payment, a return of the overrun territories could be arranged. To be sure, Mexico might prefer not to have them back. She might prefer a permanent connection with the United States. That was a possibility never to be ruled out.[57]

This campaign had no apparent effect for months. The public had little taste for a complete overwhelming of Mexico. The expansionist press did not rally to the cause; the Whig press remained hostile to it. Some Whigs were circulating rumors that

[56] Quaife (ed.): *Diary of Polk,* II, 471–5.
[57] New York *Sun,* June 10, July 19, 20, 1847.

Beach had been on a secret mission to Mexico City on behalf of the administration. They even were asserting that his editorials were trial balloons of the administration to test out public sentiment regarding complete occupation. He finally felt obliged to meet such slurs on his reputation as an independent and fearless editor head on in his own columns. On May 27, 1847, he wrote: "It has been suggested that we went on a secret mission from the Administration to Mexico. We went on our own business, and when that was concluded, returned, having neither the fear nor favor of cabinets before us. So far from having been on a mission from the Administration, we here say, that it has no office in its gift that we would accept, as our own business is of more profit and importance than any Government diplomacy." [58] This was independence, boldly proclaimed, and neither the President nor Buchanan felt it desirable to say him nay.

Late in the summer of 1847 Beach published an editorial captioned, significantly, "Mexico Annexed to the United States." He introduced it without explanation, in discussion of the related slavery issue, as a kind of aside. He denied that Mexico, if annexed, would swell the ranks of the slave states. The Mexican people and the Mexican state legislatures would never agree to enter the Union as slave states. If they were admitted by Congress they would come in free, and Congress would have no power to impose slavery on them either as states or as territories. "Mexico will be occupied and eventually annexed, such is the great and determined purpose, as well of the Mexican people as our own." [59]

This editorial may be said to have opened formally the campaign to annex Mexico. It enlisted, it is true, few followers at first. The hour for followers to gather was yet to come. Trist's mission had not collapsed; news of the insulting peace terms offered by Mexico had not yet become known; General Scott had not yet electrified the nation by his triumphal entry into Mexico City. Undaunted, however, Beach pressed the standards forward. His flow of editorials urging annexation became incessant. Every phase of annexation

[58] Ibid., May 27, 1847.
[59] Ibid., August 12, 1847.

was examined repeatedly in detail. He had become an expert on the subject by virtue of the time he had spent in Mexico City. He was not loath to let this be known. He referred repeatedly, if always casually, to his stay in the city, describing it first as lasting several months, then expanding it genially into a winter's sojourn.[60] He wrote of the state of affairs in that unhappy land with an authority rivaled only by that of the famous war correspondents of the New Orleans press. He had penetrated the inner wishes, emotions, and needs of the Mexicans, the subterranean sources of their politics, the inner spirit of their institutions, and, above all, the desperate need of the people for a change in their oppressed state. The impression he was able to give was of firsthand knowledge of Mexican affairs, and this was of great value to the cause and even to himself financially. It was sufficient compensation for all his labors for peace even had he received no compensation from his government at all. It gave authority to his impassioned crusade, first for occupation, then for annexation. If he overrated his achievements he did so only a little, when he wrote, in the autumn of 1847:

> Whether our government in Mexico shall be military, territorial or other, is not for us to decide. We were the first to strike for occupation; that being accomplished, we leave details to the authorities at Washington. And now that the press and the country, following our lead, have declared for occupation, and even the European press has acknowledged its expediency and justice, we may briefly review the results that will follow the consolidation of Mexico with the United States.[61]

Beach believed he was actually shaping programs for the President. When he read, in the message of December 1847, the recommendations for imposing a stringent peace settlement on the stubborn Mexicans, he confided this idea modestly to his readers in the words: "We can almost detect our own thunder reverberating in the Message."[62]

An item naturally emphasized, among the gains a well-drawn peace would bring, was a future canal at Tehuantepec. This was

[60] Ibid., May 22, June 7, 1847.
[61] Ibid., October 22, 1847.
[62] Ibid. (w.), December 11, 1847.

pronounced one of "the results that will follow consolidation." But nowhere was it set forth with more feeling than in an editorial in the early autumn of 1847:

> THE GREAT COMMERCIAL NECESSITY of this age and most particularly of our Union, is a short passage to the Pacific. . . . Whether it is gained by breaking asunder the Isthmus of Darien or cutting through the nearer route of Tehuantepec, this republic should stand by her interests with watchful eye and ready hand. . . . At this hour the Cabinet . . . have the power to secure to our citizens the precious, the priceless right of way across the Isthmus of Tehuantepec, and bitter and heavy will be the judgment of the nation upon their negligent servants if they throw away this all-important advantage. . . . Let them not dare to tell us that Tehuantepec is of no value—that it is an impractical route for navigation—that the harbors are useless—for none of this is true. . . . From the commencement of our controversy with Mexico, we have hoped the administration had its eye on two vital points, the prevention of a new monarch on our borders, and a passage to the Pacific. If the United States fails in either, it would be better for Mr. Polk, and better for the nation, if he had never held the reins of government.[63]

The old haunting fear that the priceless right would get into British hands before the United States acted remained with Beach. He had heard rumors, already in Mexico City, of a transfer of the right. He believed that except for the intrigues of "the McIntoshes and their co-laborers Mexico would not have resisted us as she has." He thought:

> It will be ten chances to one when we commence the passage across the Isthmus of Tehuantepec that this same McIntosh will show a title from the Mexican government to a strip of land the whole way from thirty to sixty miles wide, for which he will demand his own price from the United States. To our positive knowledge a single individual, an Irish subject of Great Britain, holds a title to the great valley of California, sixty miles in width and over one hundred and sixty in length, which has been, like McIntosh's Tehuantepec strip, and mines, obtained as collateral security for Mexican bonds.[64]

[63] Ibid. (d.), September 30, 1847.

[64] Ibid., November 20, 1847. The reference to an Irish subject of Great Britain holding title to the great valley of California is a garbled version of the MacNamara affair. Eugene MacNamara was an Irish priest who applied to the au-

No less intent than Beach upon acquiring the Tehuantepec strip for the United States was Matthew C. Perry, Commodore of the Gulf Squadron. He had been appointed to that charge just prior to the assault on Vera Cruz. He was a brother of Oliver H. Perry, of War of 1812 fame. An aggressive expansionist, he was destined to achieve repute by forcing Japan to open her doors. He used that opportunity to proclaim American sovereignty over the Bonin Islands, a group southeast of Yokohama. After the capture of Vera Cruz he took the first opportunity to send a craft to the Coatzacoalcos to learn the depth of water over the bar and the navigability of the river inland. He obtained, through the adroitness of his brother-in-law, Commander Alexander S. Mackenzie, the loan of a map of the entire Tehuantepec route that had been made by a surveyor in the employ of the Mackintosh company. By what inducement the loan was obtained was not disclosed, but a copy was sent at once to the Bureau of Hydrography and was published. The Commodore had three surveys made of the river's mouth under differing flow conditions. He himself was in and out of the river several times.[65] What he thus learned, and hoped still to learn, he reported in May 1847 to Washington:

> On my next visit to the River [Coatzacoalcos], I propose to ascend it a much greater distance, perhaps as high as Sitio de Morelotitlan, and shall be careful to transmit to the Department an ac-

---

thorities in Mexico City and at Santa Barbara in California, in 1845–6, for an *empresario* privilege to settle as many as 10,000 Irish people in the inner valley. His application was sent back and forth between Mexico City and Santa Barbara. In both places it was viewed with embarrassment and suspicion, and was ultimately denied. Enough of it became public to make it a basis for such rumors as Beach and other expansionists were spreading. It was used by Frémont to justify his activities in California. See Hubert H. Bancroft: *History of the Pacific States* (34 vols., San Francisco, 1882–90), XVII, 215–23; *Senate Reports,* 30 Cong., 1 Sess. (Serial 512), No. 75, pp. 19–25.

65 Published copies of the charts of survey are in Hydrographic Office, Record Group 37, National Archives. They are: 1847(1) "Sketch from the Mouth of the Coatzacoalcos River to the Town of Mina Titlan"; 1847(2) "Carta del Istmo de Tehuantepec. Copied by order of Comre. M. C. Perry, U.S. Home Squadron, Mexico, 1847, by W. May, Lieut. U.S.N. [with an inset] Plano de la Boca del Rio Coatzacoalcos"; 1848(1) "Chart of the Mouth of the Coatzacoalcos River Surveyed Jan. 1848."

count of my explorations. The persons engaged in surveying the route to the Pacific are employed by an English company, but it has occurred to me that if a Canal is ever to be opened across the Continent of North America, it should be executed by the Government or people of the United States. Destiny has doubtless decided that the vast Continent of North America from Davis' Straits to the Isthmus of Darien shall in the course of time fall under the influence of the Laws and institutions of the United States, hence the impolicy of permitting any European Power or interest to obtain a footing within the prescribed Latitudes. With such considerations in view I deemed it politic to take formal possession of the Goazacoalcos [*sic*] as far up as I ascended, and to invite the submission of the populous Towns, mostly inhabited by Indians, which are situated near its headwaters. In a treaty of Peace with Mexico I presume the exclusive right of way across the Continent could be secured by stipulation, but whether my views may or may [not] be considered visionary and chimerical, the explorations which I propose to make as soon as other occupations shall permit, cannot but contribute to some useful end.[66]

The Commodore, directed by the Secretary of the Navy to continue his good work, had repeated soundings made of the depth of water over the bar at the river's mouth. But the soundings proved uniformly discouraging. They established a depth of not over 12½ feet, as the charts sent home only too clearly showed.

This discouraging information was promptly made known to members of Congress by Lieutenant Maury, of the Department of Charts and Instruments. Other chilling phenomena of nature at the Isthmus were also described by him, which propagandists had not yet reported—the "northers," which periodically roar across the waters of the Gulf in terrific force, piling up rollers that break destructively across the bar, and hurricanes at some seasons, with like results. On the Pacific side, moreover, he reported bars which were,

[66] Commodore Matthew C. Perry to John Y. Mason, May 24, 1847, Naval Records, Home Squadron, Commodore M. C. Perry's Cruise, March 15 to July 19, 1847, National Archives. See also ibid., June 8, 27, 1847. John Y. Mason to Perry, July 23, 1847, Naval Records, Record of Confidential Letters, I, September 13, 1843, to February 23, 1849, National Archives. A report by Lieutenant Alden to Perry in 1847 of soundings at the bar and in the river is referred to in *De Bow's Review,* XXII (March 1857), 369–70.

if anything, worse. Veteran seamen described them as "truly awful." [67] Bars were thus found as discouraging to commerce and diplomacy here as they had been in the Oregon Country.

The final discouragement came in the Trist negotiation, described earlier in this chapter. Trist had suggested in this negotiation, in accordance with his instructions, that the transit right at Tehuantepec be ceded to the United States. The answer of the Mexican commissioners was brief, informative, and conclusive.

> In the 8th article of your excellency's draft the grant of a free passage across the isthmus of Tehuantepec to the South Sea is sought in favor of the North American citizens. We have orally explained to your excellency that, some years since, the government of the republic granted to a private contractor a privilege with reference to this object, which was soon transferred, with the sanction of the same government, to English subjects, of whose rights Mexico cannot dispose. Therefore, your excellency will not won-

[67] Maury was the government expert uniquely equipped to give intelligent judgments on sea routes for world commerce. He had access, as head of a scientific bureau of the Navy, to naval cruise records and often, also, to logs of commercial mariners. He was a scientist of note, a pioneer in the domain of oceanography and hydrography. He was a practical mariner, also, who knew especially the haunts and the habits of whalers. He was recognized throughout the world as an authority on ocean currents, weather, prevailing winds, and harbor and river conditions. His sailing charts were widely used, and his concept of great-circle measurements, in ocean travel, was well known and employed. He used this knowledge to inform politicians and public regarding the Tehuantepec route, but only toward the close of the Mexican War. He may have felt some diffidence about exposing the errors and exaggerations in the propaganda of powerful Northern politicians and editors. He had, however, strong supporters among Southern members of Congress. His appraisals of overland and sea routes were favorable to the South. He favored a transcontinental railroad out of Charleston, and a canal route, if a canal were undertaken, across New Granada. He revealed in his writings on the Tehuantepec route the distortions and fallacies of the Moro survey and of any cost estimates based on them. He gave vivid descriptions of dangers from storms at both ends of the route, and of the weakness of the argument of nearness as a determinant in choosing a route for a canal. He called attention to health conditions at Tehuantepec, of diseases especially prevalent there, such as the deadly "vomito" that afflicted the soldiers, a virulent form of yellow fever. Illuminating letters and articles of his in this campaign are Maury to T. Butler King, January 10, 1848, *Southern Literary Messenger,* XIV (1848), 246–54, later published in *House Reports,* 30 Cong., 1 Sess. (Serial 526), No. 596; Maury to Calhoun, March 29, 1848, *Hunt's Merchants' Magazine,* XVIII (1848), 592–601; Maury to Solon Borland, February 7, 1849, *Southern Literary Messenger,* XV (1849), 260–6; also ibid., 441–57.

der that upon this point we do not accede to the desires of your government.[68]

English subjects had stolen a march on Americans again! They had preceded Dallas, Polk, Walker, and even Beach. Nothing could be done, for English subjects were less easy to dispossess than Mexican. Trist gave up the contest. He did not even press the question in the final negotiation. But expansionists of the press had sterner stuff in them, and throughout the autumn and winter of 1847–8 they kept the issue of Tehuantepec before the American public, urging that All Mexico be taken in order that this key to the future greatness of the Republic in the Pacific should be firmly held by Americans.

[68] Mexican Commissioners to Nicholas P. Trist, September 6, 1847, *Sen. Exec. Docs.*, 30 Cong., 1 Sess. (Serial 509), No. 52, p. 337.

Chapter VI

Sectional and Party Attitudes

THE METROPOLITAN communities of the North Atlantic seaboard were the primary centers in the nation of the All Mexico drive. They were its emotional, intellectual, political, and even diplomatic base, if the penny press was a true reflection of them. They represented that remarkable combination of idealism, humanitarianism, and patriotism, which propelled the All Mexico crusade. Their enthusiasm, combined with their power, was significant. These were the great urban centers of influence in the Democratic party. They formed concentrations of voting strength unmatched elsewhere in the nation. Their leaders were accustomed to sit as chieftains in party conclaves and in Congress. To the historian of the All Mexico drive, studies of their sociological and psychological "ethos" in the 1840's would be very helpful, but none have been found,[1] and penning them would be a labor for specialists who could devote volumes to them. Here only a suggestion or two can be offered.

In these cities rank-and-file Democrats were unquestionably commoners. Their leaders were proudly, indeed, vociferously, so. They were conscious of the service they had rendered in New York

[1] Studies of immigrant elements in those cities usually deal either with their acculturation or with their connection with political machines.

and in Pennsylvania in the election of 1844, in overthrowing the pro-British Whigs. They were suspicious of monarchies, of the British especially, and of intrigues carried on by them in the New World. They were fanatically republican and fiercely egalitarian. For all the lowly in America they had high hopes. Many were immigrants or offspring of immigrants. They had affection for relatives and friends in the Old World and a corresponding indignation against the oppressions, tyrannies, and famines visited on them, especially in Ireland. They valued the swift reports of foreign news which the penny press offered and the editorials denouncing the oppressiveness of monarchical governments and monarchical institutions generally. Many spoke foreign languages. As polyglots they tended to be tolerant of recent arrivals from abroad, and not unwilling to add a few Latin American strains to the promising mixtures already in the nation's melting pot. They were likely to be affiliated with some Tammany Hall type of organization. Other than these general observations, little can be said of them with confidence. Present methods of ascertaining the attitudes and emotions of the masses by opinion polls were not yet invented. In New York City, a straw in the wind is that, at a war rally, the greatest of them all, intended to whip up enthusiasm for All Mexico, Tammany Hall was the host. The "unterrified democracy" was much in evidence there, as the press noticed. Also present were more "respectable" elements, those who discerned in Mexico profits to be derived from speculation, trade, and investments, as well as idealists and humanitarians attracted by the sublime prospect of regenerating a whole people.[2] In other cities the war rallies were of the same character.

But the historian, momentarily persuaded that the urban communities in the East were the favorite abiding places of democracy, patriotism, and vision, is rudely reminded by Democratic editors in the interior that in these cities were also Whigs in large numbers, that here were nests of stockjobbers, moneylenders, and Hunkers, who had little interest in the oppressed of other lands, who were

[2] *New York Herald,* January 30, 1848; *Cincinnati Gazette,* February 7, 1848.

cold to the idea of rescuing people in adjacent areas and giving them the freedom enjoyed by Americans, who, in short, were interested only in their own narrow concerns. The historian is further confused by recalling that on the Oregon issue the Democracy of New York City was not ready to risk war to save a promising country up to 54° 40′ from the jaws of the British lion.

In the trans-Allegheny West the Democratic press exhibited less enthusiasm for All Mexico than it did in the urbanized East. The nearest approach to it lay in the area north of the Ohio. Yet even there editorials on the issue appeared only occasionally, as compared with the steady flow of them in the penny press. The voltage in them was, also, lower. A common device of editors who were uncertain of the feelings of their public was to reprint, with little or no comment, the inspired editorials of the penny press. The exaltation, the fiery idealism, which the All Oregon cause had called forth in the Middle West, was conspicuously absent in the All Mexico cause. Some editors actually expressed a willingness to make do, for the present, with California and New Mexico. Some editors were willing to include the sparsely inhabited areas extending to the Sierra Madre Mountains. Editors showed they were aware of the fact that a heavy population of colored and mixed-breed elements encumbered southern Mexico, and that regenerating them would mean sharing with them the privileges of American citizenship. There seemed to be fear that a radical cure of the Mexican problem might have undesirable side effects for the residents already in the temple of freedom.

The editor of the *Indiana State Sentinel* noted on October 30, 1847, after a visit to New York City, that the disposition in the East as regards acquiring All Mexico was "ahead of any manifestation . . . made in the west. . . . Before travelling east we never heard a man seriously advocate the incorporation of the *whole* of Mexico into our Union; but we can assure our readers that we heard many a respectable man advocate such a measure at the east, and we are equally sure that the idea is rapidly diffusing itself among the eastern people." At this time the editor indicated his own ambitions to be the acquisition of California, New Mexico, and the Sierra

Madres. The Sierra Madres would give the United States the whole watershed of the Rio Grande. By November 13, 1847, however, he reprinted approvingly a warning from the Washington *Union,* that if Mexico would not come to terms of peace, if she would continue an unceasing war, then we must fulfill our destiny. "If nothing short of reducing the whole of that country to a province of the United States will satisfy that infatuated people, they will have to be satisfied. We must extend our conquests, even if it be for no other purpose than to obtain a satisfactory boundary and a satisfactory peace." [3]

The Detroit *Free Press,* a Cass organ in 1847, attentive to the counsels of the Washington *Union,* observed on November 29, 1847, that there would be time enough to decide the question whether Mexico should ever become an integral part of the Union, "when the actual resident population of Mexico shall seek such a connexion, and when they shall be prepared for it, both morally and politically." On February 11, 1848, under the caption "The Absorption of Mexico," it maintained, in common with the Washington *Union,* that All Mexico was a "ridiculous assertion put forth by the whig prints, to furnish whig members of Congress an excuse for refusing to vote supplies. The destruction of the national independence of Mexico was never thought of. The friends of the administration mean to carry out its measures; and that platform is laid down in the message, which avows its design of preserving the nationality of Mexico. The idea of absorbing her is, indeed, 'a painted devil,' fit only to fright 'the eye of childhood.' " [4] On June 8, the paper carried the final Senate vote on the ratification of the peace treaty without comment or pang of unhappiness over the terms.

The *Illinois State Register* spoke a language more nearly that of the Eastern penny press than was heard elsewhere in the Northwest. Illinois was probably the most expansionist of the North-

[3] *Indiana State Sentinel,* (s.w.), October 30, November 10, 13, 1847. The editor seems to have been less expansionist in 1847 than he had been in 1846. See ibid., December 8, 1846.

[4] Detroit *Free Press,* November 29, 1847; February 11, 1848.

western states, indeed, was considered the New York of the Middle West. On November 12, 1847, the editor, exchanging blows with Whig editors over the issue, whether a war for the purpose of thrashing a people into the blessings of good government was proper under the Constitution, insisted that the present war was begun solely for self-defense and was being continued merely to redress wrongs, indemnify losses, and protect national security. But if our army were now to be withdrawn without attaining those ends, we would be the laughing stock of the world. We were being forced by continued Mexican intransigence to choose between taking merely part of her territory or the whole. The latter course was preferable. It would mark the dawn of a new and glorious era for the benighted and oppressed people of Mexico. The conflict would then be proved to have been a "war of philanthropy and benevolence." [5]

The *Cincinnati Enquirer* probably expressed an honest average of Northwestern opinion. It was a faithful organ of the party and listened with respect to the views of "Father Ritchie" of the Washington *Union*. Its editor expressed on August 18, 1847, a pensive wish that Mexico would indemnify us for the expenses of this war "which by a series of aggressions she literally thrust upon us. If she is not prepared to do this otherwise, we are willing to extend the 'area of freedom,' by accepting a portion of her territory most contiguous to our own, and important to our commercial, mercantile and industrial interests." After revealing so much, the editor sat back and waited patiently for his next cue. This came with the President's Message of December, which was approved warmly. The President was cited as disavowing any desire to destroy the nationality of Mexico or to hold possession of that country longer than may be absolutely necessary to bring its government to peace. The President was determined to have full indemnity for the past and security for the future, which included acquiring a portion of territory which Mexico cannot hold or govern, and which, if ceded, would be redeemed from its present condition. To all this the edi-

[5] *Illinois State Register,* November 12, 1847.

tor agreed. He declared, early in 1848, when the issue of the annexation of Yucatán arose, that he was against it, but hoped that our armies would not be withdrawn from Mexico until a stable republican government had been established there. He thought aid should be given Mexico in this work. "The blessings that have flowed from wise laws, and will continue to swell the tide of our prosperity, should not be possessed with a selfish spirit, but all who wish to drink of the pure waters of freedom should be welcomed as brothers in the great work of regeneration." News of Mexico's action in finally agreeing to the Trist treaty of peace was reported by the editor unashamedly as "gratifying intelligence." [6]

But politicians, no less than editors, are the voice of the people, and numerous prominent Democratic politicians in the Northwest recorded themselves in Congress and elsewhere in favor of an All Mexico program. Cass, Allen, Hannegan, Douglas, and Breese all did so, and Cass, by his pronouncements, endeared himself—so, at least, the managers of the party thought—to his section. Acting on this belief, they chose him for their leader in 1848. Yet such Whigs as Corwin, Chase, Giddings, and Lincoln did represent the Northwest also and must be presumed to have known the wishes of the section. In the 1848 election Cass won all the electoral votes of the section. He won, however, only a minority of the popular vote in each Northwestern state. He was topped everywhere by a popular majority which was divided between Whigs and Free-Soilers. In the congressional elections of that year the results were likewise unclear. In Ohio, Michigan, and Wisconsin the opposing sides won about an equal number of seats. Only in Illinois and Indiana did Democrats conclusively carry off the honors, and few among those elected had been All Mexico men.[7]

The truth is, public opinion in the Northwest was sharply divided. Society was compartmentalized. Counties in southern Ohio, Indiana, and Illinois were settled by people Southern in origin.

[6] *Cincinnati Enquirer,* August 18, December 13, 1847; February 3, June 7, 1848.

[7] Edward Stanwood: *A History of the Presidency* (2 vols., Boston, 1928), I, 243; *Whig Almanac, 1850,* 4.

Counties in the north were settled from New England, the Middle Atlantic States, and Europe. Majorities in state elections were narrow and easily reversible. On all issues voters were influenced by memories and habits of the homeland. On the Mexican issue doubts and uncertainties existed, even among Democrats. Appetites for territory were dulled by reflections of what would come with the territory. Destiny called for territory to the Isthmus. Yet in southern Mexico were millions of those Mexicans, a mixed race, unfit now, and probably for a long time to come, for the privileges and responsibilities of American citizenship. The eagerness, so movingly expressed by editors in the urban East, catering to polyglot readers, for uplifting Mexicans, was not felt in the rural West. Moreover, the independence boasted of by editors of the penny press was not felt to a like degree by Western editors, who considered themselves intimately part of the communities in which they made their living. Lukewarmness in the press for All Mexico is probably accounted for by forces such as these.

The adjustment that politicians of the Northwestern Democracy made to these complex conditions, especially if they hoped to unite behind themselves the expansionism of all sections, as Polk had done in 1844, was quite standard. In speeches they thrilled audiences with visions of the American future, with high aspirations and noble ideals, with breathtaking panoramas. They did not burden listeners too much with definitions, problems, or specifications, and they dispensed sedatives on the slavery issue.[8]

In the South the press exhibited little of the extremism on opposing sides of the All Mexico issue found in the North. If the section harbored any Democratic newspaper, outside of Baltimore, with the sustained fervor for All Mexico of the penny press of the North Atlantic seaboard, the paper did not rise to notice. On the other hand, none of the passionate resistance which appeared in the Northern anti-slavery press to the extension of territory was found there either. The average temperature among Southern

[8] Cass was especially dexterous in combining a daring expansionist policy with prudence on the slavery issue. Much sentiment for the Wilmot proviso was present in his state. See pp. 178–9.

Democratic journals was more lukewarm than that in the North. Democratic editors were all aware of the undesirability of sharing the privileges of American citizenship with people of mixed blood. Some accepted the views of the President as set forth in the message of 1847 and as relayed by the venerable Ritchie. Others took the lead of Calhoun, who was vehemently opposed to any program, in whatever form, of annexing All Mexico.

In the Southwest some Democratic journals recommended lusty bites of sparsely settled Mexican territories as far southward as the Sierra Madre Mountains. The New Orleans *Delta,* the New Orleans *Mercury,* and the *St. Louis Union* had appetites of that sort. None had a sustained taste for All Mexico.[9] The *Louisville Democrat* was outspoken in rejecting All Mexico ideas and adhering to old theories of Manifest Destiny. On November 2, 1847 it wrote:

> Whenever organized resistance to our authority ceases, and the country is virtually peaceable, we can dictate our own terms. That they will be generous and beneficent to Mexico, no one doubts. As to the annexation of Mexico to the United States by force, it cannot be done. We don't take States into this Union until the inhabitants desire it, and present their republican constitution with a request for admission. We may annex territories, but the inhabitants must annex themselves by their own act. It will be time enough to annex a Mexican State, or discuss the expediency of it, when such a State applies for admission. This may not happen whilst the present population and influence govern the States of Mexico, but these will change.[10]

On March 9, 1848, in discussing the Trist treaty *projet,* the editor voiced warm approval of it and for reasons refreshingly candid:

> Besides, we have by this treaty, not the best boundary, but all the territory of value that we can get without taking the people. The people of the settled parts of Mexico are a negative quantity. We fear the land, minus the people, is not worth much. We think all Mexico will fall, piece by piece, into this government; but then it

[9] New Orleans *Delta,* September 26, 1847; New Orleans *Mercury,* November 1, 1847; *St. Louis Union,* September 25, 1847.

[10] *Louisville Democrat,* November 2, 1847.

must first be settled by a different population, and the union effected by other means than the sword.[11]

The people of the settled parts! They were the rub, even for those who cherished the noblest concepts of Manifest Destiny. If only they could be got rid of, the rest would be easy.

Politicians of the South with heavy appetites for Mexico were probably as numerous as those in the North. They were of less political stature, however, and were less often quoted. Like Northern politicians, they had a liking for imprecision of language, which left the way open for changes of mood. But they did manage somehow to convey the impression that if no really good solution to the Mexican problem appeared, they would have no insurmountable aversion to absorbing most of Mexico. Some cited destiny as authority. Others cited the danger that foreign governments might stoop to pick up scraps of the Mexican map left lying around by American scissors wielders. They showed little of the noble interest in regenerating Mexicans that dreamers in the Northeast expressed. Geographically the prominent expansionists were distributed as follows: Representative Louis McLane, Maryland; Senator Herschel V. Johnson, Georgia; Senator James D. Westcott, Florida; Senators Dixon H. Lewis and A. P. Bagby, Alabama; Senators Jefferson Davis and Henry S. Foote, Mississippi; Senators Sam Houston and Thomas S. Rusk, Texas; Senator David R. Atchison, Missouri; Senator Hopkins L. Turney and Representative Frederick P. Stanton, Tennessee. Houston and Foote were the main speakers at the great war rally in Tammany Hall in January 1848, and raised the rafters with impassioned All Mexico orations. Jefferson Davis proposed in the Senate an amendment to the Trist treaty *projet* which would have enlarged an already large cession by all or part of the states of Tamaulipas, Nuevo León, Coahuila, and Chihuahua. The amendment was supported by a number of the senators listed above.

But John C. Calhoun, outstanding in stature among Southern Democrats, opposed taking much, if any, Mexican territory. To

[11] Ibid., March 9, 1848.

him the war had seemed immoral and unconstitutional from the outset, and he had become steadily more fearful of its outcome as it dragged on, especially, of the effect on the peace of the Union and on the safety to the South of taking a great deal of Mexican territory. These fears were shared by a large part of the Democracy of the South.

Whigs were opposed not only to taking All Mexico, but to taking any, by force. They were consistent in that stand since they regarded the war as an iniquitous aggression against Mexico. One of their number, the eloquent Georgian John M. Berrien, brought a "no territory by conquest" resolution into the Senate early in 1847, for which every Whig present, except one, voted, to a total of 24. The one exception was a Senator from Louisiana.[12] However, the Whigs would have been satisfied to take, in exchange for the assumption by the United States of the prewar damage claims, the Bay of San Francisco.[13] In the Senate fight over the ratification of the peace treaty, Whigs showed a marked reluctance to take Mexican territory by force.

In the press, the Whigs adhered, for the most part, to the "no conquered territory" stand. The *National Intelligencer* and the *New York Tribune* set the pattern. They were willing to have San Francisco in exchange for the assumption of damage claims, but nothing more. A few Whig editors, protesting always that Polk had begun the war, were yet willing to end it by accepting California and New Mexico. Prominent among these were the editors of the New York *Courier,* the *Richmond Times,* and the New Orleans *Picayune*. Their wanderings from the path of party rectitude were jeeringly approved by Democrats. The Baltimore *American* was even willing to take, in addition to the Californias, territory southward to the Sierra Madre Mountains. Zachary Taylor had proposed this line in a letter of November 5, 1846, which was promptly published, and it was popularly known as "Old Zach's

[12] The tally was 29 to 24. The Whig maverick was Henry Johnson. *Sen. Jour.*, 29 Cong., 1 Sess. (Serial 492), 252.

[13] *Niles' Register,* LXXIII (1847–8), 197 ff.; *Cong. Globe,* 28 Cong., 2 Sess., 555 (March 1, 1847).

line." The editor of the Baltimore *American*, promoting Taylor for the presidency, saw special virtue in that line. It seemed to him an admirable compromise between the "no territory" and the "All Mexico" extremists. Also, he believed: "Nature having made it [the Sierra Madre] a boundary, let us accept it, and confirm the truth of nature." [14]

Editors sometimes write with tongue in cheek. Those with a literary flair, and with a feeling that they are independent of all parties, are especially prone to do so. The editor of the New Orleans *Picayune* was such an editor, who, on occasion, wrote breezily about "All Mexico." Early in January 1848, he wrote that while Congress was debating, and statesmen were building up theories, and politicians were fingering the public pulse, the Army was spreading itself over Mexico and giving a scent of Anglo-Saxonism to Mexican flowers:

> We may condemn, we may argue against the tendencies of a race of men of higher organization, bolder hearts, more enterprising minds, of superior thews and muscles, and stouter wills, to supplant weak and emasculated tribes—good authority can be evoked to show how wrong all this is—homilies to this day are written against the pilgrim fathers for ejecting the savages from the primeval forests of the North; but, until the eloquence of ethics can melt human nature and mould it anew, we apprehend the world will wag on much after the old fashion. No scrap of philosophy, nor moral essay, nor political disquisition can countervail the dangerous odor of fields in perennial blossom to an army of Anglo-Saxons.[15]

This has a distinctly All Mexico odor, and the *Picayune* has been cited as one of the Whig papers of the nation that upheld the All Mexico thesis. Yet five weeks later the same editor, referring to the Trist treaty *projet,* wrote:

> The line between conquest and indemnity is somewhat indistinct, like the point of division between the colors of the rainbow. It may be difficult to say where indemnity ends and conquest begins, but the questionable ground cannot be so broad as not to be covered by a treaty of peace which gives us New Mexico and Upper California. If the deficit in indemnity is so appalling as to require a

[14] Baltimore *American*, October 7, 12, 1847.
[15] New Orleans *Picayune*, January 8, 1848.

continuance of the war, it is doubtful if the balance, when it is made up, will not be regarded as conquest, not only by Mexico, but by our own citizens.[16]

A maverick among Whig journals was the *National Whig*, published in Washington. It is of special interest because it was so much cited by Democrats, has produced so much confusion among historians, and still creates dismay among those who would like to believe that the press is a medium of public enlightenment. The paper was ephemeral. It was established in April 1847, suspended publication for a time, and survived only to the spring of 1849. It was created to win the Whig presidential nomination for Taylor. His name appeared on its masthead from the outset, his achievements were glorified, his needs, as President, arranged for in advance. The Mexican War was denounced by the editor as a plot on the part of Polk to perpetuate himself and his party in power. Still, every American in wartime must rally to the flag. Polk had deliberately made the subjugation of Mexico inevitable. The Aztec empire must accordingly fall into our arms. It was not possible to undo the Gordian knot Polk had tied except by cutting it by annexation. "The whole of Mexico is upon us. It is already ours. We have it and we know it not." Congress should declare Mexico ours by right of conquest. It is our duty to close the war by the best method of pacification circumstances will allow. It would be desirable to get out of the war without a foot of Mexican territory, but "the popular voice will so demand the entire appropriation of Mexico that no man will think of opposing it." The virtue of American institutions is to sustain themselves over an indefinite extent of country. "If there is one thing for which they are fitted, it is this very principle."[17]

Such a course of enlightenment, intended for Whigs, was unhappily used chiefly by Democrats who sought to convince the electorate, by publishing well-chosen selections, that even Whigs

[16] Ibid., February 7, 1848. A necessary rule in a study of an editor's convictions on a critical issue is to live with him in a year or two of his files. Every editor indulges moods on occasion.

[17] Washington *National Whig*, April 7, October 8, 9, 15, 23, 1847. The editor was Charles W. Fenton.

were demanding All Mexico. These selections came, in later years, under the eyes of historians and the myth became established that the All Mexico agitation was actually bipartisan.[18]

[18] John D. P. Fuller: *Movement for the Acquisition of All Mexico, 1846–48* (Baltimore, 1936), passim.

Chapter VII

Problems

THE PROSPECT that a vast foreign territory would come to the United States at the end of the war and would be integrated into the Union generated problems. These were of unusual magnitude whether the acquisition was to be All Mexico or less. They became subjects of dissension between the sections, between the parties, and within the parties. They were under incessant debate in the press and in Congress during the war, and especially after the entry of Scott's army into Mexico City.

One of the gravest of the problems was the size and character of the population which would come with the territory. The Mexicans were estimated to number about eight millions. The greater part, by far, were colored. Half or more were Indian. A large fraction were mixed-bloods: mestizoes, samboes, Negroes, and mulattoes. Mestizoes were a union of Indian and white; samboes, of Indian and Negro. Only a sixth of the population was white, descendants of the conquering Spanish. Could such a mixture ever be regenerated? If it could be, how long would it take? What, in the meantime, should be the status of those people? What would be the effect on American institutions of admitting them to American citizenship? Who would become the owner of their ineffectually used lands? These were some of the problems raised.

Answers were usually sectional or partisan. But by no means was this always the case. Indeed, within sections and parties, answers diametrically opposite were sometimes given. Thus, the penny press of the Eastern seaboard, on the issue of regeneration of the Mexicans, was confident, as editorials cited above have indicated, that the process would be speedy. But the *New York Evening Post,* a liberal Democratic sheet, edited by a poet, was gravely doubtful. Indeed, it was impatient of images, drawn by the starry-eyed, of Mexicans as a people of Spanish or European descent and capable of easy regeneration. It wrote:

The Mexicans are *Indians*—Aboriginal Indians. Such Indians as Cortez conquered three thousand [*sic*] years ago, only rendered a little more mischievous by a bastard civilization. The infusion of European blood whatever it is, and that, too, infused in a highly *illegitimate* way, is not enough, as we see, to affect the character of the people. They do not possess the elements of an *independent* national existence. The Aborigines of this country have not attempted, and cannot attempt to exist *independently* along side of us. Providence has so ordained it, and it is folly not to recognize the fact. The Mexicans are *Aboriginal Indians,* and they must share the destiny of their race.

Now we ask whether any man can coolly contemplate the idea of recalling our troops from the territory we at present occupy, from Mexico . . . and thus, by one stroke of a secretary's pen, reconsign this beautiful country to the custody of the ignorant cowards and profligate ruffians who have ruled it for the last twenty-five years? Why, humanity cries out against it. Civilization, Christianity, protest against this reflux of the tide of barbarism and anarchy.

How we are to maintain our control over the Country—on what terms, under what contingencies—is a matter of detail, and subject to future events; but we do not believe there lives the American, with a true understanding of this country's interests and duties, who, *if he had the power,* would deliberately surrender Mexico to the *uncontrolled* dominion of the mongrel barbarians, who, for a quarter of a century, have degraded and oppressed her. . . .

No party in this country contemplates the dismemberment of Mexico proper, or the annexation of any portion of her population to our own. It would be a disastrous event for the whole confederacy. But we owe it as a duty to ourselves and the general cause of freedom, to keep our flag flying . . . till the progress of time, and the silent effect of our presence, our customs, our busy commerce, our active intelligence, our press, shall have breathed a new life into this unfortunate country, and we have some security that she will not be a curse to herself and to her neighbors.[1]

Western views concerning Mexicans and their regeneration were also pessimistic on the whole. The editor of the *Cincinnati Gazette*, for instance, discussing the problem early in 1848, brought the testimony of a Swiss scholar, Johann J. von Tschudi, regarding the mixed races of Peru to bear on the Mexican problem: "As a general rule they [mixed races] unite in themselves all the faults, without any of the virtues of their progenitors; as men they are generally inferior to the pure races, and as members of society they are the worst class of citizens." [2]

Cass was a believer in those views. Early in 1847 he said: "We do not want the people of Mexico, either as citizens or subjects. All we want is a portion of territory which they nominally hold, generally uninhabited, or, where inhabited at all, sparsely so, and with a population which would soon recede, or identify itself with ours." [3] He felt that a union of Americans and Mexicans would be an evil amalgamation, which would be deplorable in its results. His one comfort was that he did not believe it could happen in his day.

A year later he no longer looked upon amalgamation as so remote. He found comfort, however, in another reflection. Denying that he had ever advocated the annihilation of Mexico, he maintained that "if we were to obtain Mexico by absorption through the pores, or by swallowing through the throat—deglutition—it would not destroy us. He admitted it would be injurious; but if the obstinacy of the Mexican people should lead to that result, he had

[1] *New York Evening Post*, December 24, 1847. At the end of the war the editor approved the Trist treaty, though lamenting the folly of the Polk government in bringing on the war and expressing the conviction that California could have been peacefully obtained; ibid., June 9, 1848. Statistics on the racial composition of Mexico's population were estimates. A work sometimes cited was Thomas G. Bradford: *Comprehensive Atlas, Geographical, Historical and Commercial* (Boston, 1835).

[2] *Cincinnati Gazette*, January 26, 1848.

[3] *Cong. Globe*, 29 Cong., 2 Sess., 369 (February 10, 1847).

enough confidence in the intelligence of the American people to be assured it would not destroy us."[4]

Another Middle Westerner, Breese, of Illinois, thought much better of Mexicans as a result of readings he had done. He was able cheerfully to agree with Cass, therefore, that swallowing them would not prove fatal.

> Could they be brought under the happy influences of such a Government as our own, having all their rights, civil and religious, protected, what might we not hope from them? The Indian population, numbering about four millions, are reputed to be very gentle and quiet in their dispositions, apt to learn, and willing to improve, and, if not possessed of all the manlier virtues, have at least those which fully ensure their cheerful acquiescence to our control and rapid advancement under it. Take the population as a whole, and there is not a people on the globe more capable of advancement in the arts and sciences, and of assuming all the forms of the highest civilization. . . . I do not suppose, sir, the Mexicans are at this time fitted for an equal union with us; and much is to be done before they will be. By the infusion of our population among them (and they are now there in great numbers) . . . together with emigrants from Europe, who will not be slow to avail themselves of the unsurpassed advantages such a country enjoys, a gradual change in their manners, customs, and language, will ensue. Education will be diffused among the masses. Speech, the press, and religion will be free, and high opinions of themselves speedily generated; and considering the . . . aids to knowledge, and for its rapid spread, which the world now possesses, the period of their pupilage will be of short duration.

Breese added a touching picture of the eagerness of many Mexicans to reach the high levels of advancement which union with the United States would make available to all. The Puros, or republican elements, were, he disclosed, fighting our troops for no other purpose than to make sure those troops would not be called home. Nothing was so feared by the better elements as withdrawal of our forces, which would have the effect of delivering the people over to their native oppressors. "They see, in our advance, the dawnings of a brighter day for them and their children, and in glad anticipa-

[4] Ibid., 30 Cong., 1 Sess., 321 (February 8, 1848). See also ibid., 184, 216.

tion behold our azure studded with their stars. They see no refuge but in our free institutions, no shield but our power, and desire no nationality but that which an union with us will give them. This party, sir, may submit for a time [to a treaty refusing annexation], but will not agree [to it], and if they obtain power, true to their original design, they will become embroiled with us to effectuate it. They have always been, and are now, the most clamorous for war, and will oppose any accommodation which withdraws our army. . . ."

Breese asked a rhetorical question: "Were we to exclude men from the blessings of free institutions merely because of a difference in the color of the skin? The Mexicans are willing to give up their nationality in exchange for our free institutions; and he hoped to see, or, that his children would see, the extension of these institutions from one end of this continent to the other. He wished to know if Senators on the other side [Whigs] would give their consent to any act by which Texas should be given up. The enemies of free institutions [Whigs] were to be found in large cities; they were not to be found in the broad prairies of the West." [5]

In the South sentiment was more unified than in the North on questions involving the colored races, their characteristics, and their admissibility as citizens into the Union. Indeed, Southern feeling was solid, irrespective of party. The tendency was to fuse attitudes toward Mexicans and free Negroes and the ethics of the enslavement of a race into one conglomerate of emotion. On race issues Calhoun was the trusted spokesman of the section, and his postulates, even if not always his conclusions, went unquestioned. His views were expressed vehemently in Congress early in 1848:

[5] Ibid., 30 Cong., 1 Sess., App. 344–50 (February 14, 1848). The Breese view was held also by Buchanan; Philadelphia *Pennsylvanian*, December 25, 1847. It was spread widely in the United States through the writing of the war correspondents of the New Orleans newspapers, especially George W. Kendall of the New Orleans *Picayune*. See issues of November 27, 1847, January 9, 16, 1848. War correspondents lived with the invading armies and, of course, heard only one-sided reports. See also New York *Sun*, June 8, 1847; Baltimore *American*, October 16, 1847, January 8, 1848; *Illinois State Register*, November 26, 1847; *National Intelligencer*, January 20, 1848.

I know further, sir, that we have never dreamt of incorporating into our Union any but the Caucasian race—the free white race. To incorporate Mexico, would be the very first instance of the kind, of incorporating an Indian race; for more than half of the Mexicans are Indians, and the other is composed chiefly of mixed tribes. I protest against such a union as that! Ours, sir, is the Government of a white race. The greatest misfortunes of Spanish America are to be traced to the fatal error of placing these colored races on an equality with the white race. That error destroyed the social arrangement which formed the basis of society. The Portuguese and ourselves have escaped,—the Portuguese at least to some extent—and we are the only people on this continent which had made revolutions without being followed by anarchy. And yet it is professed, and, talked about to erect these Mexicans into a Territorial Government, and place them on an equality with the people of the United States. I protest utterly against such a project. . . .

But . . . suppose all these difficulties removed; suppose these people attached to our Union, and desirous of incorporating with us, ought we to bring them in? Are they fit to be connected with us? Are they fit for self-government and for governing you? Are you, any of you, willing that your States should be governed by these twenty-odd Mexican States, with a population of about only one million of your blood, and two or three millions of mixed blood better informed—all the rest pure Indians, a mixed blood equally ignorant and unfit for liberty, impure races, not as good as the Cherokees or Choctaws?

We make a great mistake, sir, when we suppose that all people are capable of self-government. We are anxious to force free government on all; and I see that it has been urged in a very respectable quarter,[6] that it is the mission of this country to spread civil and religious liberty over all the world, and especially over this continent. It is a great mistake. None but people advanced to a very high state of moral and intellectual improvement are capable, in a civilized state, of maintaining free government; and among those who are so purified, very few, indeed, have had the good fortune of forming a constitution capable of endurance. It is a remarkable fact in the history of man, that scarcely ever have free popular institutions been formed by wisdom alone that have endured. . . .

It is a very difficult task to make a constitution to last, though it may be supposed by some that they can be made to order, and

[6] The reference is unclear.

> furnished at the shortest notice. Sir, this admirable Constitution of our own was the result of a fortunate combination of circumstances. It was superior to the wisdom of the men who made it.

Calhoun called attention to the transformation which administration leaders had allowed to take place in the professed objectives of the fighting. They had, at the outset, disavowed any intention of extinguishing Mexico. They had assured the public that indemnity and peace were their sole aims. Now they were preaching conquest as the inexorable outcome of the hostilities. Calhoun protested against the change. He gave solemn warning of the calamitous effects the conquering of Mexico and reducing her to a province of the United States would have on the institutions of the Union.

> There is not an example on record of any free State even having attempted the conquest of any territory approaching the extent of Mexico without disastrous consequences. The nations conquered have in time conquered the conquerors by destroying their liberty. That will be our case. . . . This Union would become imperial and the States mere subordinate corporations. But the evil will not end there. The process will go on. The same process by which the power would be transferred from the States to the Union, will transfer the whole from this department of the Government (I speak of the Legislature) to the Executive. All the added power and added patronage which conquest will create, will pass to the Executive. In the end you put in the hands of the Executive the power of conquering you.[7]

Of the dangers an absorption of Mexico would pose for the institutions of the Union, Calhoun had earlier issued warning. He had given in the Senate a year before his prophetic admonition that Mexico is to us forbidden fruit to eat of which is to die.[8] Such a warning even expansionists, if reflective at all, could not entirely ignore.

One of them, Louis McLane, a friend of Calhoun, proposed to the House, a fortnight after Calhoun's speech, a plan which would have stopped short of the absorption of Mexico. It would have preserved, as far as still possible, her territorial integrity. It would

[7] *Cong. Globe*, 30 Cong., 1 Sess., 98 (January 4, 1848).
[8] Ibid., 29 Cong., 2 Sess., 356 (February 9, 1847).

have retained for the United States, however, some of the practical advantages of an absorption by reducing Mexico to a protectorate status. As part of a peace settlement a perpetual commercial treaty would be signed with her, by which she would thereafter be a satellite revolving helpfully in the orbit of the United States.[9] But this interesting proposal was never given real consideration, for in a matter of weeks the Trist *projet* reached the Senate and overshadowed it.

On the question of the amount of time needed to effect a regeneration of the Mexicans, there were wide differences of opinion. Racists of the more extreme sort felt the answer was "never." O'Sullivan, in his more idealistic moments, had thought it might be a century. Dreamers in the penny press believed it would take relatively little time.[10] A useful rule of thumb to apply, if a study should ever be made of these estimates, is this: the more intense the eagerness for annexation, the shorter the period needed for regeneration. Breese and others thought ten years would be ample time.

Similar diversity of opinion appeared regarding the opportunities land-hungry Americans would have to acquire farms in an incorporated Mexico. The opportunities were, by some, loosely described as "immense" and "limitless." Senator Foote, of Mississippi, described them more specifically, as millions of acres of the richest land in the world.[11] But a Whig diplomat, Waddy Thompson, who had spent years in Mexico and had some knowledge of the facts, described them in depressing terms. In a speech delivered in South Carolina, which was republished in full in the *National Intelligencer,* he said, after pausing long enough to protest, on moral and other grounds, to taking any Mexican territory:

> I would take no more Mexican territory—first, because we have no right to it; none is pretended but the ruffian—the robber right of conquest; it is the bandit's right . . . who is stronger than the traveller, and takes his purse. . . .

[9] Ibid., 30 Cong., 1 Sess., 201–2 (January 19, 1848).
[10] Philadelphia *Public Ledger,* May 25, 26, 1846.
[11] *Cong. Globe,* 30 Cong., 1 Sess., App. 128 (January 19, 1848).

Secondly, I would not take more territory, because it will be worse than valueless. It will be a heavy charge upon our Government instead of an indemnity to our citizens who have claims upon Mexico. A friend said to me today that we will not take the people, but the land. Precisely the reverse will be the case; we shall take the people, but no land. It is not the country of a savage people whose lands are held in common, but a country in which grants have been made for three hundred and twenty-five years, many of them two and three hundred miles square; nothing paid for these grants when they are made, and no taxes upon the lands afterwards; it is all private property, and we shall get no public domain which will pay the cost of surveying it. I speak of the country beyond the Rio Grande. We shall get no land, but will add a large population, aliens to us in feeling, education, race, and religion—a people unaccustomed to work, and accustomed to insubordination and resistance to law, the expense of governing whom will be ten times as great as the revenues derived from them.[12]

But to such gloomy views Ambrose Sevier, chairman of the Senate Committee on Foreign Relations, and friend of the President, gave answer. He did so by way of reply to a charge of a Tennessee Whig, John Bell, that circumstances in the Mexican War were so arranged as to compel us to hold the whole of Mexico by right of conquest, and that this had been looked to by the President himself.[13] Sevier maintained that all the President had ever wanted was an indemnity, that he had never thought of taking the whole of Mexico, that until the beginning of this session such a thought had never been even imputed to him or to his Cabinet, and that "if things are [now] taking this tendency, it will be because of the course of the argument which has been pursued here."

As to what the Senator from Tennessee had said on the . . . impossibility of civilizing the [Mexican] mass, he reminded the Senator of his own system for the removal of the Indians to the West. In carrying out that system, bills had been passed locating some of these Indians on the borders of Arkansas, where they had formed themselves into a government, and had since flourished, and had become an orderly, prosperous, and easily-governed people. He did not see any greater difficulty in civilizing and governing the mass of Mexicans. As to the right of voting, he did not know

[12] *National Intelligencer* (t.w.), October 21, 1847.
[13] *Cong. Globe,* 30 Cong., 1 Sess., App. 191–201 (February 3, 1848).

that the Mexicans would gain it from the Constitution. The Indians had not gone up to vote that he knew of.[14]

Sevier did not think it necessary to point out what result would follow a removal of Mexicans to reservations. That was self-evident —a public domain for the land-hungry. Nor did he make a distinction between removals from northern Mexico and from southern Mexico. But, as it turned out, in northern Mexico, after it had been acquired by the United States, Indians were removed to reservations and the expected result came to pass—a public domain for the land-hungry.

A problem more divisive even than race was raised in the All Mexico discussion—the extension of slavery. It was precipitated early in the war. A proviso appeared in Congress in August 1846 as an amendment to the Two Million bill.[15] It provided that in any territory acquired by the United States as a result of the war, neither slavery nor involuntary servitude was ever to be permitted. The man who moved it, David Wilmot, was a Pennsylvania Democrat of free-soil convictions. He had not boggled at the annexation of Texas, for Texas had been slave territory prior to its annexation and so its admission would involve no extension of slavery. But Mexico was free, and an annexation of any of her territory would probably result in an extension of slavery.

The Wilmot proviso was provisional. It was to go into effect if, and when, territory was acquired. Whether territory would be acquired, whether all of it or part of it would be suitable to slavery, whether, in a ceded territory, Mexicans would consent to slavery, whether slavery could be excluded there by Congress under the Constitution—all these were questions wide open. The proviso was an adventure into the unknown. It was hardly more than a moral abstraction. Yet for these very reasons it released emotions, pro and con, so deep and so violent as almost to destroy the Union.

Among the unknowns one of the most controversial was the extent of the expected cession. California and New Mexico were anticipated almost from the beginning. As American armies moved

[14] Ibid., 30 Cong., 1 Sess., 302–3 (February 4, 1848).
[15] Ibid., 29 Cong., 1 Sess., 1214–17 (August 8, 1846).

deeper and deeper into Mexico, more and more territory appeared on the horizon and the awful fear grew among anti-slavery men that All Mexico might become part of an empire of slavery. If Mexico were absorbed, would Cuba come next?

In expansionist journals, and especially in Beach's and Bennett's, the Pearl of the Antilles was coming into increasing notice. It was also attracting Polk and his Cabinet. It fascinated O'Sullivan.[16] In the spring of 1848 he and Senator Douglas had an interview with Polk, and tried to enlist him in the cause of taking Cuba. At a second interview O'Sullivan confided to the President his relations with a filibustering group that was intent on freeing the island and bringing it to the United States. He was obviously sounding out the President. But Polk balked at the idea. Purchasing the island from Spain was what he favored and this was the course he recommended to his Cabinet. Walker embraced the idea at once; he was ready to pay as much as $100,000,000. Buchanan was reluctant. He feared the effect of opening the Cuban issue on the fortunes of the party in the presidential election.[17] To anti-

[16] The increased agitation for Cuba was a reflection largely of the activity of three incorrigible New York City expansionists—O'Sullivan, Beach, and "Montgomery" (the wife, now, of William L. Cazneau). O'Sullivan had a brother-in-law in Cuba, an important planter who desired annexation of the island to the United States, and O'Sullivan, as secretary of a junta in New York City, worked toward that end constantly, in 1847 and later, flitting back and forth between his home and Havana. Beach and the New York *Sun* were equally active. "Montgomery" was an editor (the only one, for a time) of *La Verdad,* the organ of the junta, which was printed on the presses of the *Sun.* Hope was high that soldiers of the American Army in Mexico, on being mustered out, would be induced to help free the island. General William J. Worth, one of their commanders, had visions of that sort. The action of the French revolutionary assembly, early in 1848, in freeing the slaves in the French West Indies led slaveholders in Cuba and in the United States to fear that Spain might take a like step in Cuba. This helps to explain the filibustering from the United States to Cuba, and the famous Ostend Manifesto of 1854, a declaration by three American diplomats, including Buchanan, in Europe, that the United States would be justified in seizing Cuba to ward off the emancipation danger. Basil Rauch: *American Interest in Cuba: 1848–1855* (New York, 1948), ch. 2.

[17] Quaife (ed.): *Diary of Polk,* III, 446, 469, 475–93. In the spring of 1851 O'Sullivan furnished and equipped a vessel for a filibustering attack on Cuba. The plan was to join other vessels, from New Orleans and elsewhere, on the Georgia coast, and thence to proceed to Cuba under the command of Narciso López. Spanish authorities in New York City were informed, and O'Sullivan's vessel, the *Cleopatra,* was seized by federal agents as she was about to depart with several hundred Hungarian and German revolutionaries aboard. Indictments were brought against

slavery men the agitation for Cuba seemed a new menace. They saw in press discussion of it an extension of the All Mexico agitation. They clung to the Wilmot proviso all the more desperately.

Another of the unknowns unsettling the public was whether, and to what extent, California, New Mexico, and Mexico proper, were suited to the growth of slave crops, whether the climate and soil there were attractive from the point of view of a slave economy? Testimony pro and con was before the public. Some Northern Democrats thought sections of Upper California well suited to cotton. Buchanan, early in the war, believed that slavery was inevitable in a Mexican cession and that, therefore, too big a slice ought not to be demanded. He was ready to take land as far south as a line projected from El Paso on the Rio Grande to the Pacific—the line, in short, of latitude 32°. If more were taken, he told the Cabinet, embarrassment, national and international, would follow; the anti-slavery opinion of the world would be alienated. Walker objected. He wanted to go to a line at 26°—a projection from the mouth of the Rio Grande. He was willing to fight the world rather than submit to outside meddling. The President believed that none of the Mexican territory would support slavery, and certainly not California or New Mexico. His personal preference was a line at 26°, but he was willing to be satisfied, if necessary, with 32°.[18] Outside the Cabinet, Calhoun held that no part of Mexican territory was suited to slavery. He was charged by his critics with opposing a Mexican cession solely because freedom

---

O'Sullivan and two others for violation of the Neutrality Act of 1818. The case came to trial a year later. The position of the defendants was that the recruits aboard the *Cleopatra* were "colonists" heading for Texas. Some of the "colonists" turned state's evidence. The leaders did not deny that the colonists would have had an opportunity at sea to change their minds and set a course for Cuba. Juries in such cases in New York and in New Orleans always included enough loyal Democrats to render conviction impossible. O'Sullivan's jury was hopelessly divided, and he was freed. Subsequently the expansionist press carried on an agitation to extract teeth from the Neutrality law. For the record of O'Sullivan's trial, see *U.S.* v. *John L. O'Sullivan et al.*, O.D., cr. 267, National Archives; *New York Tribune,* April 25, 1851–April 3, 1852; *Democratic Review,* XXX (1852), 314; XXXI (1852), 209, 352, 553. See also Robert G. Caldwell: *Lopez Expeditions* (Princeton, 1915), ch. 6; J. F. H. Claiborne: *Life and Correspondence of John A. Quitman* (2 vols., New York, 1860), II, 218–25.

[18] Quaife (ed.): *Diary of Polk,* I, 495–7.

was ineradicably settled there and he wanted no territory that would spawn free states.

Whigs also were in disagreement over the question whether Mexican soil would support slavery. Northern anti-slavery Whigs of radical views believed it would, and wanted none of Mexico, therefore. Moderates on the slavery issue were willing to have the port of San Francisco, but no more. Southern Whigs, of nearly all convictions, saw virtue in an analysis made of the problem by the pro-slavery protagonist from South Carolina, Waddy Thompson. In a speech to his South Carolina constituents on October 15, 1847, he declared that Mexico was decidedly not a New Canaan, though, even if it were, none of it should be taken if its taking would set our children to war. "He would stake his life that no part of the territory could or would be occupied by slaveholders. He would consent to be gibbeted, or, if dead, that his bones should be dug up and made manure of, if ever a slaveholding state were formed out of any portion of it." His speech was given wide circulation by the *National Intelligencer,* a Whig journal of moderate views on slavery.[19]

Southern Whigs believed, also, that the Mexican inhabitants of ceded territory would be unwilling to establish slavery. Mexicans were predominantly a colored people and would have compunctions about slavery for Negroes. They had made slavery illegal in Mexico. As part of the United States they would adhere to that decision, assuming they were to have any voice in the matter. Also, the labor of peons was so much cheaper than slave labor could be, that, competitively, slavery would be ruled out.

A maverick among Whigs on all this range of issues was Gamaliel Bailey. He was a Northern Whig of moderate anti-slavery views. His position resembled that of John Quincy Adams. He disliked slavery, but, as a supporter of the Constitution, was willing to tolerate it in the states. He was implacably opposed to its extension. He had been incensed by the annexation of Texas, which he thought an unholy conspiracy of the slave power. He

[19] *National Intelligencer* (t.w.), October 21, 1847; *National Era,* November 4, 1847.

considered the Mexican War another conspiracy of the same sort. He had once been associated with James G. Birney in editing the *Cincinnati Philanthropist*. He was made editor during the Mexican War, on January 7, 1847, of the *National Era*, newly established in Washington as a Whig journal, under the auspices of the American and Foreign Anti-Slavery Society. His corresponding editor was John Greenleaf Whittier.

A half year after the *National Era* was founded, Bailey became convinced that in no part of Mexico, from its northernmost limits in California to its southernmost in Central America, could slavery ever establish itself. Nature there was too unfavorable to it. If all Mexico were to be acquired, it would be for all time free. Inasmuch as this was so, any territory obtained from Mexico could be considered a *cordon sanitaire*, preventing a seepage of the evil system to adjacent regions. More important, such a *cordon* would serve to weaken, and ultimately destroy, the disease in our own Southwest, where it had only a tenuous hold. The more territory obtained from Mexico, therefore, the better. The only question was: How could it be justly acquired? Forcing a cession would, of course, be unthinkable. That would be sheer conquest. The United States should declare peace. Invitations should then be issued to each of the Mexican states to voluntarily enter the American Union. The Mexican states, reassured by safeguards to their right of choice, would vote to come in. They would come in on a basis of full equality with the older states of the Union. Here was O'Sullivan again!

The *National Era* first presented these ideas in a four-column editorial on August 19, 1847. The editorial was entitled: "Plan of Pacification and Continental Union." It pointed out that the conquest of Mexico was virtually completed. What was next? If, by virtue of conquest, we take a third of her territory, a conflict over slavery will convulse the United States. In that conflict slavery will win. "The Curse will move like a pestilence over the new territory." As for Mexico, she will remain an embittered enemy. Our armies will have to stay there to enforce peace. Peace should, instead, be unilaterally declared by the United States. A proclamation to that effect should be issued, together with an invitation to each Mexican state to become an American state. That friendly invitation would be accepted. The blessings of the American system would be extended over the new states—freedom of trade and of religion, education, security, efficient use of Mexican resources, a free market for America's manufactures, a transit across the Isthmus. Nineteen of the Mexican states—those having an adequate population—would become sister states of our Union. All would remain non-slaveholding. Their Mexican population would see to that. These people are as well fitted for the responsibilities of republican government as the hordes of immigrants now pouring in upon us every year. Under American rule they would be rapidly educated and assimilated. Here was Bailey's answer to the question "What shall we do with Mexico?" The answer was further spelled out in attractive detail in later issues of the paper.[20]

The "Plan of Pacification and Continental Union" had a reception in the press less than favorable. The reception in the Southern press was uniformly hostile. The Southern conviction was that this was an insidious abolitionist plot to multiply free states on the borders of the South and thus to destroy the power of the South. Most Northern Whigs were convinced that the scheme was utterly chimerical; anti-slavery Whigs, that its expansionist temper was a "pandering" to the robber spirit of conquest. The only newspapers that took it seriously were those of the penny press on the Eastern seaboard, which thought it a variant merely of their own ideas. Bailey was driven, in self-defense, to reprint gossip, which originated in Washington and was circulating in the expansionist press, to the effect that even John Quincy Adams favored annexing Mexico and hoped thus to submerge the Southern slavocracy in a sea of free Mexican votes.[21]

[20] *National Era,* August 19, 1847.

[21] Ibid., December 23, 1847. The facts concerning Adams's views were the opposite of those set forth here. Adams wanted none of Mexico. His position was embodied in a resolution for which he and forty other Northern Whigs voted on January 3, 1848. The resolution called for withdrawal of American forces from Mexico, peace without any indemnities, a southern boundary that should run through the desert between the Nueces and the Rio Grande (Benton's proposal), and Mexican payment of any just damage claims of American citizens. See *Cong.*

Of all the questions rising out of the Wilmot proviso the one most ominous and basic was constitutional. It was whether the Constitution, with all its restrictions on congressional power, extends to the territories—any territories, present or yet to be acquired. Calhoun thought it did so extend. The Constitution follows the flag into the territories. Under the Constitution Congress is without the right to forbid slavery in the states. It is similarly without the right to do this in the territories, which are the common possession of the states. The Wilmot proviso, which would prevent people of the slave states from taking property in the form of slaves to the territories, is, therefore, patently beyond the power of Congress to adopt. Congress, Calhoun recognized, had adopted the Missouri Compromise in 1820, but he believed this had been an unconstitutional exercise of power.[22]

Webster set forth the Northern anti-slavery point of view. He denied that the Constitution follows the flag into the territories. Territories, though they belong to the United States, are not part of the United States in the constitutional sense. They resemble the colonies of England, which are possessions of, but are not part of England. Congress has greater powers in the territories than it has in the states—its powers are not inhibited there by the ordinary limitations of the Constitution. Slaves, moreover, are not property in a legal sense. They are human beings held in servitude. Congress has long exercised a power over slavery in the territories. It excluded slavery from certain territories by the Compromise of 1820 and it has complete authority to do so again under the Wilmot proviso.[23]

The Wilmot proviso thus opened conflicts of law and theory

Globe, 30 Cong., 1 Sess., 93–4 (January 3, 1848). Gossip in the press attributing All Mexico desires to Adams originated, characteristically, in the irresponsible New York *Sun*. See New York *Sun* (w.), December 4, 1847, a letter from a correspondent signed "Seneca."

22 The Calhoun view is set forth in *Cong. Globe,* 29 Cong., 2 Sess., 453–5 (February 19, 1847); ibid., 30 Cong., 1 Sess., 875–6 (June 27, 1848); and ibid., 30 Cong., 2 Sess., App. 272–5 (February 24, 1849).

23 The Webster view is set forth in ibid., 30 Cong., 1 Sess., 1060, 1077 (August 10, 12, 1848); ibid., 30 Cong., 2 Sess., 579–80 (February 21, 1848); ibid., App. 259–60 (February 23, 1849); and ibid., 272–5 (February 24, 1849). This is the famous Webster-Calhoun clash. A good analysis of the issue in a wider setting

which became more heated as the debate progressed. It became a threat to the unity of the two sections. More immediately, it became a threat to the unity of the two political parties. It threatened to break each into a Northern and a Southern wing. In the Democratic party the Northern wing was deeply infected with Wilmotism. Its congressional representatives wavered between loyalty to the administration and loyalty to their free-soil constituents. William Sawyer, of Ohio, who remained loyal to the administration, graphically described the predicament of his colleagues. Many of them would vote for the proviso and then confess to him privately afterwards that "it was the bitterest pill they had ever swallowed." [24] Southern Democrats, on the other hand, considered Wilmot, and any who gave him countenance, traitors, little better than abolitionists.

The Whigs were in the same predicament. "Conscience Whigs" considered Wilmot a prophet to be followed. Regular Whigs, especially Taylor boosters, who had plans of campaigning in 1848 without a platform and with only a candidate, considered him a radical who was raising troublesome issues. They gave wide circulation to the Waddy Thompson speech which had pointed out that Mexico was utterly unsuited to slavery. Southern Whigs were certain that Wilmot was a firebrand, and that any Northern Whigs, who lent him countenance, were traitors. In both sections Whigs, devoted to the party, thought it best, therefore, to take cover under a policy of "no more territory." Here was a tent sheltering all. In both sections it would keep Whig clothes dry in the storm that was rending the Democratic party over the issue of slavery in the Mexican cession.

One means to safety in the storm adopted by regulars of both parties in the North was a program of "hush" in the press, a conspiracy of silence almost. This had been forming ever since the dangerous brawling began over the Texas issue. On the Democratic side, O'Sullivan had muted the slavery issue regularly in his

---

is Arthur Bestor: *State Sovereignty and Slavery 1846–60* (Springfield, Ill., 1961). Calhoun had once thought the Missouri Compromise constitutional.

[24] *Cong. Globe,* 29 Cong., 2 Sess., 427 (February 15, 1847).

philosophic writings on Manifest Destiny. Father Ritchie had committed himself to the same program in his writings in the *Union*. On the Whig side the *National Intelligencer* regularly kept discussion of slavery in connection with the territories to a minimum. Other regular party journals imitated this forbearance as widely as was possible in a quarrelsome world, and it was mentioned by Calhoun hopefully in an address at Charleston as reflecting the attitude of the more responsible portions of the Northern press.[25]

A further way of avoiding the troublesome issue of congressional power in the territories was to make use of a bypass. This started off from the unquestionable right of states to decide whether or not to have slavery within their borders. The only debatable ground was whether Congress had a similar right in the territories. If, now, all territories acquired from Mexico were simply admitted as states into the Union, without ever going through a territorial stage, the whole disruptive question of congressional power could be avoided. This avenue to peace was thought of by the *National Whig*—the Taylor organ—and was triumphantly proclaimed there in August, 1847.[26] It was widely approved by Whig regulars and was remembered later, in the crisis of 1850, by the party leaders, including Taylor himself.

But the Northern public stubbornly favored the Wilmot proviso. It distrusted the maneuvers of the two parties on the slavery issue. It was not persuaded by propaganda designed to show that slavery was impossible in the Mexican cession. As late as 1850, when Webster declared in the Senate, in an effort to preserve the Union, that slavery could not be established in the Mexican cession and that the Wilmot proviso was a mere taunt and reproach to the South for its way of life, and ought to be silenced, all he got was abuse and disbelief.[27] The Northern public clung to the proviso as a warning to expansionists in both sections of the Union that if

[25] *National Intelligencer* (t.w.), May 27, 1847.

[26] *National Whig*, August 18, 1847.

[27] As recently as 1847 Webster had laid claim to the proviso as his invention, his "thunder," in a speech to his constituents; *Writings and Speeches of Daniel Webster*, XIII, 359.

Manifest Destiny was ever to be fulfilled, at least slavery was to have no part in it, and that slavery was, in any case, never to be spread by the sword. The proviso was the Northern conscience giving answer to expansionist demands for an advance southward.

The congressional record of the Wilmot proviso reveals the hold it had on Northern opinion. In the House the proviso was attached as an amendment to the Two Million bill on August 8, 1846, by a vote of 85 to 79. The vote was significantly sectional. Those in the majority were all Northerners except two from Kentucky. The breakdown in party terms was: 53 Democrats, 28 Whigs, and 4 Native Americans.[28] In the Senate the amended bill was abandoned. In February 1847 the Three Million bill came before the House and the proviso was attached to it by a margin of 115 to 106.[29] On this occasion every "aye" vote came from the North. The majority was composed of 57 Democrats, 53 Whigs, and 5 Native Americans. But the Senate struck out the proviso and then adopted the bill. The majority here was chiefly Southern, though it was attained only with the help of a few Northern Democrats, the so called "dough-faces," who deserted their section. The bill was returned to the House, where, by a similar combination of Southern Democrats and Northern "doughfaces," it was enacted.[30] The *National Era,* bemoaning the result, bitterly attributed it to executive patronage, the "invisible force which moves mountains." [31] Eight state legislatures in the North, in the meantime, passed resolutions protesting against the admission of any territory unless it had been closed to slavery. These gathering evidence of Northern sectionalism led Calhoun to despair of the Union.

Since Wilmotism could not be made to subside, a compromise was obviously in order. Buchanan had one—partition of the expected territory by the line of the old Missouri Compromise [36°

[28] *Cong. Globe,* 29 Cong., 1 Sess., 1214–16 (August 8, 1846).

[29] Ibid., 29 Cong., 2 Sess., 425 (February 15, 1847).

[30] Ibid., 555 (March 1, 1847). The Northern Democratic senators who shifted were William Allen, John A. Dix, John Fairfield, John M. Niles, and Daniel Sturgeon; ibid., 573 (March 3, 1847).

[31] *National Era,* March 4, 18, 1847.

30′] extended to the Pacific. He proposed it to the Cabinet early in 1847, where it was unanimously approved.[32] From the point of view of politics it had much to be said for it. The 1820 line had been lived with in peace for more than a quarter century in the two sections. It symbolized a spirit of neighborly accommodation. Extended to the Pacific, it would divide approximately in half the territory generally expected then—California and New Mexico. The northern part of the territory would go to one side, the southern to the other. Considering that in neither part was slavery likely to be established, this solution of an abstract ethical problem was one which no reasonable man anywhere could quarrel with.

To spread this humane view Buchanan sent a letter late in August 1847 to a meeting of his admirers and to the general public. His thesis was that the Northern Democracy ought to favor such a compromise rather than quarrel over the harsh principle of the Wilmot proviso, especially since slavery could not possibly establish itself anywhere in California or New Mexico. The letter was shown to the President before mailing, and he approved it. Its thesis was the opposite of the one which had been urged by Buchanan on the Cabinet a few months earlier, but so accustomed had the President become to these shiftings by his Secretary that he did not even take the trouble to mention it. The letter, published in *Niles' Register*,[33] was widely regarded as an early shot fired in the battle for the Democratic nomination in 1848.

As such, it was not much of a success. Buchanan's Whig opponents, especially in Pennsylvania, pointed out at once that earlier in his career—in 1819, in the fight over the Missouri Compromise—he had eloquently opposed any extension of slavery to the territories. He had been a leader in the cause. This information they gave wide circulation.[34] Also, the *National Era* published a caustic analysis of the letter in an article captioned "The Secretary of State in the Field." Its mode of attack was to quote, first, the

[32] Quaife (ed.): *Diary of Polk*, II, 305, 308–9.
[33] *Niles' Register*, LXXIII (1847–8), 4.
[34] *National Whig*, September 20, 1847.

smooth generalizations offered by the distinguished author, and then to cite his *non sequiturs* and contradictory applications. Thus:

> "Let us leave the question of slavery where the Constitution has left it, to the States where slavery exists"—*therefore,* use the power of the General Government to extend it *where it does not exist!* "We compromised the Missouri question by allowing slavery to continue, where it already existed in United States territory, south of 36½ degrees"—*therefore,* let us allow it to be introduced into new territory, *where it is now prohibited!* "We admitted a sovereign State [Texas] applying for admission into the Union, with slavery established under her Constitution"—*therefore,* let us anticipate State action, and, under the sanction of the General Government, introduce slavery into *dependent territory,* over which Congress will have exclusive jurisdiction! "Slavery, in all probability, cannot exist in New Mexico and California"—*therefore,* the South will establish it there, or dissolve the Union, and so we had better let her do the former! "The question is not one of practical importance"—*therefore,* the Democratic party is in danger of being divided, if not destroyed, by it, and the Union is in danger of being dissolved! [35]

But the North's chief objection to Buchanan's plan was that, in dealing with a problem highly fluid and rapidly changing, it relied on a line fixed and predetermined. It proposed to divide an acquisition which might get as big as All Mexico, by the static old line of 36° 30′. Such a scheme would give the South, conceivably, four-fifths of the ultimate spoils of the war, for slavery, and the North, one-fifth for freedom. An even more serious objection was inherent in the plan. If Congress were to establish 36° 30′ as a set line between slavery and freedom in the Far West, expansionists in the North and South might feel impelled to add Central America and Cuba to the land of freedom. Tactically as well as strategically, Buchanan's letter was defective. In the campaign for the nomination it made its appearance too soon. Buchanan had been too eager. When the All Mexico movement got well under way, it was superseded by a more comprehensive, better contrived plan, that

[35] *National Era,* September 9, 1847.

of Lewis Cass, and Buchanan's sank into the background.

The plan of Cass was set forth in the famous Nicholson letter, sent to the public the day before Christmas 1847. It came late enough to take cognizance of the All Mexico movement. It was the popular-sovereignty plan. Its theme was that the power of Congress over the territories is not well defined in the Constitution. No express power is given Congress by the framers to do anything except dispose of land in the territories. No general legislative power is given at all. Since this is so, Congress should do nothing respecting local matters in the territories. It should leave local matters, such as slavery, to the people of the territories acting through their local legislatures. It should merely set up governments. In particular Congress should avoid the Wilmot proviso.

Cass observed that a great change had come recently over the mind of the public and even over his own.[36] The public had become persuaded that the issue should be kept out of Congress. It was, in any case, already settled. Slavery is impossible in California and in New Mexico for physiographic reasons. Reference was made by way of proof to the recent letter of the Secretary of State. Nor could slavery go into any area beyond the Rio Grande. To support this contention Cass cited a letter which Secretary Walker had published in 1844, which had made clear that slavery was unacceptable to the colored race of that region. Slavery is a question, thus, which, for any area hereafter acquired from Mexico, could be en-

[36] Cass could not have been judging public sentiment by that of his own state. Early in 1847 the Michigan state legislature resolved that it was the duty of the federal government to extend the principles of the Northwest Ordinance of 1787 to any territory thereafter acquired by the United States. On January 31, 1848, the lower house resolved by a vote of 52 to 3 that it would be repugnant to the moral sense of the nation for Congress to extend slavery to any area acquired by conquest, cession, or purchase, from which slavery had previously been excluded. Cass shifted his position repeatedly on the issue. In the summer of 1846 he declared himself favorably disposed toward the Wilmot proviso. Later, according to Buchanan, he took the view that Mexican territory should not be taken south of 36° 30′, to avoid the slavery issue. In the autumn of 1847 he moved toward an All Mexico position and also toward popular sovereignty. His shiftings received unfavorable comment in anti-slavery journals. See Michigan *Senate Journal 1847,* 166; *House Journal 1847,* 171; ibid., *1848,* 155–6; Moore (ed.): *Works of Buchanan,* VII, 286–7; *New York Evening Post,* January 3, 1848.

trusted to the people there in perfect confidence that the answer would be everywhere negative.[37]

The letter was a masterpiece of its kind. It gave something to every shade of opinion worth placating at the coming Democratic convention, and it took an offensive stand on nothing. It particularly pleased expansionists, East, West, North, and South. It hinted to them that territory beyond the Rio Grande, even, was on the way. It eschewed all controversy over the slavery issue. It left that issue to an authority which could do no wrong—the sovereign people. Most of all, it pleased the West. The doctrine of local self determination was political gospel to that section. The constitutional exegesis of the letter was open to question. To Calhoun, who was a profound constitutionalist, it seemed beneath contempt. For if authority over the territories was not vested in Congress, how could it get vested in a territorial legislature, a creation of Congress? Practical politicians are, however, urbane. What's the harm of a difference over the Constitution among friends! The letter was a platform of great promise on which to go before a nominating convention and, afterwards, before the people.

[37] The Nicholson letter is in *Niles' Register*, LXXIII (1847–8), 293–4.

Chapter VIII

The Demise of All Mexico

AN UNEXPECTED development occurred in Mexico while the American public was wrestling with problems rising from the coming territorial cession. Peace negotiations with the Mexicans were reopened late in 1847 by Nicholas Trist. He was acting irregularly in this matter. He no longer had the authority to negotiate. His powers had been canceled and he had been ordered home early in October 1847, after the failure of his negotiation with Santa Anna. A rebuke and a more peremptory order to return home had been sent him later by direction of the President. He had angered the President by taking for reference to his government a Mexican proposal that the disputed region between the Nueces and the Rio Grande be established as a buffer state. He should have rejected that proposal out of hand, the President felt. In accepting it for reference home he had shown weakness regarding the sensitive issue of the origins of the war. He had made concession to the Mexican contention that the Nueces was the boundary between the two countries. He had cast doubt on the President's contention that the boundary was the Rio Grande, and that the Mexicans, in crossing it, had invaded American territory, had forced war on the United States, and had shed blood on American soil. He had virtually given aid and comfort to the enemy.[1]

[1] The letters to Trist of October 6, 25, and 27, 1847, are in Moore (ed.): *Works of Buchanan,* VII, 425, 442, 444.

Dispatches to Trist were slow in arriving. Those canceling his powers, recalling him, and rebuking him had piled up on the way and finally had come through together, but only on November 16, 1847. They had been forty-one days in transit. By the time they arrived a new Mexican government had been set up, and this one was really ready to negotiate. Santa Anna, broken by his defeats, had resigned. His successor was Manuel de la Peña y Peña, the Presiding Justice of the Supreme Court, who had become Provisional President. Peña believed a prompt peace was essential if Mexico was to survive as a nation; that, if peace failed, the country would be overrun by the enemy with results which could not be undone. Reopening negotiations required courage. But Peña was a man of courage and integrity. He was supported by one of the Mexican parties, the Moderados, and also by Edward Thornton and Mackintosh, British intermediaries, who saw to it that Trist and the Mexicans stayed in touch with each other. Trist had sent Peña notification of the cancellation of his powers. He had offered, as a courtesy, to take back to Washington any proposal for peace the Mexican government might care to make. Peña, in turn, had asked Trist, shorn of powers though the latter was, to remain for renewed negotiations. Trist had refused, but had postponed his departure, partly to obtain an armed escort. He was asked to reconsider his refusal; he was assured that a settlement could be reached. He was encouraged by Scott to remain. A warm friendship had developed between those two men, based on a mutual antipathy for Polk. Trist hesitated, then stayed on.

Trist was an idealist. He had visions of the kind O'Sullivan had seen in earlier days. He was confident that Mexico, left to herself, would some day gladly enter the temple of freedom. It was inevitable, foreordained. But it could happen only when she was better prepared for entrance. A reconciliation between the two peoples must, in any case, come first. A forced union would be a disaster for both, especially for the United States. It was likely even to destroy the Union. A quick peace with Mexico was essential. If it were not made, all of Mexico would be overrun, and the government would disintegrate; then would come anarchy and, worst of all, a forced absorption by the United States, with all its attendant disasters. Politicians in distant Washington, surrounded by self-seeking advisers, did not know the great opportunity and great need for peace as well as did someone on the ground. The opportunity lay partly in the confidence the new Mexican leaders had in him. Trist was too modest to say this, but Peña did rely on the good will the Commissioner had displayed toward the people of Mexico as distinguished from their tyrannical and corrupt former leaders. The longer Trist reflected on these things, the clearer became his conviction that opportunity was rapping at his door, that it should not go unheeded, that it would probably never return if allowed to go by. "Now or never" was the word. On December 3, 1847, he withdrew his refusal to deal further with the Mexicans. He entered into negotiations with them, shorn though he was of authority to do so, and defiant of the orders he had received to return at once to Washington.[2]

The negotiation thus commenced extended over two months. On both sides its progress was precarious; it was a searching test of how much each side wanted peace. On the Mexican side, the negotiators persevered amid turbulent cross currents of military, factional, religious, and personal rivalries and fears. Any treaty acceptable to Americans would be, to Mexicans, a humiliating defeat, a capitulation to a conquering army, a forced transfer of a major part of the national patrimony to an aggressor. It would rub raw every nerve of the national pride. On Trist's side, the negotiation, in defiance of authority and in violation of law, was a labor of anxiety, also. Trist could never be sure but that he might look up from his work to find, beside him, an Army officer with Presidential orders for his arrest and expulsion in disgrace from the country.

Yet Trist, despite his predicament, was in a position of extraordinary bargaining leverage vis-à-vis the Mexicans. He was backed

[2] Trist's dispatch justifying his decision to renew the negotiation is a sixty-five-page document dated December 6, 1847, a copy of which is in the Trist Papers, Library of Congress. Part of the dispatch is printed in *Sen. Exec. Docs.*, 30 Cong., 1 Sess. (Serial 509), No. 52, pp. 231–68.

by Scott. He spoke for a conquering army. The Army, relatively inactive during the negotiation, was ready, on a failure of it, to fan out over the country. Also, Trist's very predicament strengthened him. His weakness was a source of power. His canceled instructions, still the basis on which he was negotiating, were less harsh than any that might replace them. They reflected a military situation long since passed, which could not, by Mexico alone, be restored. If the terms he required were declined, if the negotiation broke down, if a question were but postponed for reference to Washington, the result would be only a worsening of the outcome for Mexico, and the Mexican negotiators realized it. A mere threat to terminate the negotiation was terrifying to them. It was a threat of worse things to come. On the Mexican side the one great element of strength was, likewise, weakness—the prospect of anarchy if negotiations broke down, of guerrilla war, which in this case would be fought in desperation and would last indefinitely.[3]

Out of this composite of weakness and strength on both sides came peace. Peace, to be sure, was highly contingent and uncertain. The terms of the *projet* were merely a hope. They were subject to repudiation by an outraged President or by a deeply divided Senate. The terms of greatest importance concerned the boundary. A line was drawn along the Rio Grande from its mouth to the southern limit of New Mexico (just below El Paso), thence along New Mexico's southern boundary to its western extremity, thence north to an intersection with the Gila River, thence via the river to a confluence with the Colorado, and finally, by way of the boundary between Upper and Lower California, to the Pacific.[4] By this line territory comprising about a third of Mexico's domain was ceded to the United States. It was the minimum Trist had been authorized in April 1847, to accept. Within this cession, grants of land legally made prior to the opening of the war by Mexican authorities, were recognized and protected. Mexican sub-

[3] The course of the negotiation is fully described in documents submitted to the Senate by the President on February 23, 1848; ibid., No. 52, pp. 70–348.

[4] A useful map of the line, illustrating its relationship to the disputed Texan boundary which led to the war, is in Rives: *United States and Mexico, 1821–48*, II, opposite page 726.

jects who resided in the area became eligible for American citizenship. A sum of fifteen million dollars was given as payment for the cession. In addition, unpaid damage claims of American citizens against Mexico, to a maximum of three and a quarter million dollars, were assumed by the United States government. This figure was the sum total of the financial grievances of the American government against the Mexican government prior to the fateful crossing of the Rio Grande by the Mexican army. It had been deemed by the President and his Cabinet of sufficient dimension to justify a recommendation of war prior to the crossing. The negotiated *projet* was, on February 2, 1848, approved at Guadalupe Hidalgo by both sides and signed.[5]

On February 19, it came before the President. It had been brought to Washington by a special courier—a war correspondent of the New Orleans *Delta*. It created in Washington, and especially in Polk, perplexities equal to those of its negotiators. A settlement of territory reflects a military situation normally. This one did not. It reflected what had been a military situation ten months earlier. Of the tremendous victories won by American armies in those months, and of the great expenditures of blood and treasure which they had cost, it took no account. It made payments, actually, at old rates, for territories that had been conquered. An additional annoyance to the President was the nature of the dispatches Trist had written during the negotiation, justifying his conduct. Knowing full well he had worked himself out of a job, he had become actually insolent to the President.[6]

Yet something could be said for accepting the *projet* despite its

[5] A good account of Trist's role in the negotiation is Louis M. Sears: "Nicholas P. Trist, a Diplomat with Ideals," *M.V.H.R.*, XI (1924–5), 85. Valuable for the general account is Justin H. Smith: *War with Mexico* (2 vols., New York, 1919), II, chs. 28, 32. A more objective work is the older one of Rives, cited above.

[6] *Sen. Exec. Docs.*, 30 Cong., 1 Sess. (Serial 509), No. 52, pp. 231–301. Trist proposed impeachment of the President in a letter addressed to the Whig Speaker of the House on August 7, 1848; *Cong. Globe*, 30 Cong., 1 Sess., 1057–8 (August 10, 1848). He also submitted documents bearing on the case, which the House, by a vote of 96 to 83, refused to print. Trist not only was discharged from his post by his angry chief, but was denied pay for his services from the date on which he received notice of his recall. He was obliged to wait for his pay until 1870. *Senate Reports*, 41 Cong., 2 Sess. (Serial 1409), No. 261.

insubordinate origin. It came clearly within the terms of previous instructions. If it were to be rejected, force would be given the charges of the Whigs, and even of some Democrats, that the war had been begun and continued to acquire All Mexico. In Congress Whigs held the purse strings. Many Whigs objected to taking any territory. Moreover, the war was producing fiscal strains. Edward Everett wrote Lord Aberdeen on December 15, 1847, that the "tax gatherer" was making peace desirable and would help to ward off the disaster of incorporating the "outlandish population" of Mexico into the Union. "We are paying about 100,000,000 dollars for the luxury of conquest." [7] Democrats feared changes in the method of tax gathering as the price of a continuance of the war. They were proud of their recently adopted Walker tariff, which had reduced rates to a low level. They were fearful that the continuing drains of the war might induce Congress to return to Whig principles of high rates, which even some Democrats (Buchanan and Dallas, for instance) would have liked.[8] The country's burgeoning debt troubled conservatives, including some in the Democratic ranks, such as Calhoun and Gallatin. Calhoun, in his great anti-war speeches, predicted fiscal disaster if the war did not come to an early end. In 1847 and 1848, in his attack on the war Gallatin gave fiscal as well as moral reasons. Gallatin might be dismissed, without danger, as an old fogy by Polk Democrats. He was described in the Washington *Union,* and in other journals, as still an alien at heart. In some Western journals he was referred to as a "Mexican Whig," which was a double insult, and even as a "Mexican Secretary of the Treasury." [9] But Calhoun was another matter. Among Southern Democrats his name was potent, and he could not be disposed of thus summarily.

[7] Edward Everett to Lord Aberdeen, December 15, 1847. Aberdeen Papers, British Museum.

[8] The Irish famine and short crops throughout Europe were important elements in financing the Mexican War. Exports of American grain in large volume, paid for at high prices, encouraged imports from Europe. Thus the Treasury prospered, despite cuts made by the Walker tariff in the rates.

[9] Washington *Union,* February 8, 1848; Detroit *Free Press,* March 1, 1848. The Gallatin articles referred to are Albert Gallatin: *Peace with Mexico* (New York, 1847), and *Expenses of the War* (Washington, 1848).

Other party considerations weighed heavily on the side of accepting the *projet*. The presidential elections were approaching. Taylor was enormously popular. In 1840, Whigs, under a military hero, had been able to unhorse the Democrats. More recently they had won the House elections. If their candidate in the election of 1848 were still in shining armor, they might sweep the country. Discontent among the Democrats was on the increase, sadly enough, especially over the issue of admitting so many Mexicans into the Union. More frightening still, the Wilmot proviso was regarded with favor by Northern Democrats. If the war continued, the issue might break the party asunder, and more than that—the Union.

Polk was resolved, even before his Cabinet was called together, to submit the *projet* to the Senate for approval. He had called the Cabinet merely to say yes, and to share a responsibility he did not like to carry alone. He let the Cabinet know at once that he thought the *projet,* even though irregular, should go to the Senate. He would himself, he said, have preferred to acquire more territory, perhaps to the Sierra Madres. But he doubted whether the Mexicans would ever have agreed to this. He feared that the American public, which was aware of the *projet,* would not sustain the administration in rejecting it. The House was controlled by the Whigs, who would charge, if the *projet* were rejected, that the war had been begun for conquest. The probability was that the House would refuse grants of more men or money for the war. The Army would have to be withdrawn. Should the coming election be won by the Whigs, the nation might lose even California and New Mexico, which were now in hand.

The President had barely concluded his remarks when Buchanan began protesting. He was especially vehement against withdrawing from the Sierra Madre line. Walker took the same position. The President became annoyed. He had respect for such unswerving loyalty to a cause as Walker showed. But for the shiftings of a Buchanan he had none. He proceeded to read Buchanan a lecture on the evils of shifting, right there before the whole Cabinet. It was such a lecture as is not often heard, even in the frank privacy of an official family. He entered into the most painful detail. The Secretary's proposal, on the evening of the declaration of war, to inform foreign governments that the United States intended to acquire no Mexican territory, was recalled. His opposition to taking Mexican territory was alleged to have continued to April 1847. He had shifted in drafting the Trist instructions. He had fully consented to those instructions. Now he was demanding yet more territory. The embarrassed Secretary finally got in a word. He had been satisfied, he said, with the Trist instruction, but the situation had altered. A great deal of money and blood had been spent since then, and he was no longer satisfied with the indemnity then demanded. During this altercation the other members of the Cabinet sat silent, only to vote, afterward, for the President's proposal to send the *projet* to the Senate.

Later the President entered in his diary thoughts he had only intimated to the Cabinet. He thought the true explanation of his Secretary's last shift was that he was a candidate for the presidency, who knew all the time that the *projet* had to go to the Senate; who wished to throw the full responsibility for the decision onto other shoulders; who, if the decision were approved by the public, would share in it; who, if it were objected to, would disown it. The President reflected further that no candidate for the presidency ought to remain in the Cabinet—that such a man was an unsafe adviser. This reflection had occurred to him before, in the spring of 1846, when Buchanan had shown similar vacillation in the Cabinet on the Oregon issue. When the question had then arisen of sending the Senate a compromise *projet,* he had suddenly displayed a covetousness for everything to 54° 40′.[10]

[10] Quaife (ed.): *Diary of Polk,* III, 346–51. Polk's reasons for sending the *projet* to the Senate are a valuable commentary on public opinion regarding the war at this time. They reflect a national reluctance to take more territory than the sparsely populated provinces of California and New Mexico. They suggest Polk's fear that the war's prolongation might imperil retention of even these two. They reflect anxiety in his mind concerning the revolt in his own party against taking more. The picture drawn here differs considerably from the one editors of Manifest Destiny journals were painting of a public desire to annex All Mexico. It casts doubt on the inevitability of any such annexation if the war had continued, which some historians have assumed. It weakens the defenses of Trist by his biographers, who credit him with having preserved the nation from such a disaster. But see Fuller:

In submitting the *projet* to the Senate the President recommended changes. The most important of these was the elimination of Article X, which dealt with grants of land made by Mexico in Texas before the war and which was so phrased that it might have been later construed to revive extinct claims there. The President sent the Senate, also, the documents exposing Trist's behavior. He did not explicitly recommend ratification of an amended *projet*, but he implied that he was in favor of it.

The Senate showed a disposition to accept the *projet* with a minimum of change. It rejected proposals to alter the territorial core of the *projet*. Jefferson Davis would have liked an enlargement of the cession by adding all or part of Tamaulipas, Nuevo León, Coahuila, and Chihuahua. Crittenden, on the other hand, representing eighteen Whigs, would have reduced it. He would have provided for the assumption by the United States of the damage claims of its citizens in return for a cession by Mexico of only the port of San Francisco and a compromise as to the Texan boundary. The Senate rejected both proposals. Article X was struck out. Article IX was also eliminated. This article gave special security to the Catholic Church in the ceded area, a provision which seemed a reflection on American religious tolerance, and also provided for statehood for California and New Mexico as soon as possible, which seemed an intrusion on the discretion of Congress in admitting new states. Then, by a majority of 38 to 14, the Senate voted to advise and consent to the ratification of the amended *projet*.[11]

Mexican acceptance of the modifications was necessary. A commission of two, Sevier and Attorney General Clifford, was sent to Mexico to obtain acceptance. As a prod to Mexico to act promptly the administration pressed forward a large new war loan in Congress and sent reinforcements to Scott's army.

News of the prospect of peace became public promptly. It pro-

---

Movement for the Acquisition of All Mexico, passim, and Sears: "Nicholas P. Trist," *M.V.H.R.*, XI, 85.

[11] The President's message and the accompanying documents are printed in *Sen. Exec. Docs.*, 30 Cong., 1 Sess. (Serial 509), No. 52. The *projet* and the Senate proceedings are in the same document.

duced a national sigh of relief. It gave both political parties and all sections some sort of satisfaction. Speaking for the Whigs, the *National Intelligencer* repeated a comment which Sir Philip Francis, an English writer, had made in 1802 on the expected peace with Napoleon, that it was "a Peace which every one would be glad of, but no one would be proud of." [12] In the New York *Tribune* Horace Greeley, regretting that so much land had been taken from Mexico (so little of it worth taking), also took refuge in a quotation. He quoted Benjamin Franklin's observation on the peace of 1783: "There never was a good war or a bad peace." [13] Among the Democrats a common observation was that the peace was at least honorable. Implicit in some of the editorials was the suggestion that the President had been taken, by the *projet*, "off the hook." A number of editors followed Ritchie, of the Washington *Union*, who was happy that the land taken from Mexico was encumbered by only 100,000 Mexicans.[14]

The penny press responded favorably, on the whole, to the treaty, which is surprising in view of its crusade for All Mexico. It demonstrated its remarkable ability to adjust to new situations. The *Boston Times* comforted itself with the reflection that, even if only a third of Mexico's territory had been obtained, the rest would come later. "If we do not come to Mexico, Mexico will come to us, with or without a treaty." [15] A flighty response was made, characteristically, by the *New York Herald*. It pronounced the treaty at first "a monster"; then, three days later, "an abomination"; three days later, "satisfactory"; and, finally, after a lapse of

[12] *National Intelligencer* (t.w.), March 14, 1848; Thomas Moore: *Memoirs of Richard Brinsley Sheridan* (3rd ed., 2 vols., London, 1825), II, 300.

[13] New York *Tribune*, February 25, 26, 1848. The longing for peace in the Whig portion of the community is reflected in the New Orleans *Picayune*, which wrote almost lyrically, on March 19, 1848: "There is something cheerful in the sound of peace. There is a charm in the word which soothes the chafed and bruised spirit. Kinder and more charitable thoughts displace the revengeful fancies which usurped the mind of the nation, and gentle reveries succeed the rude impulses which possessed the people. After all, battles are hard purchasers and glory the luxury of cruelty. We have heard so much of the cannon's roar, that the tinkling bell is a welcome change."

[14] Washington *Union*, February 28, 1848.

[15] *Boston Times*, March 13, 1848.

three more days, "a sublime spectacle of national magnanimity in not keeping possession of all of Mexico." [16]

Some penny-press editors did lament the shortcomings of the treaty. But it can be said with confidence that such lamentation as the New York *Sun* permitted to escape its lips was heard nowhere else in the nation. Its editor suffered torments while the *projet* was before the Senate. Under the caption "The Ordeal," he wrote: "The men who adopt, in blind haste, an imperfect, inadequate and but semi-legal treaty, at the sacrifice of the most splendid and enduring advantages already paid for, and in our possession, will never be forgiven by the masses." [17]

When the sacrifice so unforgivable had been made, the editor poured out his grief in a long piece entitled "The Losses of the Treaty." He believed the boundary should have been nothing short of the Isthmus of Tehuantepec. As it was, the nation had lost a hundred million dollars and ten thousand lives. It had lost the shortest and most easily defended boundary in that country. It had given up the precious passage—the gateway to supremacy in the Pacific; control of the Asiatic trade; the market there for our manufactures, now monopolized by Britain; the mines of gold and silver in Mexico, worth an annual income of twenty-five millions; an independent supply of silk, coffee, sugar, cocoa, fine woods, cochineal, and pigments, essential to our commerce and manufacturing, which would have employed more than five hundred sail and steamers; public land sufficient to grant parcels to our soldiers and to pay the war debt. "This is what *we* have lost. . . . We desire

[16] *New York Herald,* February 6, 9, 12, 15, 1848. Bennett was able, during the Senate's deliberations on the treaty, to score one of his typical journalistic scoops. His Washington correspondent, John Nugent, by devices unknown, established an inside connection with the secret treaty proceedings of the Senate. He sent Bennett a detailed report, which was triumphantly published in the *Herald* on March 15, 1848. The Senate summoned Nugent and sought to extract from him the source of his information. He refused to give it, was cited for contempt, and was remanded to the custody of the sergeant-at-arms for several days. He was released when he complained that he was "seriously indisposed." Bennett in the meantime denounced the Senate's questioning as interference with the freedom of the press. Ibid., March 15, 16, April 1, 1848; *Jour. Exec. Proc. of the Senate,* VII, index, under entry "Nugent, John."

[17] New York *Sun* (w.), March 4, 1848.

not the possession of Mexican territory, not the destruction of her nationality (if she possess any):—we only require the above conditions to be complied with. But we shall not hesitate to say, that making a treaty which does not secure these rights is an act of treason to the integrity, position, and honor of this Empire."[18] Here was real feeling, and incidentally, also, retribution visited on Polk. Polk had charged Whigs with treason earlier in the war. Now he was himself charged, at the end of the war, with the same crime by a journalist who was powerful in his party and who had even been employed by him during the war on the quiet.

A striking aftermath of the ratification of the treaty was the swift disappearance of the idea of All Mexico from the press. As a balloon collapses at the touch of a needle, so the idea of All Mexico collapsed at the touch of the Trist *projet*. This is such an extraordinary phenomenon, in view of the energy of propaganda which had gone into manufacturing the program, and in view of the program's attractiveness to the administration, that the historian is confronted with the question: How is it to be accounted for?

In groping for an answer the historian stumbles upon the conclusion that the All Mexico doctrine, like its parent, the Manifest Destiny doctrine, underwent some real testing in the efforts to apply it. The testing was conducted in the full hearing of the public in the discussions of the practical problems involved. One practical problem was citizenship. If All Mexico were taken, citizenship would have to be conferred on colored people—on Indians, on Negroes, on mixed races. This seemed to editors of the penny press no formidable problem. But to Calhoun, to the South, to the West, and even, it must be confessed, to many persons in the East, it seemed a formidable problem indeed. Everywhere in the land, colored people—notably Negroes, free or slave—were considered weak candidates for citizenship. Keeping Negroes in slavery might be objected to by some Northerners, but raising them to citizenship was, even by them, opposed; and the idea of a whole-

[18] Ibid. (w.), March 15, 1848. See also June 5, 1848.

sale raising to citizenship of the mixed races in Mexico, which seemed inescapable if they were to be absorbed, was horrifying. A cheerful optimism was felt by Americans concerning the power of man over physical nature. This was part of the theory of Manifest Destiny. With the aid of science a continent could be spanned, mountains overleaped, deserts reclaimed, space and time annihilated by rail and wire, mighty lakes and rivers joined by canals, continents torn apart in order to wed oceans in the service of commerce. But of human nature little was expected. Not even a wrinkle could be ironed out.

Testing was given, also, to other theses so attractively presented during the All Mexico crusade. One favorite thesis had been that democracy, republicanism, and those special forms of freedom embedded in Anglo-Saxon constitutions, are universal ideals, and natural to man. Or, conversely that disorder, misgovernment, and exploitation are breaches of nature, thrust on virtuous people by such malefactors as the war lords in Mexico and the tyrants in Europe, and that nothing more is needed than to overthrow the tyrants and offer nature's man the gift of the freedoms and protections of the American Constitution. This idealism had been thought naïve by realists of the Calhoun type, who were not democrats, except in name. Calhoun thought that the capacity for good government varies among the races of mankind; that it is an error to regard the institutions and privileges of the American Constitution as a suit of clothes to be made to order and presented indiscriminately to all people to ensure their happiness; that the American type of government is a white man's affair—indeed, is not even suited to all white men. The Constitution is a product of historical growth; even more, it is a special gift of Providence to the American people. It is certainly not to be offered ready-made to other races and expected to fit well. Here again was conflict regarding Providence and its intentions, conflict in this case between an O'Sullivan, who considered Providence equally friendly to all, and the great Southern philosopher, who considered it partial to the elect. The disintegration of the All Mexico crusade seemed to mean that the Southerner and his ideas had triumphed.

In yet another respect, theory and fact seemed to collide in the All Mexico crusade and to have registered the outcome of their collision in the distintegration of an idea. The theory of the All Mexico crusaders was that the press is the voice of the people, and that, judging people's sentiments by their voice, the great American majority was eager to take the whole of Mexico. This theory Bennett and Beach, whose papers had the greatest circulations in the world, undoubtedly subscribed to. And yet the view is somewhat difficult to reconcile with the swift withering of the All Mexico sentiment on the appearance of the Trist *projet*. Is it permissible for the puzzled historian to conclude that the Bennetts and Beaches and their like were mistaken in believing they represented the inner thoughts of the masses; that they grossly exaggerated their sway over the masses, and even over the masses in the big cities of the Atlantic seaboard? Is it conceivable that the *New York Herald* and the *Sun* and their equivalents elsewhere were read by the masses on account of their freshness and coverage of news, on account of their sensationalism; or even because they satisfied their reader's earthy tastes, and not at all because their editorial views had deep-seated popular support? Is it possible that such popular sentiment for continentalism as they did arouse was transitory, that editorial propagandizing, however persistent, did not fix it, and that, on the contrary, it might have produced boredom and even what is termed in modern parlance "sales resistance"?

Few of the editors who preached the All Mexico crusade seemed prophets to Americans in their own day. Many had careers in journalism that were brief and were followed by careers in other occupations of not much distinction. Even the editors of the penny press were respected more for the range and swiftness of their news gathering than for their editorial greatness. Certainly they were not held by Whig editors, nor by all Democratic editors, in high esteem. A judgment passed on Bennett, for instance, by the distinguished editor of the New Orleans *Picayune*, George W. Kendall, is to the point: "Bennett can say more about nothing, spin a longer yarn with less of the raw material to commence with, than any other editor in the country." [19] The same journal, though not at all of the quarrelsome type, publicly castigated the editor of the New York *Sun* as a notorious fabricator of news and hoaxer of the public.[20]

Of the politicians who preached the All Mexico doctrine on the floor of Congress, a popular suspicion was likewise entertained that they were not among the great intellects of the world. No Webster or Calhoun or even Clay was to be found among them. Such figures as Cass, Allen, Hannegan, Douglas, and Dickinson, seemed to many observers orators rather than intellectual giants. An observation made by Webster in a speech in Boston during the agitation for All Mexico, was, doubtless, to the point: "It is not the noisiest waters that are the deepest." [21] Such intangible factors may help to account for the puzzling phenomenon, that a concept of unrestrained expansionism, which seemed frightening to some and attractive to others, evaporated so swiftly on the appearance of the Trist *projet.*

Also helpful in accounting for this phenomenon was an honored American tradition—that the American people never had acquired territory, and never would, except by peaceful purchase or by the request of a neighboring people to enter the Union. This tradition had been emphasized by philosophers of Manifest Destiny in the case of Texas, and it remained alive in the public consciousness throughout the Mexican War. It was embodied in the Two Million and Three Million bills suggested by the President to Congress, and it was embedded in the payment proposals of the Trist instructions. Payments to an enemy in war were recognized by some expansionists to be unusual. They were grumbled at a little as a purchase of goods already in our possession. Still they were recognized as helpful in bringing about peace and preserving a valued ideal. Payments to Mexico did not harmonize well with concepts associated with indemnity requirements, but the two could be reconciled. If peace were made soon, indemnity

[19] Fayette Copeland: *Kendall of the Picayune* (Norman, Okla., 1943), 37.
[20] New Orleans *Picayune,* October 14, 1847.
[21] *Writings and Speeches of Daniel Webster,* XIII, 348.

would not need to be so great for the wrong Mexico had done, and the purchase price could be larger. When Trist agreed to rates of payment his government had proposed nine months earlier, he simply exhibited ineptitude as a business man, if not as a diplomat.

The Whigs considered the purchase money "conscience money" —atonement for a wrong done Mexico. What a libel, Democrats replied, on the President! It questioned the sincerity of his message to Congress regarding the origin of the war. The money given was purchase money, paid at a forced sale perhaps, but, after all, Mexico had only nominal possession of the territory anyway, even before the war began. A great Democratic historian, George Bancroft, who knew well the theory of Manifest Destiny and the inner history of the coming of the war, gave a correct view of the payment to Mexico. Writing Buchanan from London late in 1848, he referred happily to California and New Mexico as "purchased."[22] This tenacity on the part of Americans in adhering to an old ideal is evidence of the failure of expansionists to convert much of the American public to the concept of conquest and absorption of All Mexico.

Events of world-wide importance occurred while the Trist *projet* was before the Senate. Revolution overturned the government of France, toppled the monarchy of Louis Philippe, and replaced it with a provisional republic. These events were reported in the United States on March 18, 1848, a few days after the Senate had acted on the Trist *projet,* and before the terms of the *projet* were officially made public. They produced a sensation throughout the country, a tremendous outburst of enthusiasm and joy, beside which the reception given the news of the *projet* seemed anemic. They were, according to the *New York Herald,* "on every tongue and palpitating in every bosom." The excitement they created was "most tremendous"; public feeling expressed itself in celebrations, flag raisings, congratulations, and speeches. A theme stressed in all Democratic speeches and editorials was that this revolution was the fruit of seeds planted by the American Revolution of 1776.[23]

[22] Bancroft to Buchanan, December 15, 1848, Bancroft Papers, M.H.S.
[23] *New York Herald,* March 20, 21, 1848.

More European revolutions were expected, and this added to the glow of enthusiasm in the press and to the exhilaration of the public. The shaky state of monarchy in Germany, Austria, Italy, Spain, and elsewhere was noted with satisfaction. From London, George Bancroft predicted that in twenty years not a monarchy would be left standing in Europe.[24] A pious hope was expressed in the *New York Evening Post* that all remaining monarchies would die a death as happy and peaceful as the French.[25] The last to go, according to some commentators, would be the English. Yet hopeful signs of its demise were observed—famine in Ireland, agitation for repeal of the Act of Union, Chartist demonstrations in London. Speculation on such happy events and prospects engrossed American attention, and helps to account for the quick passing from the front pages of journals (even of Democratic journals) of the concept of All Mexico. This illustrates, again, the transitory nature of public interest in certain causes.

The Polk administration gained real advantages from this European upheaval. It was lifted off the hook of problems left by the war less painfully than might otherwise have been the case. Also, Polk was well served by his agents in Europe and in America. In Paris, Richard Rush, the American minister, instantly recognized the provisional republic. He acted without instructions in doing so, and at the risk of recognizing a child that would not live. But it turned out to be just the right thing to do. It showed the natural affection of American parents for their French child. In Congress there was fast work also. Allen, in the Senate, promptly introduced a joint resolution congratulating the French people on the success of their "efforts to consolidate liberty by imbodying its principles in a republican form of government." [26] This was followed some days later by a special message from Polk, who pointed out that our sympathies were naturally enlisted on the side of a people who, "imitating our example, have resolved to be free." He thought the world had seldom witnessed a more sublime spectacle than the

[24] Howe: *Life and Letters of George Bancroft,* II, 33.
[25] *New York Evening Post,* April 6, 1848.
[26] *Cong. Globe,* 30 Cong., 1 Sess., 549 (March 28, 1848).

peaceful rising of the French people to increase their liberty and to assert the great truth that "man is capable of governing himself." [27] In the Senate an unpleasant rivalry developed over the question, whose joint resolution of congratulation, Allen's or one offered by Hannegan as new chairman of the Committee on Foreign Relations, should be made the order of the day. But even this rivalry had the virtue of permitting Democratic orators, one after another, to rise and point to the beauties of republicanism, the inevitability of the collapse of tyranny, and the great contribution made to the freedom of the world by the example set by the United States. The senators who shone in these efforts were Cass, Allen, Hannegan, Douglas, and Dickinson, precisely the ones who had fought so valiantly to extend freedom southward.[28]

The Whigs were less impressed than the Democrats with the need to send congressional congratulations, and their reserve was shared by conservative Southern Democrats. Alike, they complained that the adoption of a joint resolution for such a purpose was unprecedented, that it was unnecessary, and, even more to the point, that it was premature. Calhoun, in particular, objected on the ground of prematurity. He pointed out that little was known yet of the course of the revolution, that the irregular government set up in Paris was highly provisional, that no harm would be done by waiting a little before sending congratulations.[29] Some Whigs became almost ribald in commenting on Allen's fine compliment to the French on the success of their efforts to "consolidate liberty." William L. Dayton, of New Jersey, for instance, observed:

> If we are to congratulate a people on consolidating liberty, we should first be sure that liberty is consolidated, or perhaps when we send them out, the return may be *non est*. It was said that it was right to offer congratulations when a child was born. True; but he would wait until it was born. France had not yet been delivered—she may miscarry.[30]

[27] Richardson (comp.): *Messages and Papers,* IV, 579.
[28] *Cong. Globe,* 30 Cong., 1 Sess., 580–1, 590.
[29] Ibid., 568–9.
[30] Ibid., 592 (April 6, 1848).

Objections of other sorts to congratulations were offered. The French had a way of carrying revolutions to extremes, to reigns of terror, to religious infidelity, to wars. Also, disquieting reports were coming in of crude economic heresies appearing in Paris, of extremist ideas—socialism, appeasement of the mob—and strange new notions of Christianity. Bennett, of the *New York Herald*, felt obliged to take notice of these reports. But he reassured his readers. "Here [in America] we have Fourierism, Communism, infidelity, anti-sabbath movements, Mormonism . . . all sorts of sects . . . striving to overturn all general opinions hostile to the principles of these sects. . . . Yet when the general mind is left free to combat all these extreme notions . . . we see how vain have been all the efforts of those enthusiasts." [31]

In Congress, after days of oratory designed for audiences back home, votes were finally taken on Allen's resolution in both houses. They were overwhelmingly favorable to sending the congratulations. In the Senate the vote was unanimous; in the House there were only two votes in the negative. Whigs and conservative Democrats once again made clear that they did not consider it necessary to carry to extremes their objections to momentary popular impulses.

Predictions in the American press of further revolutions in Europe speedily materialized. In one European state after another monarchs were dethroned, or their powers were diminished by constitutional changes, or republics were established. These developments were given tumultuous welcome in the United States, especially in the cities. Editorials favoring extending help to the newborn infants if monarchical reactionaries should try to destroy them, appeared in the Democratic press. Bennett was among the first to express such sentiments. The idea was discouraged, however, by the President. A broad suggestion was made by Bennett and other expansionist editors, that, while tyrants were busy in the Old World just staying alive, freedom might be extended in the

[31] *New York Herald*, March 31, 1848.

New. It might be extended to Canada, Cuba, and to all the West Indies. "Wake up, Congress!" Bennett exhorted.[32]

But such suggestions found little response. The labor of extending freedom to Mexico had left Americans quite weary. The feeling elicited in most Democratic journals when the good news arrived was just a relaxed contentment, a happiness at seeing the prospect of a cluster of European republics, with ours as the sun about which they would all revolve. The *New York Evening Post* phrased the idea nicely: "Asia had her day; Europe has had hers; and it remains to be seen whether the diadem must not first be worn by the new world, before it reverts again to the old." [33]

The same idea was put forth by the *Sun*, in an editorial in April, under the caption "The World a Republic," a rapturous piece, even if sometimes tangled a little in its metaphors.

> The enthusiastic vision of Independence, and the daydream of suffering humanity, is being rapidly realized. Since the might of the human mind is aroused in Europe; since Freedom has unfurled her banner, and the voices of glad millions are echoing in thunder tones our own dear watchword of Liberty, the field is open, the time has come, and the occasion is ripe. France, beautiful France, leads the van, with one hand bearing aloft the republican tri-color, and the other pointing to our own stars and stripes as the polar light of Liberty. Italy, Germany, Switzerland, Prussia and Belgium, respond to her call, and her loud shout, "Vive la Republique," has found an echoing pulse in the bosoms of millions in our Fatherland [England]. Ireland has groaned under the oppressor's rod till patience has ceased to be a virtue, and further endurance will but add another stigma to her long list of humiliations. England feels this truth, and is redoubling her energies to keep down the ardor of myriads, who like Tantalus, chained to the rock, see their hearts-longing within their reach, but cannot grasp it. England's incubus of five thousand millions of dollars, in the shape of public debt, is the mill stone that must sink her, and drag with it, a throne. Freedom, from her home in the West, has a charter-deed of Liberty to offer to the isles of the ocean, and majestically sublime is the idea that the daughter, with all due respect for the mother, with all kindness and love, tenders her a post, side by side with herself, in

[32] Ibid., March 20, April 18, 1848.
[33] *New York Evening Post,* April 26, 1848.

> the ranks of Liberty. The human being now breathes who will see this consummation—cannot we *all* see, the whole Anglo-Saxon race, with feelings and impulses in common, striving each, who shall outdo the other, in God's own righteous cause of Human Liberty.[34]

An even more sublime idea occurred to the *Sun* as news continued to pour in of the revolutions in Europe. It was the idea—the old idea—of the Mission of America. It had struggled for expression, already, in the metaphorical welter of the April editorial; it found clearer form on May 6, 1848:

> Our republic, firm as the immutable principles on which it is based, happily stands so far aloof from the revolution now transforming Europe that we can look calmly upon the struggle, and by our sympathy and counsel, nerve and help guide the sinews of liberty-seeking masses, without breach of faith with nations. We are the reserve corps to consummate the triumphs of freedom, as our fathers were pioneers to strike for and win its first fruits. Our example has been leaven to the millions of the old world—a light and fire, illumining their souls and warming their hearts and hands until they have dared to shout in the ears of their tyrants, "we too, are men—we will be free!" Say not to us any more, they cry, that liberty is a fable, behold the fruit of her seed planted in a wilderness beyond the ocean seventy years ago—twenty millions of people, free, intelligent, prosperous and happy. Nor is our influence forgotten now that it has ripened and burst in the heart of Europe. Amid the waving banners and the flash of uplifted sabres, whether in Italy, France, Germany, Poland, or our own fatherland, Britain, the finger of revolution points to us as its example, its cloud and pillar of fire! As we vowed, so are the masses of Europe vowing—as we struck, so are they striking, and as we cast out the tyrant, so will they cast him out, him and his heirs forever!
>
> Better for us and the world that we stand thus aloof; at present the work goes bravely on, promising to freedom a perfect victory without an appeal to arms. We are the watchword, the pole star of their struggle, without mixing in the conflict or dipping our fingers in blood. Yet if freedom were in *danger*—if she should call to us for succor, there is not an American hand or heart but would fly to her rescue.[35]

[34] New York *Sun* (w.), April 15, 1848. On April 28, the *Sun* happily reported, in reference to the revolution, that "England shivers in every limb."

[35] Ibid. (w.), May 6, 1848. This editorial and the one of April 15 were perhaps from the pen of Beach's favorite reporter and editorial writer, "Montgomery,"

Set forth here in abundance is the concept of America's Mission. America is the light, the leaven, the fire, the polestar of liberty for Europe. She has been this ever since 1776. One aspect of Mission is, however, understressed—its relationship to Manifest Destiny. But the relationship is clear. America's Mission is to hold a light aloft to Europe in the great struggle for freedom. The light ought to have a maximum brilliance. It will attain this if Manifest Destiny is fulfilled, if American freedom extends from arctic to tropic, if it is continentalized in the New World. When that has been achieved, the light will guide the Old World more clearly than ever. The image of half a hemisphere smiling in the sunshine of freedom, peace, and security will be seen by the downtrodden of Europe sooner, will ignite the fires of their revolutions quicker, will topple their gory tyrants earlier, than the image of a radiant but hemmed-in United States. Unfortunately the fulfillment of Destiny was delayed by Mexican stubbornness and Whig treason. But why worry? The image of even a hemmed-in freedom has proved quite sufficient. Europe has seen the light, the fire, the polestar, from the depths of her darkness, and is successfully shaking off her chains. Here is, perhaps, another element in the explanation of the cheerful resignation with which American expansionists accepted the failure of their crusade into Mexico.

---

already identified here as Mrs. Jane M. Storms. Its vivid imagery and style resembles that of a series of wild, self-important letters she sent Bancroft in these years which are in the Bancroft Papers. Bancroft, on first receiving one, signed "Storms," made inquiry of William L. Marcy: "Who is Storms?" The reply was: "*She* is an outrageously smooth and keen writer for the newspapers in N.Y. Principal contributor to the *Sun*." Endorsement on a letter of July 23, 1846, Bancroft Papers, M.H.S.

Chapter IX

A *Caribbeanized Manifest* Destiny

IN THE MIDST of these pleasurable excitements news arrived which gave reason for hope that the cause of All Mexico might even yet be revived. It came from Yucatán after the Trist *projet* had been modified by the Senate but before the modification had been submitted to the Mexican Congress. Yucatán was a province with a history of restlessness and separatist tendencies within the Mexican confederation. During the 1830's she had objected to the centralism of the Mexican authorities, and in 1839 had staged a revolt and had declared her independence. She had actually maintained independence until 1843. Then, under a treaty that recognized her autonomy, she had returned to an unsteady allegiance. She was considered by American expansionists an especially promising candidate for the Union; indeed, almost as promising as California and New Mexico. When, in 1846, she seceded from Mexico again, Walt Whitman predicted that she would add a bright star to the "Spangled Banner." In 1848 her white governing class was threatened with extermination at the hands of her Indian population, and her authorities offered themselves to the American, British, and Spanish governments for protection.[1]

[1] A brief account of Yucatán secessionism is Mary W. Williams: "Secessionist Diplomacy of Yucatán," *Hispanic American Historical Review*, IX (1929), 133–43. The Walt Whitman editorial is in the *Brooklyn Eagle*, June 29, 1846.

Her offer was referred by Polk to his Cabinet. There it aroused in the incorrigible Walker hope of retrieving losses suffered in the Mexican treaty. He urged an occupation of Yucatán with a view to ultimate annexation. He was opposed by Buchanan, whose bones still ached from the drubbing he had received at the Cabinet meeting when he had ventured such ideas. The President on this occasion tentatively aligned himself with Walker, but he made clear that he would agree to annexation only to forestall a British seizure.[2] He sent a special message to Congress, in which, refraining from any recommendations, he pictured vividly the predicament of the whites in Yucatán; emphasized the value of the peninsula for controlling the Gulf of Mexico and Cuba; warned of the danger of a foreign (meaning British) seizure; referred to "authentic information" he had that, if aid were denied by the United States, it would be given by some European power, which might, thereafter, assert dominion over Yucatán; and declared that under no circumstances could the United States permit Yucatán to become a colony of a foreign power. Unfortunately, he could not, he continued, withdraw troops from the rest of Mexico for Yucatán without serious danger. Then, having fulfilled his duty by merely transmitting facts, he dropped the problem into the lap of Congress.[3]

In the Senate, Calhoun listened to the reading of the message with deep suspicion. He was distrustful, for one thing, of its mixing of purposes, its uniting of humanitarianism with policy, concern for imperiled Yucatecos with concern for the interests of the United States in the Gulf of Mexico. He was always put on the alert by mixing of that sort. Also, he was distrustful of the heavy emphasis in the message on the danger of European (meaning British) intervention, and of the President's assertion of having authentic information that some European power, if the United States did not act, would give the Yucatecos the aid they requested, and then would claim dominion and sovereignty over them. Noted quietly, too, was that this information was not shared with Congress, and

[2] Quaife (ed.): *Diary of Polk*, III, 430–47.
[3] Richardson (comp.): *Messages and Papers*, IV, 581.

that Congress was expected to act without it. Furthermore, Calhoun added a grain of salt to the President's assurance of having no intention of acquiring "dominion and sovereignty" over Yucatán. He noticed, also, that it was Hannegan who moved immediately that his Committee on Foreign Affairs be the one to which the message be referred for purposes of preparing a bill.

Though not given to speaking hastily, Calhoun spoke out on this occasion at once. Before Hannegan's motion had even been laid before the Senate for debate, he was on his feet. He deemed it essential to give early warning to the Senate and the nation of the dangers he perceived in the trend of the message. He protested as a matter of prudence against intervention in the affairs of a Latin American state on the mere request of one portion or another of it. This would establish a principle far broader and more dangerous than any laid down by President Monroe in 1823. Where would it lead, if adopted? As for the justification that some European government would intervene if we did not, could anyone believe that those governments, engrossed as they were with issues bearing on their very survival, would embark on predatory excursions to the New World? Calhoun warned, at the end, against a repetition of the precipitate and rash experiment, which the nation had entered into in the Mexican War in response to the President's recommendation, which had cost so dear in blood and treasure.[4]

Polk's message went to Hannegan's committee, and a bill came back from it soon, authorizing a "temporary" military occupation of Yucatán. Hannegan and others exerted pressure at once for a quick—an emergency—adoption of the measure.[5] Emergency action was necessary to prevent the extermination of the suffering Yucatecos, and to prevent other dangers, which Hannegan spelled out:

> England cherishes the design, at this moment, to secure the most practicable route for an artificial means of communication between the two oceans, and to effect that object she is gradually and rapidly

[4] *Cong. Globe*, 30 Cong., 1 Sess., 712–13 (April 29, 1848); ibid., App. 592–607 (May 8, 1848).

[5] The bill appears at ibid., App. 591.

absorbing the entire Isthmus. Unless we act, she will accomplish her purpose. Does any one suppose for a moment that the miserable traffic in dye-woods, which is the principal article of commerce there, is what is leading England so steadily and regularly to seize, foot by foot, all the territory of which she can obtain possession in that quarter of the globe? No! It is the great and mighty object which I have just indicated. In Yucatan she has another and a higher object. She has, in fact, a double purpose. The first relates to herself, but the second strikes directly at us. Look at the position of Yucatan! . . . See how she stands out in almost juxta-position with Cuba! She shakes hands with Cuba! The possession of Yucatan by England would soon be followed by the possession of Cuba. . . . I doubt it no more than I doubt that the trees will put forth their leaves, and that the grass will renew itself next spring. It is inevitable. . . . We have, I may say, authentic information, that at this very hour, she is taking steps to accomplish that object. Give her Yucatan and Cuba, and what will be the result? That very instant the Gulf of Mexico will be under her control. It becomes *mare clausum!*

Here was "authentic information" again, even if not shared with the Senate. Also, stated right in the title of the bill was assurance that a military occupation, if voted, would be only temporary. But Hannegan was forced to admit, though speaking only for himself, that circumstances might change.

No man has dreamed as yet, so far as I know, of the permanent occupation of the territory of Yucatan. There are motives, however, which may lead us to such a result. As the Senator from South Carolina has remarked, we may be led we know not where. Considerations may arise which will lead us beyond our first intentions and render it imperative that we should convert this temporary occupation into something more.[6]

The bill thus introduced was kept in debate nearly two weeks, despite its emergency character and the pleas of administration spokesmen for immediate passage. Its passage was most earnestly pressed by frustrated All Mexico men, by Cass, Jefferson Davis, Houston, Foote, Bagby, Westcott, and others. A speech made by Cass was the longest and most eloquent on his side. It was a mixture such as had seemed so distasteful to Calhoun in Polk's mes-

[6] Ibid., App. 596–7 (May 5, 1848).

sage—humanity, the value of Yucatán to the United States, the greed of the British. The Indians of Yucatán were actually being armed, Cass said, by the British. "When she [England] lays the lion's paw on Yucatán, it will be difficult to displace it. . . . Let England get possession of Yucatán, and she will make the Gulf a *mare clausum*. . . . England wants Cuba for commercial purposes; we want it for our very existence as a nation."[7] Westcott, asked by Crittenden whether the administration intended to hold Yucatán permanently, joined Hannegan in saying it depended on circumstances. If England made attempts to hold it, or the region ceased to have a government, we certainly would retain it. It was of the utmost importance to us. Houston emphasized the humanitarian element in the discussion. The Indians who were menacing the whites in Yucatán were like those who had beset Texans in an earlier day. They were of "gigantic size, ferocious in their dispositions, loathsome in their habits, and rioted on human flesh."[8] Bagby (admitting that he had been for All Mexico) could not resist the temptation to twit Cass, who "is disposed that the temple of Janus shall be always open, and he would have his park of artillery always playing."[9]

The Whigs contented themselves with restating and amplifying points raised by Calhoun before the Hannegan bill had even been presented. Their principal speakers were Clayton; Crittenden; John Davis, of Massachusetts; Reverdy Johnson, of Maryland; and Jacob W. Miller, of New Jersey. They pointed out that two important agreements with Mexico would be violated by an occupation of Yucatán—the treaty currently before the Mexican Congress and the armistice which had ended the fighting in Mexico. They maintained that an intervention in Mexican affairs would be an unwarranted and an unwise extension of the principle enunciated by Monroe in 1823. They denounced the mixing of aims in Polk's message. They insisted that the charge of British interference in the affairs of Yucatán was a diplomatic humbug of the sort

[7] Ibid., App. 613–20 (May 10, 1848).
[8] Ibid., App. 604 (May 8, 1848).
[9] Ibid., App. 635 (May 16, 1848).

practiced in connection with Texas and California, and without a particle of sound evidence to sustain it; that the one actual item of evidence offered—the British make of guns carried by the Yucatán Indians—was spurious. Those guns were outmoded models sold by the British at auction in London, which had been picked up by speculators and disposed of at a profit in Yucatán. The guns actually were imperiling England's position, it was pointed out, in British Honduras. This may have been the "authentic information" referred to in the President's message.[10]

The bill did not progress well for the administration. A pressured vote, such as had followed Polk's recommendation of war against Mexico, proved unattainable. The opening speech of that renegade Calhoun had blocked it.[11] Also, the Democratic big guns, other than Cass, "with parks of artillery playing," did not appear. The public was apathetic. The Democratic press did not lead well; it merely echoed voices heard in Congress. Worst of all, the alliance of Whigs and conservative Democrats, which had been Polk's cross from the beginning of his administration, was bearing down again. On May 17, Hannegan learned of a peace treaty made between the Yucatecos and the Indians. He withheld this information from the Senate long enough to allow a Democratic colleague from New York, Senator Dix, to deliver a carefully prepared, impassioned plea (designed to be heard by the folks back home) for action, an example of senatorial courtesy of the right sort. Then he disclosed the news of the treaty, and himself proposed that his bill for an occupation be dropped. Without even a vote, the bill was dropped, and that hope of reviving the corpse of All Mexico vanished.[12]

When Mexico's Congress accepted the peace *projet* in its amended form and the Army came home, the corpse was decently buried. It was never exhumed. Successive administrations, however, nibbled at Mexico's territory. Disputes over the boundary

[10] Ibid., App. 630–3.

[11] Calhoun was now attacked with real vigor as a renegade by Southern Democratic colleagues.

[12] *Cong. Globe,* 30 Cong., 1 Sess., 777–8 (May 17, 1848).

arose. A discovery was made that the gateway for a transcontinental railroad to the Pacific lay in territory south of the Gila. Claims for damages against Mexico had accumulated again. In 1853 a proposal to buy the whole southern watershed of the Rio Grande and the peninsula of Lower California, for good measure, was made to Mexico by the Pierce administration, with a view to removing irritants in the relations of the two countries. Santa Anna was again in power, and, as always, in need of money. After negotiations, conducted for the United States by James Gadsden, a railroad man, a bargain was struck, whereby a rectification of the boundary was made, a triangular tract of territory south of the Gila, containing the desired gateway, was ceded, the right of transit across the Isthmus of Tehuantepec was conferred, and other problems were settled, for a payment of $10,000,000.[13]

Nibbling was tried further during the Buchanan administration. It was directed at territory down to the Sierra Madre line, for which Buchanan still had a taste. In December 1858, in his annual message to Congress, he reported that claims had accumulated against Mexico once more, to the extent of over $10,000,000, and called attention to chaotic conditions in Mexico, especially along the northern border. He requested authority to establish a "temporary protectorate" over northern Chihuahua and Sonora. He was sure that the state governments and people there would view such a step in a friendly spirit. Congress was less sure, and nothing was done. In the next annual message the President returned to the theme. He believed that if the United States did not restore order in Mexico, some European government would. He asked permission to employ military force in Mexico for the purpose of "obtaining indemnity for the past and security for the future." That phrase revived memories in the minds of many people; it was not well chosen. Also, the House of Representatives was controlled by the Republicans, the

[13] These later phases of the Tehuantepec question are well discussed in Paul N. Garber: *The Gadsden Treaty* (Philadelphia, 1923), and James F. Rippy: "Diplomacy Regarding the Isthmus of Tehuantepec, 1848–1860," *M.V.H.R.*, VI (1919–20), 505–32.

spiritual heirs of the Whigs, and this recommendation, like its predecessor, fell on deaf ears.[14]

These designs on Mexico in the postwar era were actuated by a petty materialism. They were imbued with little of the lofty spirit of the All Mexico crusade and none of its altruism of regenerating a benighted people and lifting them to the heights of American citizenship. Nor did they have the sweep, the grandeur, the sublimity, of the doctrine of Manifest Destiny which had been the parent of the All Mexico idea. Times had changed. The poetic forties had given way to the prosaic fifties.

After death, frustrated ideas sometimes walk the earth at night as ghosts. The deceased All Mexico idea was one of these. It sent adventurers on filibustering expeditions from the American border southward, such men as William Walker, who sought to win the lightly inhabited parts of northern Mexico—Sonora and Lower California—and, later, Central America.[15] It generated talk of a new republic of Sierra Madre. But such ideas collided with repugnance more strong than ever now to conferring citizenship on a mixed race of millions. That sentiment kept the All Mexico corpse tied down. It redirected Manifest Destiny thinking. It turned attention more strongly than before to the Caribbean—to Cuba and to the white-controlled Dominican Republic.

In Cuba whites were a minority. Colored and mixed elements formed well over half the population. Most of them, however, were, happily, slaves.[16] These would not become American citizens if Cuba were annexed. Whites would, of course, become citizens. They would increase the power of the South in Congress. The slaves would add their bit, too, under the three-fifths provision of the Constitution. Accordingly, while All Mexico moldered quietly

[14] James M. Callahan: *American Foreign Policy in Mexican Relations* (New York, 1932), ch. 8.

[15] A good account of Walker is Wallace: *Destiny and Glory*, chs. 7–11. An older standard is William O. Scroggs: *Filibusterers and Financiers* (New York, 1916). Walker paved the way for the introduction of slavery into Nicaragua. William Walker: *The War in Nicaragua* (Mobile, 1860), 262–3.

[16] Ramón de la Sagra: *Histoire, Physique, Politique et Naturelle de l'Ile de Cuba* (Pt. 1, Paris, 1842–3), I, 328.

in the grave, Manifest Destiny, its parent, became, in the fifties, Caribbeanized.

In 1860 Manifest Destiny was less inclusive than it had once been as a concept. Geographically and racially it had become selective. British North America was now less inevitably part of Heaven's design for the United States. Canadians were less restless under their yoke than they had been, and the lion was still around. Mexico was ineligible. Her mixture of races, combined with her tradition of freedom for them, was unattractive. Cuba, where whites were in firm control and where slavery was well established, attracted the South but not at all the anti-slavery Republicans of the North.

In 1860 how strangely reversed since the forties were the sections in their response to Manifest Destiny! What a transformation had the dozen short years since the doctrine had come to fruit wrought in this respect! In 1846–8 the South had shown only a limited enthusiasm for Manifest Destiny. It had accepted Calhoun's idea of a "wise and masterly inactivity" on the issue of Oregon to 54° 40′.[17] It had lacked strong desire for "expansion to the arctic and to the tropic." In the Senate, Calhoun, and in the House, the Whig, Alexander H. Stephens, had gone on a virtual crusade against the All Mexico idea. In the same period, most disciples of Manifest Destiny—certainly the most ardent—and most crusaders for its related creed, All Mexico, had come from the North. New York and Illinois had contributed more, and indubitably more active ones, than any other states. Illinois had the singular honor of being represented in the Senate by two leaders of the creeds, Douglas and Breese, each of whom had a nation-wide audience. A Whig congressman from Illinois, Abraham Lincoln, had expressed disapproval of the Mexican War, though he had always voted for war appropriations. He had failed of re-election.

In 1860 Jefferson Davis occupied the niche in Southern respect and affection once occupied by Calhoun. He demanded the acquisition of Cuba. He favored congressional measures that

[17] Merk: "Presidential Fevers," *M.V.H.R.*, XLVII (1960–1), 3 ff.

would protect slavery rather than merely tolerate it in the territories. He wanted removal from federal statutes of prohibitions on the African slave trade, leaving the matter to the states. His wing of the Democratic party supported the first two of these proposals and wrote planks favoring them into its platform in 1860. John Slidell, of Louisiana, in 1859 brought a bill into the Senate to purchase Cuba, which had wide support in the South. It drew from Senator Stephen R. Mallory, of Florida, the observation that if Spain should reject all reasonable terms of purchase, he would think well of "taking Cuba and talking about it afterwards, as Frederick did with Silesia."[18] Already in 1854 the Southerners Slidell and Pierre Soulé and also Buchanan had indicated in the Ostend Manifesto that they would subscribe, if need be, to a seizure of Cuba.[19]

In 1860 Abraham Lincoln was President-elect. He was the successful leader of a party consisting of former Whigs and Free-Soil Democrats. The party had grown in protest against such developments as the Kansas-Nebraska Act of 1854 (which overturned the Missouri Compromise), the Ostend Manifesto, the Dred Scott decision, and the episode of Bleeding Kansas. It was a party strictly Northern, strictly sectional. Its victory at the polls in 1860 had been followed by the secession of the Southern states, one after another, from the Union. In 1860 the nation faced the possibility of a sectional war.

To save the Union, compromise proposals of various sorts were brought into Congress, and to the notice of the President-elect. One of the most sweeping was brought into the Senate by Crittenden, the former Whig. It tendered large concessions to the Southerners as a means of reassuring them. It would have drawn, as an amendment to the Constitution, a compromise line across the territories

[18] *Cong. Globe,* 35 Cong., 2 Sess., 1332 (February 25, 1859); Stanwood: *History of the Presidency,* I, 287.

[19] For Southern efforts to annex Cuba and the Dominican Republic during the Pierce administration, see G. B. Henderson: "Southern Designs on Cuba," *Journal of Southern History,* V (1939), 371–85, and Sumner Welles: *Naboth's Vineyard, The Dominican Republic 1844–1924* (2 vols., New York, 1928), I, 136–210; II, 939–56. See also below, page 230.

at 36° 30′. This would have served as a permanent guarantee of slavery south of that line. It would have extended the guarantee to territories "hereafter acquired," as well as to those currently held. It would have riveted the dubious Buchanan plan of 1847 permanently into the Constitution. It would have riveted into the Constitution, also, perpetual guarantees regarding slavery in the District of Columbia, the domestic slave trade, and the recovery of fugitive slaves.[20] It was a desperate bid for preserving the Union.

Its concessions to the slaveholding states on issues such as slavery in the District of Columbia, the domestic slave trade, and the recovery of fugitive slaves, seemed grievous to Lincoln. Utterly unbearable were its guarantees of slavery in territories south of 36° 30′—in territories to be "hereafter acquired" and those currently held. On this issue Lincoln was adamant. On December 17, 1860, he wrote that if we were to surrender on that issue, "filibustering for all South of us, and making slave states of it, would follow in spite of us . . ." On January 11, 1861, he wrote: "Either way, if we surrender, it is the end of us, and of the government. They [the Southerners] will repeat the experiment upon us *ad libitum*. A year will not pass, till we shall have to take Cuba, as a condition upon which they will stay in the Union." On February 1, he wrote William H. Seward of New York:

> I say now, however, as I have all the while said, that on the territorial question—that is, the question of extending slavery under the national auspices,—I am inflexible. I am for no compromise which *assists* or *permits* the extension of the institution on soil owned by the nation. And any trick by which the nation is to acquire territory, and then allow some local authority to spread slavery over it, is as obnoxious as any other.[21]

[20] *Cong. Globe*, 36 Cong., 2 Sess., 112–14 (December 18, 1860).

[21] Roy P. Basler (ed.): *Collected Works of Abraham Lincoln* (9 vols., New Brunswick, N.J., 1953–5), IV, 154, 172, 183. The Constitution of the Confederacy (Article 4, Section 3) provided: "The Confederate States may acquire new territory. . . . In all such territory, the institution of negro slavery, as it now exists in the Confederate States, shall be recognized and protected by Congress and by the territorial government; and the inhabitants of the several Confederate States and Territories shall have the right to take to such territory any slaves lawfully held by them in any of the States or Territories of the Confederate States."

In 1860, as in 1848, the issue involved more than territory actually in the Union. It covered everything to Darien. That was the rub—that jungle of uncertainty. It was the jungle from which Northerners had fled to the moral security of the Republican platform. The Republican platform had declared, as the Free-Soil platform had in 1848, that, if Manifest Destiny ever was to be fulfilled, slavery should have no share in it.

This sectional reversal of attitudes on the issue of Manifest Destiny was a product of changes in the Union's foundations. The changes included remaking of the sections. In the mid-forties the Union had been composed of three sections, the Northeast, the Southeast, and the West. The West had a unity formed by a great river and by mountains that divided it from the parent sections of the East. It was unionist. It maintained a balance in Congress between the attitudes and interests of the older sections.

By 1860 the West no longer had this unity. It had become northern and southern. The northern half was tied to the Northeast and formed the North. The southern half was tied to the Southeast and formed the South. The Father of Waters now went vexed to the sea. North and South nursed bitterness against each other, bitterness which was a product of memories of the past, current conflicts, fears for the future.

From the past the North remembered the betrayal, in Polk's day, of Northern interests by Southern Democrats on the Oregon issue; the repudiation of a sacred intersectional bargain (the Compromise of 1820) in the Kansas-Nebraska Act of 1854; and Bleeding Kansas. The South remembered the rise of Northern abolitionism, or what looked like it; the support the North had given the Wilmot proviso during, and after, the Mexican War; the adoption of the Personal Liberty Laws, which seemed a repudiation of the Compromise of 1850.

This bitterness was intensified by current issues. They included issues of slavery in the territories—both the old territories and those acquired in the Mexican War. Northerners were demanding that slavery be excluded from all of them; Southerners, that slavery and even guarantees of slavery be extended to all of them. Both sections brushed aside the thesis that slavery was ruled out by nature from all of them. Both ignored the fact that in Bleeding Kansas at the time of the census of 1860, there were only two slaves.

The most ominous issues related to the future. One related to territory "hereafter acquired." Territory "hereafter acquired" meant Cuba. Did it mean more? How were the territories to be acquired, and where would the limit be placed? Who would decide such questions? Would a government controlled by the North decide them? By the election of 1860 the presidency and the control of one house of Congress had passed to the Republicans. Northerners rejoiced over the end of a long control of the national government by Southern Democrats abetted by Northern doughfaces. Southerners thought of Northern control with dread. For the first time in the nation's history, government of the Union would be dominated by a party utterly sectional, a party for which not a single Southern electoral vote had been cast in the 1860 election.

In 1860 pressures, past, present, and future, blasted the Union apart. Not least were past, present, and future expansionist pressures. Combined, they brought the Southern states, after the election of 1860, to secession, to attack on Fort Sumter, and to sectional war. The doctrine of Manifest Destiny, which in the 1840's had seemed Heaven-sent, proved to have been a bomb wrapped up in idealism. The explosion it helped set off seemed likely to snuff out even the beacon light of Mission, which America had been holding aloft to the world.

Chapter X

The Demise of Continentalism

THE PROGRAM OF Manifest Destiny was never consummated. Though the Pacific was reached the acquisition of the rest of the continent from the frozen north to the torrid south remained an uncompleted enterprise. Set in motion by John Quincy Adams, the program had limped for a quarter century. Even under Polk it had not attained the momentum of a national drive. In its later stages it was impeded by roadblocks of slavery and race. But from the beginning it suffered from other handicaps such as the character and personality of its leaders, and, even more fatally, from its own inner contradictions.

These disabling forces were epitomized in John Quincy Adams. He was utterly unfit to lead a movement requiring political support on a nation-wide scale. His unfitness lay in his lack of the accommodating spirit any politician must have to win agreement among sections and parties. He was too austere, too brittle, too far in advance of his age in his thinking to have many admirers. As Secretary of State, he was surrounded by rivals for the succession. As President, he lacked patronage, since he refused to employ office for his own ends. His domestic and foreign programs became a football of politics. His grandiose concept of a continentalized republic hardly got off the ground before the 1840's.

One of his gravest weaknesses as an expansionist was his New England conscience. Unlike most Manifest Destiny spokesmen of the 1840's, he could not subordinate the moral problem of slavery, and its extension, to a getting of land. Indeed, when Manifest Destiny became tied to the extension of slavery in Texas, he was ready to repudiate it. The annexation of Texas, he declared in a public statement of March 3, 1843, to which he had obtained the signatures of twelve other Whig congressmen, would be illegal as well as a conspiracy, would be unauthorized by the Constitution, and would, if agreed to by the federal government, "be identical with dissolution" of the Union.[1] Even worse, from the point of view of territorial acquisition, he soured on all southward expansion after 1845. In compensation, he emphasized northward expansion. Prior to 1845 he had reconciled himself to an Oregon settlement at the line of 49°. He had repeatedly offered this himself in his earlier years. When the annexation of Texas triumphed, he came out for 54° 40′.[2] He sought, like other near-abolitionists, to neutralize, by a seizure of All Oregon, the wrong done freedom by the slavery oligarchy in the theft of Texas. But this only accelerated sectionalism.

From the outset Manifest Destiny—vast in program, in its sense of continentalism—was slight in support. It lacked national, sectional, or party following commensurate with its bigness. The reason was it did not reflect the national spirit. The thesis that it embodied nationalism, found in much historical writing, is backed by little real supporting evidence. Evidence in the form of nation-wide votes is not, of course, to be expected. On an abstraction a national referendum is not held—at least none was ever held on this one. But other factual evidence ought to be adducible. The factual evidence is, however, against the thesis. In 1844 a presidential election testing expansionism as limited to the Texas and Oregon issues was held. The test was not one which would please laboratory scientists, confused as it was by slavery and other issues of domestic politics. A social scientist is content, however, with less than perfection, and proceeds on the theory that the dominant issue in the election was

[1] *Niles' Register*, LXIV (1843), 173–5.
[2] *Cong. Globe*, 29 Cong., 1 Sess., 340 ff. (February 9, 1846).

expansionism. The majority vote in that election was anti-expansionist, but was divided between the Whig and the Liberty parties. Polk won without a majority.[3]

Evidence of congressional voting on issues of expansionism is revealing. In the spring of 1844 a vote was taken in the Senate on Tyler's treaty annexing Texas. The treaty was defeated by a vote of 16 to 35. In the following year a victory was won for annexation by a joint resolution. The vote was 27 to 25. It was won in the Senate by a discreditable trick, if Benton, who supplied the swing vote, is to be believed.[4]

On the issue of Oregon to 54° 40′ a decisive test was taken in 1846, when a treaty, based on a line at 49°, came before the Senate. The number of senators holding out for 54° 40′ was 14 out of 55.[5] While the Senate was considering the Mexican treaty of 1848, a proposal of Jefferson Davis, demanding more territory than the treaty gave, was voted on. It was supported by 11 votes out of 55.[6]

The attraction of individual parcels of territory to voters was probably greater than any general expansionist aspiration would have been. Thus, Texas was attractive on the ground that its people were true-blooded Americans with a right to dispose of themselves as they wished after nine years of independence, that they were eager to be annexed and would bring with them valuable real estate conveniently located. In the Oregon settlement many persons happily accepted a line at 49° who had been troubled by the attempt of war hawks to stretch it to 54° 40′. In the Mexican case many persons voted for a war declaration who regretted it a few months later and voted, in the elections of 1846 and 1848 against the administration responsible for it. Many persons accepted the treaty ending the war, in spite of, rather than because of, the immense tract of territory it added to the Union.

On the issue of an All Mexico step toward continentalism, sup-

[3] Stanwood: *History of the Presidency*, I, 223.
[4] See above, pp. 44–5.
[5] *Senate Journal*, 29 Cong., 1 Sess. (Serial 469), 555.
[6] *Senate Journal*, 30 Cong., 1 Sess. (Serial 502), 627.

port can be tested in the party press. It is alleged to have transcended party lines and to have been nation-wide. Whig support is said to have appeared in such journals as the *National Era*, the *National Whig*, the New York *Courier and Enquirer*, and the New Orleans *Picayune*. This evidence has already been questioned. The editor of the *National Era*, it will be recalled, was fervently opposed to the extension of slavery. He conceived the idea that if the Mexican states—all of them non-slaveholding—were invited to enter the Union on a perfectly voluntary basis, and did so, as they probably would, a cordon of freedom would be drawn around a diseased slavery area, and an unrighteous war would be brought to an honorable and happy end. Again and again the editor repudiated with horror the allegations of irresponsible Democrats that he favored an All Mexico program such as they favored. His paper was primarily a literary and philosophical journal, to which Whittier, Theodore Parker, and Harriet Beecher Stowe contributed. The mere mention of these names will indicate how far wide of the truth is a thesis that Gamaliel Bailey was an All Mexico crusader. Of other Whig papers cited as promoters of the All Mexico crusade—the *National Whig*, the New York *Courier and Enquirer*, and the New Orleans *Picayune*—all were Taylor papers, content with the line as ultimately drawn by the treaty. Not one went for All Mexico; indeed, all opposed it. A search through newspapers as wide as the preservation of files, and as deep as frailties of eyesight and temper permitted, has uncovered not a single Whig party paper which supported or even encouraged the All Mexico crusade. The thesis of bipartisan support for that cause is based, in truth, on unguarded acceptance of Democratic press propaganda, a propaganda as low in its standards of accuracy as it has ever been.[7]

One other contention of like frailty for the thesis that continentalism was fueled by nationalism is the temper—allegedly nationalistic—of the period of its greatest vogue. That argument has been earlier examined in terms of a variety of issues fought over and decided

[7] But see Fuller: *Movement for the Acquisition of All Mexico.*

then. It might be further examined in terms of the political creed of those pressing the doctrine. Who would have maintained in other connections that Cass, Buchanan, Allen, or Douglas, in the North, or Walker, Jefferson Davis, Atchison, or even Polk, in the South, were nationalists in this phase of their careers? And who would maintain that nationalism was expressed in the form of a doctrine that was a virulent and chauvinistic form of states' rights?

Early in this narrative the opinion was expressed that believers in the doctrine of a continental destiny for the United States were, prior to the 1840's, inconsequential in number. It is now in order to estimate how large a part of the public had been converted to it at the height of its vogue in the Mexican War. The estimate is that a small minority of a minority gave continentalism support in those years. Yet this minority, despite its diminutive size, was significant. It could be swelled as the need arose, by appeals to chauvinism, which is latent in all societies. Its spokesmen, in all sections, played for high personal stakes in politics, were exceedingly vocal, and in the years 1845–9 had the blessing of the Polk administration.

On February 21, 1848, John Quincy Adams, official initiator of the program, fell insensible to the floor at his seat in the House. Two days later he died. On the Senate agenda at the time was the Trist *projet*. Death overtook, thus, at almost the same moment, the initiator and the program itself in its All Mexico phase. The death of Adams was marked by a welling up of national emotion. It came from the press, the pulpit, and the rostrum. Such a manifestation had not been witnessed in America since the death of his ancient foe, Andrew Jackson. Eulogies were directed especially to the integrity, the fearlessness, the ability, the dedication to ideals and to the nation, of a great son of New England. Factional rancor, which had assailed Adams throughout life, was hushed, and gave way to praise from almost every faction. The Whigs did their leader honor as a champion of their ideals. Democrats of free-soil convictions praised him as a leader in their battles, though he had refused to join them. Democrats in the Northeast and Northwest honored him for the great expansionist concept he had given them and for much more. They praised him for a closely related concept—that a continent which the American republic was destined to occupy was shut to new European colonization—a concept formulated by him for Monroe as early as 1823. They praised his vigilance against the British, his early triumphs in the cause of American expansionism, and his later championship of the cause of 54° 40′. Praise from such a variety of sources was a tribute to his greatness as a public figure. But it could not altogether conceal the contradictions and incompatibilities which lay unresolved in his program. Only the Democrats of the South, to whom slavery was all-important, found in the man and in his program little to praise.

An epilogue to this drama was a speech in the Senate delivered by Hannegan several months later on the Yucatán issue. The speech gave warning that a European occupation of Yucatán was imminent, that it would violate the non-colonization principle of the Monroe Doctrine, and that it could be forestalled only by a United States occupation. Hannegan took this occasion to deliver a eulogy on Adams as a statesman whose foresight had given the nation a needed shield to protect its rights.[8] The speech and the eulogy were part of a process by which a supposed shield was converted into a staging platform for an active extension of American territorial and other ambitions in the Caribbean.

An important element in the continentalist doctrine was the theory of consent. Consent, expansionists held, must always be cheerfully given by a people about to be absorbed, and in advance of the absorption. The theory was as old as the doctrine itself, indeed, it was older. It had figured in the case of West Florida in 1810, and also, in the case of East Florida, as developed during the War of 1812. In 1823, it seemed applicable to Cuba. Cuba, John Quincy Adams then held, was "indispensable to the continuance and integrity of the Union itself." Its annexation would occur, he thought, by reason of political and physical laws, automatically, and despite any obstacles encountered at home or abroad:

[8] *Cong. Globe,* 30 Cong., 1 Sess., 728 (May 5, 1848).

> But there are laws of political as well as of physical gravitation; and if an apple severed by the tempest from its native tree cannot choose but fall to the ground, Cuba, forcibly disjoined from its own unnatural connection with Spain, and incapable of self support, can gravitate only towards the North American Union, which by the same law of nature cannot cast her off from its bosom.[9]

The concept of apples ripening and gravitating to the bosom of the North American Union was cited in the mid-forties with deserved confidence in the case of Texas. It seemed to Lieutenant Maury, in 1845, applicable to the case of his proposed "State of Toronto." He thought the people there "would be glad to join the Union." He appears not to have known that much of the population there consisted of United Empire Loyalists and their descendants, who were far from being admirers of the United States. In Mexico the people of New Mexico, Sonora, California, etc., were generally believed by editors of the expansionist press to be panting for annexation to the Union.

Ripening is a time-consuming process. It cannot be waited for in some cases. A gentle shaking of the tree becomes necessary. Tree-shaking instructions to be used in California were the Buchanan and Bancroft orders to Larkin and to Sloat in the autumn of 1845. Similar instructions were given commanders of the American military and naval forces in northern Mexico and California after the opening of the Mexican War. Consent now went hand in hand with force. To General Stephen W. Kearny an instruction was sent early in the war as a guide for New Mexico and California. Civil governments of a territorial sort were to be established. Existing officials were to be retained in office, if they were friendly to the United States and willing to take an oath of allegiance. Customs duties were to be reduced, and the people were to be assured that they would have free governments similar to those of the American territories. Kearny's orders were to "act in such a manner as best to conciliate the inhabitants, and render them friendly to the United States."[10]

[9] Worthington C. Ford (ed.): *Writings of John Quincy Adams* (7 vols., New York, 1913–17), VII, 373.

[10] William L. Marcy to General S. W. Kearny, June 3, 1846, *House Exec. Docs.,*

These instructions were carried out well. At Santa Fe, Kearny issued, on arrival, a proclamation for New Mexico. He announced that another American military force as powerful as his own was in his rear and that resistance would therefore be madness. Then he offered all the assurances authorized by his instructions and, in addition, assurances concerning freedom of worship, peaceful possession of property, and protection against Indian enemies—the Eutaws, Navahoes, and others. New Mexicans were absolved of allegiance to Mexico and were claimed as citizens of the United States. This was followed up by a detailed organic law of a "Territory of New Mexico." [11]

In California the same technique was enjoined by Bancroft in his instructions to Sloat. Sloat was commanded to take possession of Monterey, San Francisco, and other ports, in a sequence set down in his instructions. He was ordered to do this, however, if possible "without any strife with the people of California." The people were "rumored" to be well disposed, and the Commodore was ordered to encourage them "to enter into relations of amity with our country." If they should separate themselves from our enemy and establish a government of their own under the auspices of the American flag, "you will take such measures as will best promote the attachment of the people . . . to the United States, will advance their prosperity, and will make that vast region a desirable place of residence for emigrants from our soil. . . . You will bear in mind generally that this country desires to find in California a friend, and not an enemy; to be connected with it by near ties; to hold possession of it, at least during the war; and to hold that possession, if possible, with the consent of its inhabit-

---

29 Cong., 2 Sess. (Serial 499), No. 19, p. 6. An order to Taylor of July 9, 1846, in the drafting of which the President had a personal part, is of special interest: "Availing yourself of divisions which you may find existing among the Mexican people . . . it will be your policy to encourage the separate departments or States . . . to declare their independence of the central government . . . and either to become our allies, or to assume, as it is understood Yucatán has done, a neutral attitude. . . . In such . . . you will give the inhabitants assurances of the protection of your army until the return of peace." Ibid., 30 Cong., 1 Sess. (Serial 520), No. 60, pp. 333–6; Quaife (ed.): *Diary of Polk*, II, 16–17.

[11] House Exec. Docs., 29 Cong., 2 Sess. (Serial 499), No. 19, pp. 20–1, 27–73.

ants." [12] "Consent of its inhabitants" was as much in Bancroft's mind in 1846 as it had been in Buchanan's in 1845. This order, also, was obeyed as far as possible.[13]

Later a suspicious Congress requested to see the instructions the Executive had issued to the armed forces. The documents were submitted. They were complained of by Whigs for what seemed an encroachment by the Executive on functions of Congress. The setting up of civil governments by military order in a conquered province seemed to Whigs an assumption that a cession had occurred without a treaty. The authorization of a territorial government by a military order seemed even more clearly an encroachment on a function of Congress. Such complaints were dismissed by administration Democrats as sheer factionalism. Whatever their motivation, it is clear that the instructions and the proclamations based on them were an advanced stage in the evolution of a theory of consent. The first stage was ripe fruit; the second, a gentle shaking of the tree; the third, consent at the point of a sword.

An unusual form of consent appeared with regard to Mexico proper in 1847–8. It took the shape of an assumption that the best elements in Mexican society desired incorporation of their nation into the North American Union. This assumption was not altogether without basis. It rested on views held by some Puros. The Puros were a radical group in Mexican politics. They were reformers, or purists, in respect to administration, and anti-clericals in respect to the relations between church and state. They admired the tradition, honored in the United States, of the separation of church and state. Some, despairing of Mexican reform from within, were prepared to accept it from without—by incorporation of their country into the United States. Annihilation of Santanistas, the military element, by the American army was the hope of numbers of them, and led them to wish a continuation of the war. A cessation of the war, they felt, should come only on annexation to the United States. It is not easy to ascertain how many Puros held such views. Their patriot leader, Gómez Farías, was certainly not

[12] Ibid., 80–1.
[13] Ibid., 102–3.

among them. Quislings usually do not advertise their views, for they fear that the conqueror may depart and that his identifiable friends, who cannot flee with him, will become uncomfortable. Their number in Mexico was naturally thought to be high by expansionists, such as Breese, who were eager for the absorption of Mexico. It was thought to be low by non-expansionists. Too much reliance was not placed by the Polk administration on hopes that the true feelings of the Mexican people were heard in the whisperings of these elements. American reenforcements were sent to Scott's army even after the Trist *projet* had been approved, to prepare for the contingency of rejection by the Mexican Congress of the changes made in the *projet* by the American Senate and of a subsequent long guerrilla war, supported by all Mexican elements. Thus the theory of annexation by consent cheerfully given, was less successful in the heart of Mexico than it had been in California and in New Mexico.

Fact and fancy make the fabric of history. They should be interwoven systematically if the fabric is to have credibility. An obvious fact in early American history is the steady flow of population from the Atlantic seaboard westward, a continuous movement from 1607 to the 1840's and after. In the course of this flow a frontier population was brought to the eastern edge of the Great Plains by the 1840's. Its outposts were in the Willamette Valley of Oregon and in the inner valley of California. Westerners considered those valleys and the areas surrounding them desirable future homes for themselves and for their children. They had a similar liking for Texas, though some Westerners might have wished that the Texas issue had not included the problem of the extension of slavery. Such are the facts, the grass roots, of American expansionism. They give meaning and vitality to the history of a process.

But where does fancy enter the fabric? What was the role of continentalism in this history? Was it a weighty article carried by a frontiersman in the rude baggage he took to the upper or lower Mississippi Valley? Frontiersmen carried politics with them. In the period of the 1840's they were Whigs or Democrats. Some were troubled about the extension of slavery over new country; others were not. Some were sensitive to issues of race in a new country; others were less so. Some were pleased with the thought of expansion "northward to the arctic and southward to the tropic." Others —probably most—were troubled about a war with England which 54° 40′ was likely to generate, or a party clash over Texas, or a sectional conflict over the extension of slavery. An idea, even a fanciful idea, looms larger to politicians than it does to humble citizens at the grass roots. It does so naturally. Politicians gather harvests from fancies. And historians, who make a business of gathering fancies, philosophies, and ideologies from orations, speeches, and newspaper editorials, and setting them forth in neat order without reference to hard facts such as votes, sectionalism, partisanship, and the ambitions of politicians, are likely to overemphasize the "idea" in history. They are likely to do so especially when the idea is as tenuous and as extensive as the doctrine of continentalism.

Ideas are spread by propaganda. The greater the resistance to an idea, the greater the need for propaganda. If the core of an idea is the taking of another's property, it may stir up moral objections. In that case, the quantity, the vigor, and the repetition of the propaganda has to be abnormally great. Also, the propaganda must be of a special sort. It must surround the taking with an aura of reasonableness and good conscience. Emphasis must be directed to the end to be achieved, especially if the end is desired by Providence. The means employed (to get consent, for instance) must not be inquired into too closely. Particularly are such rules to be applied in a democracy, where public opinion has to be coddled. But it holds true even, to some extent, in a police state.

Propaganda designed to prepare for a seizure of territory has a characteristic language. It comes interlarded with stereotypes, parallels, and figures of speech. The stereotypes of the forties were "war of liberation," "protection of the better classes," "regeneration of the downtrodden," "better use of the gifts of Providence," "superior rights of God's elect." Parallels and figures of speech were numerously used—too numerous to mention here. They did not always fit well at the joints. Another characteristic of the language was that it was upside down. Old and familiar words and phrases took on meanings opposite to those they had once had. Thus a term frequently used—"extending the area of freedom" —came to mean "extending the area of slavery." "A war of liberation" came to mean "a war of acquisition;" "a government of a colony by a monarchy" became, *ipso facto,* "a government by a tyranny." "Monarchy" was a term redolent of decay and suggested a prompt burial.

Counter-propaganda was, of course, resorted to by the opposition. It took the form of challenging the idealism in expansionist projects, and, also, the honesty of the language employed in furthering the projects. Questions were raised, for instance, as to the truth of predictions that neighboring peoples would cheerfully consent to annexation. The truth seemed to be that those peoples were, in most cases, in terror of such proposals. Questions as to the disinterestedness of extending citizenship to neighboring peoples were raised. If Indians in neighboring Latin America were to have citizenship thrust on them, why was it not conferred on the noble red man in the United States? Extension of American citizenship was thought to be a perverted ideal—perverted to the uses of aggrandizement.

A favorite method of deflating propaganda was dissecting its terms. The dissection was designed to expose shiftings of meaning. Shiftings were shown to be always in the same direction, always demonstrating that the pronoun "thine" really meant "mine." Usually dissection was limited to some single word or phrase. But a more general operation was performed by the *National Intelligencer* early in 1848, in an editorial entitled "Political Clap-Trap." The "Clap-Trap" was designed, according to the editor, to hold the entire land "spell bound, as if the lies of magic were realities and a syllable or two of gibberish could reverse all the laws of nature and turn human intelligence into brutishness." Illustrations of "cabalistic" phrases intended to perform these miracles were given.

> One of these is "Our manifest destiny," a shallow and impious phrase. Who shall assure us that it is not of the "Devil's fetching."

> Another is "Anglo Saxon race." This patronymic is meant for those who know as much about who the Angles and who the Saxons were as they do of those Jewish affiliations which run back to the twelve sons of Jacob. Oh, miserable humbug of History! Another perverted phrase is "Our country, right or wrong," which justifies supporting an iniquitous war.[14]

Yet phrases and slogans do serve politicians and are not to be overlooked in the writing of history. "Manifest Destiny," "Anglo-Saxon race," "All Mexico," and "Monroe's principle," rendered valiant service to Polk. They were trumpeted to the electorate while he went ahead with the business of extending American territory to the Pacific. They were a factor in the surge to the Pacific, the greatest territorial advance achieved by a single administration in the history of the Republic.

In a recapitulation of the reasons for the virtual disappearance of continentalism from American thought after 1848, one, in particular, may be explicitly stated now, which has only been intimated before—that continentalism was just a rider on an aspiration to reach the Pacific, a rider that dropped off after Americans had fixed themselves at the water's edge by the treaties of 1846 and 1848. But probably other explanations are more fundamental—a national reluctance to add peoples of mixed blood to a blood that was pure, and an unwillingness in some parts of the population to have unfree blood added as well. Only those people should be admitted to the temple who would qualify someday for equal statehood in the Union, and this requirement the colored and mixed races to the south could not meet. These are the principal reasons why continentalism was allowed to die, and why, later, another concept had to be devised to take its place.

[14] *National Intelligencer* (t.w.), January 15, 1848.

Chapter XI

The Rise and Fall of Insular Imperialism

A FEW POLITICIANS of lively imagination still sought, after the demise of continentalism, to resurrect it. One of them was William H. Seward, of New York. He was a Whig, a close associate of Thurlow Weed in politics, and a leading Northern supporter of Taylor for the presidency in 1848, though an ardent foe at the same time of the extension of slavery. He toyed with the idea that the United States would someday become a continent-embracing republic, simply by consenting to requests of neighbors for annexation. He did not make this a dominant article of his faith, however, in the manner of the idealist O'Sullivan. He objected vigorously to the annexation of Texas, to insistence on All Oregon, and to the Mexican War. Concerning Canada he publicly expressed the view in 1857 that she would always maintain, when she had become an independent republic, a mere sisterly relationship to the United States. Yet he pronounced a blessing on Manifest Destiny in all its breath-taking inclusiveness in the presidential campaign of 1860. In a speech delivered at St. Paul, Minnesota, he declared that the United States would extend in the future from the frozen North to the burning South. He had ideas, even, where the capital would be. He had once thought it would be in the great valley of Mexico, where the Aztecs had ruled. Now he thought it would be right near where he stood, at St. Paul. The fervor with which he expressed these ideas was inspiring even if somewhat contrived. Perhaps the oratorical flights were intended to set listeners throughout the nation to watching the stars at a time when the foundations of the Union were dissolving.[1] Or it may be that the orator was simply indulging a propensity for striking pronouncements.

In 1867 Seward obtained Alaska from Russia. More correctly, perhaps, he received it from Russia. The province was thrown at him, much as Louisiana had been at Jefferson. It had not been negotiated for, and the public had not desired it. The transfer was hardly known to the public before it was on its way to completion. The territory was offered because it had become an encumbrance to the Russian Tsar. The American public received it with considerable grumbling. It seemed a vast glacier and became known as "Seward's Folly," because Seward had thought it worth taking. It was accepted by the Senate as a courtesy to the Tsar, who was regarded as having been friendly to the Union during the Civil War. Chiefly it was taken because it seemed quite cheap at the price of $7,200,000. Its purchase was proof of Seward's liking for territory, but hardly evidence of a public trend toward Manifest Destiny.[2]

In the years 1865–8 Seward persisently sought insular positions, especially in the Caribbean. He sought them from Denmark, Sweden, Spain, and the Dominican Republic. He hoped Cuba and Puerto Rico would some day come to the United States. His goals were strategic in this part of the world; he felt a need for outposts of American defense. He also desired the Hawaiian Islands. He

[1] George E. Baker (ed.): *Works of William H. Seward* (5 vols., Boston, 1884), IV, 330 ff; Frederick Bancroft: *Life of William H. Seward* (2 vols., New York, 1900), II, ch. 42.

[2] Frank A. Golder: "Purchase of Alaska," *A.H.R.*, XXV (1919–20), 411 ff.; Thomas A. Bailey: *America Faces Russia* (Ithaca, 1950).

acquired the Midway Islands in 1867, two specks northwest of Hawaii, sandy, barren, inhabited by birds though not otherwise, and comprising a dominion of one and one half square miles. He got them for the price of sailing in. Except for them he went unrewarded in his insular campaign. The public exhibited a massive indifference to expansion of any sort and the Senate showed an active opposition to it. Certainly the era was a continuous demonstration of a temper in the American public the opposite of expansionism.

The same must be said of the era of Grant as president. During this era the President himself desired the Dominican Republic and made persistent efforts to obtain it. He met indifference in the public, and in the Senate active hostility from Charles Sumner, the powerful chairman of the Committee on Foreign Relations, who was not disposed to add to the voting strength of the South in Congress. Not even the wishes of a popular President could overcome the public's reluctance to acquire more territory.[3]

Charles Sumner, in these years, desired Canada. He also wanted to chastise the British for unneutral conduct toward the North during the Civil War. Which of these desires was uppermost in his mind was not always made clear. In 1869 he delivered in the Senate an inflammatory speech in which he pronounced the British liable for the direct and indirect losses arising out of a failure to perform neutral duties during the war. He believed they should be obliged to repay not only immediate losses to American commerce as a result of fitting out Confederate raiders and releasing them from their ports, but also losses arising from alleged premature recognition of Confederate belligerency, prolongation of the war "by years," and even arrest of a natural increase in the American merchant marine which would otherwise have come

[3] Sumner Welles: *Naboth's Vineyard,* I, chs. 2–5. An active American agent for years in Dominican matters was the Bostonian William L. Cazneau, the second husband of Jane McManus Storms. He was appointed special agent of the Executive in the Pierce administration, and for twenty years he and his wife were active in schemes to bring the Republic under the American flag. He had heavy personal interests in strategic locations on the island, and for that reason his campaign was regarded with suspicion in Washington. See Wallace: *Destiny and Glory,* ch. 12.

about. He believed the damages totaled in excess of two billion dollars, and he would not have objected if the British had been obliged to make a bankruptcy offer of all Canada to the United States in settlement. The British made no such offer, and the American public was uninterested. Sumner came to be regarded as a nuisance in his post of chairman of the Committee on Foreign Relations and presently was ousted from it with the active aid of the President.[4]

In the late 1880's and the 1890's major changes occurred in the life of the nation, and with them came a revival of agitation for expansion. The nation's economy reached maturity. The era of well-watered free public land ended. Pioneers moved farther and farther into areas of semi-aridity. Foods and fibers in immense quantity flowed into the markets of the world. Surpluses in other countries developed. Grain elevators and warehouses became glutted; prices steeply declined. By the mid-1890's farm prices in the United States were at their lowest levels since the black days of the 1840's. Industry also generated surpluses and corresponding price declines. The urban economy dropped from relative prosperity in the 1880's to a level comparable, after the panic of 1893, to that of agriculture. The economy as a whole sank into a prostration unparalleled since the formation of the Constitution. The sobering fact that the youthfulness of the nation had slipped away and needed somehow to be restored, was recognized by politicians of all parties. The restoratives were principally of the home variety.

Republicans, however, listed expansion among the restoratives. They considered it good in principle. It would restore youth and, by generating trade, would remove surpluses. Republicans desired it in a new, primarily insular, form. Cuba and the Hawaiian Islands were especially mentioned. Insular expansionism was not altogether new, of course. Islands had been recommended earlier. But exclusive insularism had never been in vogue before; the continent had always been preferred. Cuba had been packaged with the continent as part of the "wash" of the Mississippi River.[5] But

[4] Allan Nevins: *Hamilton Fish* (rev. ed., 2 vols., New York, 1957), II, ch. 19.
[5] New Orleans *Picayune*, October 3, 1847.

in the 1890's islands had attained in the minds of Republicans a dignity and identity of their own.

Islands in the mid-Pacific were of especial value. They seemed way stations for transporting surpluses to the boundless markets of China. Also, they were potential bases for refitting and refueling a merchant marine and a new navy. Islands, in short, were restoratives of youth and preventives of premature old age. These ideas, held by some Republicans as early as the beginning of the 1890's, were clarified, after the outbreak of the war with Spain, by a young Middle Westerner, Albert J. Beveridge, for an Eastern-seaboard audience. The thirty-six-year-old politician was then an aspirant to a seat in the United States Senate.

> American factories are making more than the American people can use; American soil is producing more than they can consume. Fate has written our policy for us; the trade of the world must and shall be ours. . . . We will establish trading-posts throughout the world as distributing points for American products. We will cover the ocean with our merchant marine. Great colonies governing themselves, flying our flag and trading with us, will grow about our posts of trade. Our institutions will follow our flag on the wings of commerce. And American law, American order, American civilization, and the American flag will plant themselves on shores hitherto bloody and benighted but by those agencies of God henceforth to be made beautiful and bright.[6]

Especially attractive were the Hawaiian Islands, which had drawn expansionist notice for generations. They had been part of an American trade to the Pacific, as old, almost, as the nation. They had been a way station in a trade to Canton in which furs, gathered on the Northwest coast, and sandalwood, loaded at Honolulu, had been taken to China and exchanged for teas, silks, and chinaware. Later they had become the focus of a whaling interest, then a missionary interest, and finally a sugar-planting interest.[7] In the 1890's they had become derelicts on the ocean, just

[6] Claude G. Bowers: *Beveridge and the Progressive Era* (Boston, 1932), 67.

[7] Harold W. Bradley: *American Frontier in Hawaii* (Stanford, Cal., 1942). The continuity of American interests in the Hawaiian Islands is traced at length in *Senate Reports*, 55 Cong., 2 Sess. (Serial 3622), No. 681, pp. 67 ff.

as California had been, a half century earlier, on land. Their government was a burlesque of monarchy, presided over by a queen, Liliuokalani, who had recently come to the throne. She was a weak, romantic, and ineffective figure. Political strength in the islands lay with the planters—the Americans. They wanted to be rid of the monarchy and annexed to the United States. Annexation would bring stability, honesty, and vigor to government, and would give, in addition, the privileges of a subsidized market for sugar in the United States. These interests had a sympathetic friend in John W. Stevens, the American minister at Honolulu. He believed the American government would readily give recognition to a regime of a republic in Honolulu, and let this be known. Early in 1893, indications of an uprising in the capital appeared. A war vessel of the United States had marines handy at Honolulu, and these, Stevens thought, should be sent ashore to guard Americans and their property in case of an emergency. They were brought ashore. On January 17, 1893, the *émeute* occurred. The supporters of the Queen, overawed by the marines, offered little fight. She was deposed and a provisional government was organized. The new government at once applied for annexation to the United States. A treaty of annexation was concluded and sent to Washington. With the treaty went a warning from Stevens that the British would be glad, if the United States should not be, to have the islands. The treaty was submitted to the Senate.[8] There, however, trouble appeared. A constitutional majority for ratification was not in sight. A severe defeat for the treaty would be ruinous. The days of the Harrison administration were drawing to a close. A Democratic administration, headed by Grover Cleveland, was on the way in. A wish had been expressed by Cleveland to have the vote deferred. He could not be safely ignored in view of the situation in the Senate and the vote was deferred.

Expansionism, as a party matter, was in a state of transition. It had lost old friends. It lacked enough of the new to be safe.

[8] Julius W. Pratt: *Expanionists of 1898* (Baltimore, 1936), chs. 2–4, is standard. A detailed account of the *émeute* is William D. Alexander: *Later Years of the Hawaiian Monarchy and the Revolution of 1893* (Honolulu, 1896).

Among Democrats, North and South, it was in disfavor. They denounced it, in its insular form, as un-American. Only a small minority of the party held otherwise. Among Republicans it had ardent friends, especially among a younger set—devotees of the strenuous life, individuals tending a little to jingoism, those who chafed at restrictions on the nation imposed by continental limits and who considered growth indispensable. But a maturer element in the party, who had great weight, adhered to older views, and disliked especially a colonialized form of expansionism. They clung to the view that unless peoples could be admitted to the Union as equal states, they should not be admitted at all, and that any other course would destroy the foundations of the Union. They had doubts about the *émeute* in Hawaii. They questioned, as did Cleveland, whether cheerful consent had been given by the Hawaiians to the overthrow of their Queen, and to the application for admission to the temple of freedom made so soon after.

An investigation was ordered by Cleveland on entering the White House. It was made with thoroughness.[9] It revealed a great deal of American complicity in the *émeute* and not much native support. It showed that the natives had been overawed into silence by the marines, and called attention to the suspiciously prompt submission to the United States of a treaty of annexation. The treaty seemed another of those cases of consent at the point of a sword. Cleveland felt obliged to withdraw the treaty from the Senate in the interests of international morality. A restoration of the Queen to her throne would have required force, and Cleveland shrank from applying it. Control in Hawaii remained with the revolutionary government, which simply sat out the Democratic years. In 1897, with the Republicans returned to Washington, a new annexation treaty was negotiated and submitted to the Senate by McKinley. Again a combination of Democrats and anti-expansion Republicans formed, and it was strong enough to discourage a test vote. It discouraged a vote even on a joint resolution of annexation.

[9] The report of the special commissioner appears in House Exec. Docs., 53 Cong., Sess. (Serial 3294), No. 1, Part 1, 467–1397. The earlier portion of this ponderous volume is devoted to background materials.

A further period of waiting for the wheel of fortune to turn became necessary.

While the wheel stood, propaganda moved. Propaganda had been resorted to earlier, as soon as the annexation issue appeared. It had come from the newer Republicans, from men such as Alfred T. Mahan, Henry Cabot Lodge, and Theodore Roosevelt, and from veterans such as Henry M. Teller. They were all believers in the efficacy of foreign remedies for domestic afflictions. Mahan especially had that belief. He was a naval officer with a strong liking for history. He was, in outlook, a realist, and an advocate of a big navy. As a historian he had outstanding gifts—a keen mind, a lucid pen, and powers of generalization of a high order. He had been detailed to lecture on naval history at the War College in Newport in 1886. In 1890 he published his lectures in a volume entitled *The Influence of Sea Power upon History, 1660–1783*. In 1892 he followed with a work entitled *The Influence of Sea Power upon the French Revolution and Empire, 1793–1812*. In the first work he traced the rise and decline of great maritime powers; in the second, the role played by sea power in defeating France in her bid for European domination. In both works he cogently analyzed elements of sea power—bases, colonies, communications, logistics. His histories took rank instantly as works of genius. They were welcomed by navalists throughout the world as lessons offered by the past to the present. They were seized upon as propaganda for the acceleration of big-navy programs already under way. They were greeted with especial enthusiasm by Lodge and Theodore Roosevelt.

As soon as the Hawaiian issue reached the stage of decision Mahan entered that propaganda campaign. He prepared for the *Forum* an article entitled "Hawaii and Our Future Sea Power," which appeared late in February 1893. He made full use in it of his now famous method of historical analysis. He took for his postulate the concept that growth is a vital necessity to a nation. Cessation of growth amounts to stagnation and decay.[10] Growth for

[10] The growth concept of national well-being was, when Mahan wrote, already an old one. It was set forth by the *Democratic Review* in May 1848, when the

the United States is possible only at sea. On land we are arrested —at the south by a race wholly alien to us, at the north by a people whose freedom to choose their own affiliations we must respect. In the Pacific, the Hawaiian Islands lie just where our routes to the Orient converge. Those islands are a halfway house to China. They will powerfully affect, hereafter, the commercial and military control of the Pacific. Our need for them will increase with the building of an isthmian canal. The people of those islands have shown a wish for union with us. If we do not take them, the British inevitably and rightly will desire them. They will desire them in order to close the circuit of their bases round the world. The article opened a series, reissued in book form in 1897, all directed to the theme of growth and the inevitability of decay if the growth is retarded.[11]

Inspired by Mahan's clarity and logic, Lodge entered the field.

Mexican cession was nearing completion, in an editorial entitled "Growth of States." The article opened with an alleged "truism" that a state must either be on the increase or decrease. This is true of all states. But a federal democracy, from its very nature, is better fitted than other forms of government for an almost indefinite increase in territory. We have to show the world that we are not only capable of carrying on war but are equal to the emergencies of victory. Clarifying this theme, the article pointed out an obvious truth. "In order that animals may grow, they first seize hold of their food, then swallow and digest it, then assimilate it. We have fairly got Mexico in our possession; shall we swallow, digest, and assimilate the entire country?"

An even better statement of the same idea appeared in the New York *Sun* (w.) on October 9, 1847:

> He [the American] is born and bred to think and act for himself almost as soon as he leaves the apron strings. And what giants have grown out of his stock. Men exalted in every act and profession of life. Heroes, sages and poets —and best of all, intelligent, hard-working men, proud of their craft and calling. Energy and endurance are synonymous with the American. These push him to the outmost verge of things. They unfurl his sails in the remotest seas and pluck imperial trophies for him. . . . By the quality of his social organism and civilization he is carnivorous—he swallows up and will continue to swallow up whatever comes in contact with him, man or empire. Whoever closely scans the aspect of the genus man on earth cannot fail to see that the Saxon on one hemisphere and the Anglo-Saxon or American on the other, are absorbing the world. But the American will yet transcend the Saxon—his instincts are nobler and his religious and political thesis better fitted for social triumph.

[11] *Forum,* XV (1893), 1–11. The article was on the stands by February, though it was in the March number. The book referred to is Alfred T. Mahan: *The Interests of America in Sea Power* (Cambridge, 1897).

He was also a historian and, in addition, an avowed politician. He adopted the Mahan thesis in an article published in the *Forum* in March 1895. He too considered growth essential to the vigor of a nation. He agreed that it was not possible in the direction of Mexico, Central America, and South America. The people and the lands there were not of a desirable kind. But he differed with his naval friend regarding Canada. There should be, northward from the Rio Grande to the arctic, but one flag and one country. Every consideration of national welfare and power demands it. As for the Hawaiian Islands, they certainly must be ours. Also Cuba, which will become an even greater necessity to us once the Nicaraguan canal is built. The Hawaiian Islands, Cuba, and the canal complement one another in a logical pattern of growth.[12]

To such an application of history to current needs Theodore Roosevelt made less contribution than his friends. He had written early in the 1880's a not too profound work entited *The Naval War of 1812*, one of the lessons of which was the need, in time of peace, to make thorough preparation for war. It sold well for a few years, then seemed to go to sleep. Mahan's writings wakened it, and in 1894 it began reappearing in new editions. Politically this was a stroke of luck, for the book, combined with the influence of Republican friends, such as Lodge, brought him appointment in 1897 as Assistant Secretary of the Navy in the McKinley administration. In that office he labored zestfully for a bigger and better navy.

The appearance of a demand for overseas colonies coincided in time with a revival of racism in the United States. As in the 1840's, expansionism synchronized with racism. In each period the postulates were the superiority of the Anglo-Saxon peoples over all others and the obligation of the superiors to give leadership to the inferiors. In the 1840's, racism had crossed party lines. But it had infected the anti-expansionist Whigs more than it had the Democrats. In the 1880's and 1890's it was especially virulent among Republicans, the party of the expansionists.

[12] *Forum,* XIX (1895), 8 ff.

It has been felt by some historians that the dual concept of racial superiority of Anglo-Saxons and leadership owed to racial inferiors was a basic force in generating expansionism in the 1890's. The concept is said to have been fathered by a number of prominent authors in the 1880's and to have gained wide acceptance. The authors especially named as such intellectual progenitors of imperialism in the 1890's are John Fiske, Josiah Strong, and John W. Burgess. Their alleged role is of such significance as to require a closer examination than it has yet had.

John Fiske was a philosopher, historian, and free-lance writer, distinguished for his range and felicity in dealing with history especially. In 1885 he published in *Harper's New Monthly Magazine* an article that was part of a lecture printed in full in the same year in a book.[13] In it he gave a graphic account of the disorders produced in Europe in early times by successive waves of Germanic, Mongolian, and Mohammedan invaders, and the gradual return to order thereafter. The race which led in the return was the Anglo-Saxon. One means it used was the concept of representative government, a major gift to the world. The race possessed physical as well as intellectual powers, as exhibited in the Old World and the New, especially fecundity and enterprise. The fecundity was so marvelous that the day was near when four-fifths of mankind would trace their pedigree to English forebears and the language of man would be the language of Shakespeare. Evidence of high talent on the American side was the development of the principle of federalism in the American Constitution. This seemed to Fiske as great a contribution, especially in its promise for the future, as representative government. The author was a racist, unquestionably, though not in the narrowest sense. The term "Anglo-Saxon" seemed to him to be a slovenly colloquialism. Anglo-Saxons were the various racial elements that had flowed into the melting pot of the United States.

But racism was not carried in the article to any anticipated con-

[13] *Harper's New Monthly Magazine,* LXX (1885), 578–90; John Fiske: *American Political Ideas* (New York, 1885), 101–52. The lectures were originally given in England in 1880.

clusion of expansionism. The central theme of the author was world federalism. The article was an early formulation of that concept as a means to future peace. It bore the arresting title "Manifest Destiny," but this was used as a foil, merely, for the bigger concept. Actually it was derisive of Manifest Destiny in the sense in which the term had been used in the 1840's. It devoted some paragraphs to poking fun at the idea of a United States extending from pole to pole. But these paragraphs had been omitted, for reasons of space, from the article in magazine form. Mankind, as a whole, Fiske thought, will ultimately form one huge federation in which peoples will manage their local affairs in independence, but will submit issues of international import to the decision of a central tribunal supported by the public opinion of the human race. Only then will it become possible soberly to speak of a "United States" stretching from pole to pole. Here was the antithesis of any concept of Anglo-Saxonism blossoming into expansionism, though portions of the article sounded otherwise. These portions were later excerpted by historians and created confusion in the thinking of uninformed readers.

Another writer listed among race propagandists was Reverend Josiah Strong. He was a Congregational pastor especially interested in "home missions" in the United States. In 1885 he wrote for the American Home Missionary Society a work entitled *Our Country,* in which he appealed for funds to evangelize the United States. The theme of his work was the perils to the Protestant way of life found in the United States, which needed to be met and overcome. The perils, described chapter by chapter, were excessive immigration from Europe, Roman Catholicism, Rum, Tobacco, Mormonism, Socialism, improperly used wealth, the City, etc., etc. They added up to a dismal total. Chapter 13, strategically placed just before the final one appealing for money, was more hopeful. Anglo-Saxonism, if preserved, would save the world. The author knew well the Darwinian concept of survival of the fittest and entirely agreed with it. He knew, also, John Fiske's concept of Anglo-Saxon superiority, with which he likewise agreed, though he maintained that he himself had given it to the world some years before. To him, the Anglo-Saxon race meant all who could speak English. He believed the race was being prepared by Providence to spread the tenets of Protestant Christianity. It was being prepared for the final competition of the races. "If I read not amiss, this powerful race will move down upon Mexico, down upon Central and South America, out upon the islands of the sea, over upon Africa and beyond. And can any one doubt that the result of this competition of races will be the 'survival of the fittest'?"

Strong spelled out in detail the method of the competition. No war to exterminate the inferior races would be necessary. The feeblest of them would be wiped out mercifully, merely by the diseases of, and contacts with, a higher civilization, for which they were unprepared. Races of marked inferiority are intended to be precursors merely of the superior. They are voices crying in the wilderness: "Prepare ye the way of the Lord!" Races, somewhat stronger, will simply be submerged. Decay already is far along in their superstitions and creeds. The dead crust of fossil faiths—Catholic, Mohammedan, Jew, Buddhist, and Brahmin—is being shattered. The pieces left in the process will be assimilated or simply neutralized by the stronger Anglo-Saxons. The plan of God is to weaken weaklings and supplant them with better and finer materials.[14]

Ideas of racial superiority were entertained, also, by John W. Burgess, a professor of political science at Columbia University. He was more broad-minded than Fiske or Strong. He was willing to include all Teutonic peoples among those possessing genius for political organization. He had been trained as a student in Germany and was, not unnaturally, desirous of including Teutons in the charmed circle. In 1890 he published a work, *Political Science and Comparative Constitutional Law,* in which he went so far as to admit that Aryans generally had talents. But still, the Teutonic nations had shown genius above all others in developing solutions to problems of modern political organization.[15]

[14] Josiah Strong: *Our Country* (New York, 1885), ch. 13.
[15] John W. Burgess: *Political Science and Comparative Constitutional Law* (Boston, 1890), I, 4, 37–45.

From writings such as these the conclusion has been reached that a causal relationship existed between the racism of the decade 1885–95 and the imperialism of the late 1890's, that racism was the climate in which imperialism flourished. Whether it did flourish then, whether it attained full growth prior to, during, or after the war with Spain in 1898–9, are questions left relatively unexplored. They deserve to be fully explored.[16]

In the late 1880's and early 1890's Americans were much concerned about their deepening economic depression, its causes, distressing effects, and cures. Political parties were likewise concerned about them. They had widely diverse views, but they agreed in one respect—that any cures to be applied should be home cures, not overseas ones. The Populists, in their famous platform of 1892, recommended among other things free and unlimited coinage of silver at a ratio of 16 to 1, public ownership and operation of railroads, graduated income taxes, postal savings banks, an eight-hour working day, and restriction of undesirable immigration. The Democrats recommended such measures as the coinage of silver and gold without discrimination between them, tariffs for revenue, and the defeat of the "force bills" Lodge was proposing to coerce the South. Republicans recommended protective tariffs, bimetallism, and more stringent laws to exclude criminals, paupers, and contract labor. No party recommended overseas expansion as a restorative or cure. A possible exception in 1892 was a Republican proposal of "achievement of manifest destiny in its broadest sense," which was in no way defined, however, and probably meant to innocent readers almost nothing at all.

In the presidential campaign of 1896 problems of domestic politics were still predominant. Free silver was the central issue. The Democrats, merged now with the Populists, recommended free and unlimited coinage of silver at the ratio of 16 to 1. The Republicans opposed it. The Republicans finally said something on the subject of expansionism. They looked forward to the "ultimate union of all English-speaking parts of the continent by the free con-

[16] Pratt: *Expansionists of 1898,* ch. 1; Richard Hofstadter: *Social Darwinism in American Thought* (New York, 1959, rev. ed.), ch. 9.

sent of its inhabitants," the "free consent" indicating, perhaps, that this was not considered a quick relief for the nation's ills. They thought, also, that the Hawaiian Islands should be "controlled" by the United States, that a Nicaraguan canal should be built and operated by the United States, and that the Danish West Indies should be secured for a much-needed naval station.[17] This reflected the views of Lodge, who had been chairman of the platform committee.

Racism bubbled up a little in these platforms. It undoubtedly was present in public opinion in the 1890's, as it had been in the 1840's. It reflected fear of competition with immigrants from southeastern Europe for jobs that were hard to find, and fear, also, regarding the dwindling of desirable free public lands. It could not be proclaimed too loudly at election time, and lurked, in platforms, behind such phrases as "criminal, pauper and contract immigration," "dumping-ground for the known criminals and professional paupers of Europe," and "alien ownership of land."

In the 1890's new theories concerning the advance or retardation of races were being developed by anthropologists. One was set forth by Franz Boaz in 1894, that any superiority held by some races in cultural matters was a product of accidents of history and opportunity rather than of innate capacity.[18] This had been suspected by many people earlier. Carl Schurz, for instance, had believed, already in the 1870's, that Indians could be regenerated and assimilated, if their tribalism were broken up. The Dawes Act of 1887 had been based on such premises. Some Republicans thought well of the possibilities of regenerating the Negro. Democrats were divided on that issue. In the big Northern cities Democrats found virtue in racial tolerance. But Southern Democrats considered Negroes innately inferior. However, Southern Democrats were not imperialists in the 1890's, and were certainly not interested in redeeming inferior races in the Pacific islands.

[17] Stanwood: *History of the Presidency,* I, chs. 30, 31.

[18] Franz Boas: "Human Faculty as Determined by Race," *Proceedings,* American Association for the Advancement of Science, XLIII (1894), 301–27. For a general survey, see William Stanton: *The Leopard's Spots* (Chicago, 1960).

Confusion of thought on the racial issue was revealed in the 1890's by Republican politicians. In the 1896 platform, for instance, they expressed unwillingness to have the mixed races of Mexico and Central America in the temple of freedom. They thought only the English-speaking peoples of North America ought to be admitted. Yet, in the same breath they proposed to "control" the brown and yellow races of the Hawaiian Islands.

On the other hand, objections on precisely racial grounds were raised by Carl Schurz to annexing the Hawaiian Islands. Himself of foreign birth and confident that European immigrants flowing into the United States could be assimilated, he drew the line at Orientals, especially mixed Orientals such as the Hawaiians. In 1893 he wrote an article on the Hawaiian issue for *Harper's* in which he declared:

> Their population, according to the census of 1890, consists of 34,436 natives, 6,186 half castes, 7,495 born in Hawaii of foreign parents, 15,301 Chinese, 12,360 Japanese, 8,602 Portuguese, 1,928 Americans . . . and other foreigners. If there ever was a population unfit to constitute a State of the American Union, it is this.[19]

On other grounds than race Schurz deemed Hawaiians ineligible for admission to the Union. They lived in the tropics, and the tropics do not produce democracy. Also, they were isolated in tight communities on their islands and, therefore, hard to assimilate. Foreign territories should be annexed only if their inhabitants could be admitted as states to the Union at no distant day on an equal footing with the older states. To do otherwise would be to undermine the foundations of the Union.

Schurz had like objections to annexing Cuba. Cubans were comparable to Mexicans. Schurz referred ironically to a speech made by Seward in 1868 in which the Secretary had predicted that "in twenty years the city of Mexico would be the capital of the United States." Schurz thought our politics would certainly become "Mexicanized" if that prediction ever materialized.

[19] Carl Schurz: "Manifest Destiny," *Harper's New Monthly Magazine*, LXXXVII (1893), 737 ff.

Even Theodore Roosevelt had racial qualms about expanding over tropical areas. In 1894 he reviewed, in the *Sewanee Review,* a work by an Englishman, Charles F. Pearson, who was a pessimist on the subject of expanding over the tropics. Pearson believed that "higher races" simply could not get established in the tropics. Only in the temperate zones did they do well. White peoples who moved into tropical or subtropical areas were inevitably absorbed and vanished. Roosevelt fully agreed with such views. He believed replacement of the tropical peoples by peoples of the temperate zone impossible. Tropical peoples throw off the yoke of their conquerors and become independent in any case. A northern race can maintain a hold in the tropics only by a complete renewal of its pure blood every generation. Surely this was no hopeful prospect for taking over Hawaii. And yet the distinguished reviewer thought very favorably, if his private correspondence of that period reflected his opinions, of taking over Hawaii.[20]

As late as June 1898, Richard F. Pettigrew, of South Dakota, in similar terms declared tropical peoples unsuitable for admission to the Union. In a clash in the Senate over the annexation of Hawaii, he declared:

> The founders of this government—recognizing the difficulty of maintaining as a unit a republic of extensive proportions—inaugurated the Federal system, a union of sovereign States, hoping thereby to extend self government over vast areas and to maintain therein the purity of republican principles—each State . . . of necessity containing a population . . . of men capable of governing themselves. Therefore the founders . . . made it an unwritten law that no area should be brought within the bounds of the Republic which did not, and could not, sustain a race equipped in all essentials for the maintenance of free civilization and capable of upholding within its boundaries a republican form of government. . . . Therefore, if we adopt the policy of acquiring tropical countries, where republics cannot live, we overturn the theory upon which this Government is established.[21]

[20] *Sewanee Review,* II (1893–4), 353 ff.; Elting E. Morison (ed.): *Letters of Theodore Roosevelt* (8 vols., Cambridge, 1951–4), vols. I, II.

[21] *Cong. Record,* 55 Cong., 2 Sess., 6228 (June 22, 1898).

Republicans of this school were reasserting, strangely enough, Calhounism.

Objection by Republicans to incorporating distant Orientals into the Union was so common, and a desire to give them racial leadership so uncommon, prior to the war with Spain, that a question concerning even Fiske, Strong, and Burgess arises. Were those writers aware of preparing the way for imperialism? In the case of Fiske the answer is clear. At the outbreak of the war with Spain, he was an anti-imperialist. He became converted to imperialism during the war, perhaps by forces unleashed in the war, though whence his "second thoughts" came he did not make evident.[22] Burgess was a vehement anti-imperialist throughout the war. He fell into the depths of despondency and despair over the course the war took. He thought he had been utterly misunderstood if any of his students believed he had, in insidious form, been teaching them imperialism. He specifically singled out Theodore Roosevelt for disapproval. He considered the imperialism generated by the war a disaster to American political civilization, and for some time after the war adhered to that view.[23]

As for the Reverend Josiah Strong, he had dealt in his book primarily with problems on the home front. His one chapter describing Anglo-Saxon superiority and its relationship to a vast world front was thrown in for inspirational purposes. He doubtless had vague hopes that the future would open a wider world front to Protestant missionaries. In 1900 he published another book, entitled *Expansion under New World Conditions,* in which he acclaimed the outcome of the war with Spain. He chided opponents of imperialism as blind and mistaken, even if well intentioned. He thought the common view, that no government can rightfully be established for a people except by their consent, outworn. Without any difficulty at all he could see a providential meaning in the circumstance that, with no design on our part, we had become a

[22] Milton Berman: *John Fiske* (Cambridge, 1961), 251–2.

[23] Jurgen F. H. Herbst: "Nineteenth Century German Scholarship in America" (Ph.D. thesis, Harvard University, 1958), p. 166.

power in Asia. The Anglo-Saxon race had been created, he thought, to assure freedom to Asia as against the tyranny of the Slav. The practical advantages of the new Asiatic front—rich markets, naval power, coaling stations, and so on—he described with a realism and with a wealth of detail that would have done credit to Mahan. He had learned of them from Mahan, whose utterances, he thought, exhibited "the insight of the philosopher and the wisdom of the statesman." [24] He especially welcomed the opening of new fields in the Orient for Protestant missionaries. In its inclusiveness of national interests to be served and in its fervor, the book was a powerful presentation of missionary expansionism.

But it is Strong's 1885 book and its impact on public opinion which are the immediate subjects of this inquiry. Its sale was considerable, as those who emphasize its significance all point out. The sale seems to have been principally in evangelical circles. Reviews of it appeared almost exclusively in such journals. They were favorable to the book on the whole, if not always enthusiastic. None of them consulted in this study mentioned the chapter on Anglo-Saxon race superiority and its relationship to the salvation of the world.[25] In that chapter Strong was endorsing Darwinian concepts that were not always greeted with applause in evangelical circles. Missionary-minded Americans of that era seemed generally to feel that the heathen should be strengthened by bringing them the Protestant gospel, not that they should be replaced with finer materials. Among Roman Catholics, little in the book could have had much appeal. In secular journals the work received scant notice. The one secular review found of it was in the New York *Nation*. It was devastating. It dealt solely with the chapters on the

[24] Josiah Strong: *Expansion under New World Conditions* (New York, 1900), 261. Mahan was a thoroughgoing racist. He believed incompetent and inferior races would go down, and ever have gone down, before the persistent impact of the superior. Mahan: *The Interests of America in Sea Power*, 166.

[25] Reviews in evangelical journals which seem to be typical are in *Christian Union*, August 19, 1886; *Zion's Herald*, May 19, 1886; *Presbyterian Review*, July, 1886, p. 584; *Congregationalist* (Boston), February 18, 1886; *Advance* (Chicago), March 18, 1886. The *Baptist Review* and the *American Church Review* took no notice of the book.

perils overhanging the homeland. The chapter on Anglo-Saxon superiority and world leadership was utterly ignored.[26]

Racism in a nation is a complex phenomenon. It varies from section to section, from party to party, and from stratum to stratum in society. If it is alleged to have contributed to imperialism and the allegation is to be tested at all levels, the complexities become bewildering. If such a hypothesis relates to a period when interest in imperialism is marginal everywhere, as it was in the 1880's and early 1890's, and when the nation is in a state of profound peace, a judgment by the historian that such a contribution was made is an act of faith rather than an act of weighing evidence. When a neighboring people, known to Americans for generations, as Mexicans had been in 1846, becomes the subject of expansionist discussion and arouses an overwhelming racial objection to having them in the Union, as it did in 1848, is it likely that an Oriental people, inhabiting islands halfway across the Pacific, were the subject of a desire in the 1890's to give them race leadership by annexation? Is it not likely that racism, prior to the war with Spain, was a deterrent to imperialism rather than a stimulant of it?

A good barometer of the climate of opinion on expansionism prior to the war with Spain is congressional voting. Voting took place in the House in 1894 on the Hawaiian issue on a set of resolutions introduced by a Southern Democrat. The resolutions condemned Stevens's actions in Honolulu in 1893 as violative of American traditions, endorsed the principle of non-interference in the domestic affairs of an independent nation, and declared the annexation of the islands "uncalled for and inexpedient." The vote was 177 yea, 78 nay, and 96 not voting.[27] In the Senate the expansionists dared not risk a vote in 1894, or in 1897, on the annexation issue in any form.

Outside Congress sentiment against annexation was equally in evidence. It appeared among Republicans, as reflected in three

[26] New York *Nation,* September 30, 1886.

[27] *Cong. Record,* 53 Cong., 2 Sess., 2007–08. The text of the resolution is on page 2001.

outstanding leaders of the older generation, George Tichnor Curtis, Judge Thomas M. Cooley, and Carl Schurz. Curtis and Cooley were eminent commentators on the Constitution; Schurz had been a pillar of the party in its early years and later was one of its great reform spirits. Curtis and Cooley assailed annexation on constitutional grounds. They maintained that the framers of the Constitution did not contemplate non-contiguous territorial additions to the Union or the creation of an overseas colonial system. They thought Manifest Destiny, if tolerated in the form of a Hawaiian precedent, would supplant the Constitution itself. Cooley assailed navalism of the Mahan type; he challenged the truth of assertions that the Hawaiian people had given consent to annexation.[28] Schurz, in the article already cited, maintained that the Hawaiian Islands would be a source of military weakness in the Pacific to the United States, not a source of strength, and expressed the conviction that annexationism found favor only among a numerically weak but demonstrative class of navalists, jingoists, and economic imperialists.[29] These elder statesmen of the party felt, apparently, that the term "Manifest Destiny" was an upside-down term in its new sense, an upsetting of everything it had once meant, another of those examples of gibberish intended to reverse all "the laws of nature and turn human intelligence into brutishness."

It is a truism of political science that an incident of startling character, occurring during an international controversy in which popular emotions have become deeply engaged, has an impact abnormally great on the public mind. Especially is this true if the incident has involved the shedding of American blood on American soil or on an American vessel innocently employed abroad. In such a case the public mind is stormed, reason departs, emotion takes over, and extremism, which is latent in every society, emerges and takes command.

On the night of February 15, 1898, an incident of this sort oc-

[28] Thomas M. Cooley: "Grave Obstacles to Hawaiian Annexation," *Forum,* XV (1893), 389 ff.; George T. Curtis; "Is It Constitutional?" *North American Review,* CLVI (1893), 282 ff.

[29] *Harper's New Monthly Magazine,* LXXXVII (1893), 737 ff.

curred. The American battleship *Maine,* on a "friendly" visit to Cuba, was blown up in the harbor of Havana. The toll was heavy —260 American lives. How the explosion was caused, whether by mine or internally, and if by mine, who set off the blast, were questions unanswered then, and have not been answered yet. Extremists in the United States had the immediate answer. The explosion, they maintained, had been ordered by the government of Spain. This is the one answer historians now consider most difficult to credit. The government having the most to lose from a disaster of that sort, in its own territorial waters, was Spain's.

News of the disaster reached an American public already emotionally on edge. For three years Americans had, from their "front windows," been witnessing a sickening exchange of bloodlettings and brutalities between Cuban insurrectionists and the Spanish military, in which the insurrectionists held American sympathies, though their brutalities were hardly less revolting than those of the soldiery. The instincts of American humanitarianism were aligned on the weaker side. The horrors were reported in the American press. They were not softened, especially in the New York press. The New York *Journal,* controlled by William Randolph Hearst, and the New York *World,* controlled by Joseph Pulitzer, were competing for supremacy in circulation in the metropolis in the manner of Bennett and Beach in an earlier day.[30] Horrors were exploited. Some, having no reality, were fabricated and vividly described. Gross exaggeration and distortion were the order of reporting. In this orgy of yellow journalism reporting standards fell to a depth of irresponsibility never before plumbed, even in the 1840's. Articles appearing in Eastern journals were taken over in sympathetic Western ones. A frenzy of interventionism was whipped up. It was not shared by McKinley, who was attentive to the voice of business and opposed intervention on the ground that it would lead to war with Spain and retard the return of prosperity so eagerly desired by all. Diplomatic pressure was applied to Spain to end the struggle by recognizing the independ-

[30] A good account of this journalistic rivalry is Joseph E. Wisan: *The Cuban Crisis as Reflected in the New York Press* (New York, 1939).

ence of Cuba. The pressure became more direct and intense as passion in the United States rose. Concessions were gained, but at a slow pace. In Spain, where it was thought that the insurrection had its secret centers in the United States, like the filibustering of a half century earlier, anything like a capitulation under threat was out of the question. A surrender to Yankee "pigs" would have endangered the monarchy.

An examination of the sunken hulk of the *Maine* by an American naval board, with Spanish permission, showed that she had been blown up from the outside. To American jingoes the report seemed proof that she had been destroyed by a mine set off on orders of the Spanish government. This was not McKinley's view. But his philosophy was that a President obeys, does not resist, public opinion. Moral courage, such as a Grover Cleveland would have shown in the face of a mob, was not part of the kindly make-up of this President. Congressional elections might be lost if action were not taken. Word had reached the President, on April 10, 1898, from the American minister in Madrid that the Spanish government had all but capitulated to American demands, that its commander in Cuba had been ordered to offer the rebels a suspension of hostilities. But the President already had a message to Congress framed recommending armed intervention. His mind had become set, as had Polk's on the eve of the Mexican War. On April 11 he sent the message—a request for authority to use the Army and Navy to end hostilities in the island. Concerning the Madrid communication he noted only that he had received word of a Spanish order "the duration and details of which have not yet been communicated to me." [31] Intervention was voted by overwhelming majorities. Spain, in turn, declared war. Once again a shedding of American blood required the shedding of more.

Fighting in the war was marked by brilliant victories on the

[31] Richardson (comp.): *Messages and Papers,* X, 56 ff. See also Ernest R. May: *Imperial Democracy: The Emergence of America as a Great Power* (New York, 1961). This work is valuable not merely for its European diplomatic background but also for new insights into American public opinion on the Cuban crisis. The distinction between the humanitarianism that produced the war and the imperialism that grew out of it is especially well drawn in it.

American side. The victories at sea were especially glorious. Off the harbor of Santiago a Spanish fleet, attempting to escape, was met by an American fleet, and in a few hours all its units were fire-blackened wrecks piled up on the Cuban coast. American casualties were one man killed and one wounded. At Manila a Spanish fleet, hopelessly outgunned, was wiped out, with total casualties on the American side of eight wounded. Land operations on the Cuban front were more costly, yet crowned with equal success. In them Theodore Roosevelt, at the head of a regiment of Rough Riders, won laurels which he made no effort to conceal and which ultimately carried him to the presidency.[32] Spanish resistance crumbled. Within a little more than three months Spain was asking for peace.

In the ensuing negotiations the issue facing the American people resembled the one facing them a half century earlier. Then it had been: What shall we do with the empire of the Aztecs? Now it was: What shall we do with the empire of Spain? But in its old form the issue had been far less difficult for a democracy to resolve. Earlier, no massive admission of colored aliens into the temple of freedom was finally involved, thanks to the restraint Trist had shown in his *projet*. The few taken in had been neighbors who had already virtually consented before the negotiations began. Now, in the Philippines alone, millions of colored aliens would have to be admitted, strangers living on the other side of the world, people who could not remotely be construed to have given consent, who were, indeed, in rebellion against their prospective benefactors, and who, if forced, would remain conquered subjects, presumably, for the indefinite future. What would all that do to a democracy?

When the negotiation began, concepts of an earlier day—Jeffersonian democracy, consent, anti-colonialism—were arrayed against the admission of these people. But the vitality of these had been impaired as a result of the incident and the war. Favoring the admission were powerful emotions, fresh and in full momentum—emotions of battle and its glories. On that side were now, also, the

[32] A fascinating account of the war is Frank Freidel: *The Splendid Little War* (Boston, 1958).

business interests of the nation, which prior to the war had been opposed to imperialism. On the same side were the evangelical Protestant churches and some Catholic clergy. They saw opportunities to serve their fellow men providentially opened in the Orient, and preferred to ignore a warning of Rudyard Kipling, repeated by Democrats, against taking up the "white man's burden."[33]

A very practical consideration shaped the thinking of many—the realization that a situation had been created in which a nation could not, without disgracing itself, let go what it had won. That sentiment was best expressed in a directive McKinley sent to the American peace commissioners on August 9, 1898:

> There is a very general feeling that the United States, whatever it might prefer as to the Philippines, is in a situation where it can not let go . . . and it is my judgment that the well-considered opinion of the majority would be that duty requires we should take the archipelago.[34]

"Well-considered" this opinion could hardly have been. The time had been too short. When the war began, virtually no one in the United States had conceived of anything more than a naval base or two as spoils of the victory. Absorption of an entire archipelago in the Orient by an Occidental democracy seemed unthinkable. To make it acceptable, forces of extraordinary potency had to be summoned to its side—national duty, honorable acceptance of the consequences of a war, inescapable destiny.

Yet another force summoned was indemnity. Indemnity had to be obtained from Spain for having thrust war on the United States, and also for the heavy losses suffered in Cuba by American investors during the years of the insurrection. This was best explained by the American Secretary of State, John Hay, in an in-

[33] "The White Man's Burden" was directed to the Philippine issue. It was written in America and published initially in *McClure's Magazine,* shortly before the Senate's final action on the treaty. It was recited in full by Senator Ben Tillman in the fight against the treaty. *Cong. Record,* 55 Cong., 3 Sess., 1531–2 (February 7, 1899).

[34] Cited in May: *Imperial Democracy,* 255.

struction of November 13, 1898, to the head of the American peace commission:

> We are clearly entitled to indemnity for the cost of the war. We can not hope to be fully indemnified. We do not expect to be. It would probably be difficult for Spain to pay money. All she has are the archipelagos of the Philippines and the Carolines. She surely can not expect us to turn the Philippines back and bear the cost of the war and all claims of our citizens for damages to life and property in Cuba without any indemnity but Porto Rico, which we have and which is wholly inadequate. . . . From the standpoint of indemnity both the archipelagoes are insufficient to pay our war expenses, but aside from this, do we not owe an obligation to the people of the Philippines which will not permit us to return them to the sovereignty of Spain? Could we justify ourselves in such a course, or could we permit their barter to some other power? Willing or not, we have the responsibility of duty which we can not escape.[35]

One of the most convincing of the voices urging the taking of the Philippines was Providence. This was admitted by the President himself in a famous interview with a delegation of Methodist clergymen in 1899:

> I walked the floor of the White House night after night until midnight; and I am not ashamed to tell you, gentlemen, that I went down on my knees and prayed Almighty God for light and guidance more than one night. And one night late it came to me this way—I don't know how it was, but it came. (1) That we could not give them back to Spain—that would be cowardly and dishonorable; (2) that we could not turn them over to France or Germany—our commercial rivals in the Orient—that would be bad business and discreditable; (3) that we could not leave them to themselves—they were unfit for self-government—and they would soon have anarchy and misrule over there worse than Spain's was; and (4) that there was nothing left for us to do but to take them all and to educate the Filipinos, and uplift and Christianize them, and by God's grace do the very best we could by them, as our fellow-men for whom Christ also died.[36]

[35] John Hay to William R. Day, November 13, 1898, *Senate Docs.*, 56 Cong., 2 Sess. (Serial 4039), Doc. 148, pp. 48–9. Hay was an imperialist in the same class with Mahan and Lodge.

[36] Charles Olcott: *Life of William McKinley* (2 vols., Boston, 1916), II, 110–11.

The treaty, signed December 10, 1898, embodied all these factors. It stipulated that Spain give up sovereignty over Cuba, and cede Puerto Rico, the Philippines, and Guam to the United States. It paid Spain $20,000,000—approximately the sum paid Mexico in 1848. It left the Carolines to Spain. Religious freedom was guaranteed to the peoples of the ceded areas. The civil rights and political status of the natives of those territories were, in the language of the treaty, "to be determined by Congress." Inoffensively and inconspicuously a principle was thus adopted, new to the Constitution and revolutionary—the principle that peoples not candidates for equal statehood in the Union were annexed and their status as colonial subjects left to Congress. This was imperialism.[37]

Ratification of the treaty by the Senate was by no means certain. Parts of the nation were reluctant, even yet, to embark on uncharted courses of imperialism. Ratification took almost as long as the fighting in the field. The margin by which it was finally achieved was narrow—one vote. What tipped the scale were memories of the war, pride in the performance of the Army and Navy, propaganda which registered now at last, of Anglo-Saxon racial superiority and the duty it imposed of giving leadership to inferior peoples, acquiescence in the treaty by business interests, and a desire for peace. A return to peace was actively supported by the President, who had not fought to prevent the coming of war. Stalwarts of the party, who had resisted the coming of war, were happy to have peace. William Jennings Bryan, the Democratic leader, recommended ratification, and delivered the crucial votes which brought it to pass.

Bryan was an embodiment of the emotionalism gripping the nation in the period from the *Maine* incident to the ratification of the treaty. He was not at all a jingoist, but after the sinking of the *Maine*, he joined in the clamor for intervention. He was no warrior, but when war came, he raised a regiment of troops and served for the duration in Cuba as a colonel. He was no colonialist, but lent

[37] The treaty terms are in William M. Malloy (comp.): *Treaties, Conventions, International Acts, Protocols and Agreements* (Washington, 1910), II, 1688–96.

his support finally to a colonialist treaty. Before entering the service he had pronounced publicly against colonialism. He took pride in having done so ahead of Cleveland. He thought the treaty an evil, but felt that good might come of it. On leaving the service he traveled to Washington and, to the dismay of his disciples, urged ratification. He saw in the treaty a transfer of peoples to the kindly protection of Congress, itself an assurance of their freedom in the long run. Having provided the votes for ratification, he opened a campaign to fasten on the Republican party the guilt of imperialism. He made that issue an important one in the 1900 presidential campaign.[38]

Emotion gave the turn to the wheel of fortune also, for which Hawaiian annexationists had been waiting. Three days after news came of the outcome of the Battle of Manila, on May 4, 1898, a joint resolution to annex the islands was brought before the House. It was approved soon after by the Committee on Foreign Affairs, and, a month later, was overwhelmingly adopted. The vote on adoption was 209 yea, 91 nay, with 49 abstentions. The Senate vote was 42 yea, 21 nay.

An analysis of this vote discloses revealingly, by party and by section, the distribution in 1898 of Hawaiian annexationism. Of the yea votes, 178 were Republican, 22 were Democratic, 9 were Populist. Of the nay votes, 5 were Republican, 78 were Democratic, 8 were Populist. Abstentions were about equally divided between the two major parties. As for sectional distribution, the states lying in the North and in the Northwest, including Minnesota and Iowa, gave 156 yea votes; those in the former slave region gave 30; those in the Great Plains and Far West, 23. Of the nay votes (against annexation), 10 were from the North, 75 from the former slave states, 6 from the Great Plains and Far West. Two of the old-time Northern strongholds of expansionism—New York and Illinois—were expansionist still. New York gave 29 yea votes, 2 nay. In Illinois the count was 16 to 2. In New York City, the

[38] William Jennings Bryan: *Memoirs* (Chicago, 1925), 119–21; Merle E. Curti: *Bryan and World Peace* (Northampton, Mass., 1931), 121–34.

Manhattan districts, and in Illinois, Chicago, went solidly annexationist. In the Senate the distribution of votes was similar.[39] The North had succumbed to Manifest Destiny in pseudo form, as it had, or part of it had, to the real article half a century earlier.

When this vote was taken, the Assistant Secretary of the Navy was Theodore Roosevelt. He had become more impressed than ever with the need for naval preparedness. He recognized the value of "looking outward," as Mahan conceived it, especially looking toward Hawaii. He was willing now to take the chance of having to renew the pure blood of Americans there every generation. In January 1898 he had written in *Gunton's Magazine:* "We must take Hawaii just as we must continue to build a navy equal to the needs of America's greatness. If we do not take Hawaii ourselves we will have lost the right to dictate what shall be her fate. We cannot play hot and cold at the same moment. Hawaii cannot permanently stand alone, and we have no right to expect other powers to be blind to their own interests because we are blind to ours. If Hawaii does not become American then we may as well make up our minds to see it become European or Asiatic." [40] This was the Roosevelt of the Navy Department who brought his former professor at Columbia to despondence and despair.

The imperialism of the 1890's is regarded by some historians as a variant merely of Manifest Destiny of the 1840's. This is an error. It was the antithesis of Manifest Destiny. Manifest Destiny was continentalism. It meant absorption of North America. It found its inspiration in states' rights. It envisaged the elevation of neighboring peoples to equal statehood and to all the rights and privileges

[39] *House Journal,* 55 Cong., 2 Sess. (Serial 3628), 637; *Senate Journal,* 55 Cong., 2 Sess. (Serial 3589), 398. An especially valuable study of the relationship between the Spanish-American War and Hawaiian annexation is Thomas A. Bailey: "The United States and Hawaii during the Spanish-American War," *A.H.R.,* XXXVI (1930–1), 552–60. The conclusion of Professor Bailey is that, if the war had not come when it did, and if Dewey had not fought successfully at Manila, "Hawaii would not have been annexed for some years to come, if ever." Pratt: *Expansionists of 1898,* is of major value, though it overemphasizes, as an element in annexation, the propaganda of Anglo-Saxon racial superiority and leadership.

[40] *Gunton's Magazine,* XIV (1898), 4. "The United States Looking Outward" was the title of an essay by Mahan published in 1890; Mahan: *The Interests of America in Sea Power,* ch. 1.

which that guaranteed. Expansionism in 1899 was insular and imperialistic. Its inspiration was nationalism of a sort. It involved the reduction of distant peoples to a state of colonialism. It was what O'Sullivan had thundered against in his writings about Rome and England. It was what he had assured his readers America would never tolerate. Manifest Destiny had contained a principle so fundamental that a Calhoun and an O'Sullivan could agree on it—that a people not capable of rising to statehood should never be annexed. That was the principle thrown overboard by the imperialists of 1899.

After the Spanish-American War, as after the Mexican War, expansionism lost attractiveness. The theory that growth is necessary to national life, as it is to individual life, that it is indispensable to vigor, and is a people's duty, even if it involves swallowing other people, fell into disfavor. A desire for an opposite course gradually replaced it, a wish to liquidate most, if not all, of the new empire as soon as was decently possible. Too much swallowing had, as usual, the effect of surfeit, weariness, and lethargy.

Cuba is a case in point. It had long been a goal of expansionists. In the 1840's and 1850's it had become a compelling attraction to them. In the 1890's some expansionists still hoped for it, though the interventionists in 1898 usually denied that they had a desire to acquire it. Senator Henry M. Teller, of Colorado, was of this group. He had been an exponent of Manifest Destiny for years. But he was unusual in his devotion to the principle of consent. He adhered to it more stubbornly than had his great predecessor, O'Sullivan. When the congressional resolution to intervene in Cuba reached the voting stage in the Senate he feared that some of his colleagues rushing to rescue the oppressed might yield to the temptation to keep the Pearl of the Antilles as reward for their labors. He proposed an amendment to the intervention resolution, pledging the United States to transfer sovereignty of the island to its people as soon as order had been restored. The amendment was easily passed in both houses without a recorded vote, a revealing evidence that as late as April 1898 Congress was not in an imperialist mood. Teller was hopeful that the Cuban people would have sense enough to ask admission to the Union after the war. They never had that sense.[41]

In 1901, Congress, preparing for the withdrawal of the Army from the island, inserted stipulations in the Army appropriation bill. Cuba was to enter into no treaty, when once free, with another power which might impair her independence. She was to lease naval bases to the United States. The United States was to have a right to intervene in Cuba to maintain orderly government. These were the provisions of the Platt amendment, which Cubans perforce accepted. In later years these provisions were used to give validity to several interventions. But in 1934, in the days of Franklin D. Roosevelt, in line with his "Good Neighbor" policy, they were replaced by a treaty canceling all special rights of the United States in Cuba, with the exception of a lease of the naval base at Guantánamo Bay. Thus, at last, in the liquidation of an empire, freedom came to the island which had been one of the earliest goals of Manifest Destiny.

The Philippine archipelago, which had been acquired as an afterthought of the war, was also kept in a status wherein its release was possible. It never was admitted into the bosom of the family with quite the warmth shown Hawaii. It was not made part of the United States by Congress in the sense in which the term "United States" is used in the Constitution. It was a possession of, an unincorporated part of, the United States. The restrictions placed on Congress in legislating for the United States proper did not apply to it. At least this is what the United States Supreme Court held in a major decision in 1904. In the decision use of the term "overseas colony" was avoided. The term used was "unincorporated territory," but it had a colonial look to it.[42]

Democrats began demanding the liberation of the Philippines as early as the ratification of the treaty. They never did become reconciled to the view that national maturity inexorably required colonialism. In successive party platforms they urged that the islands

[41] Elmer Ellis: *Henry Moore Teller* (Caldwell, Id., 1941), 308. Teller became an anti-imperialist after a break with his party over the silver issue.
[42] *Dorr* v. *United States,* 195 U.S. Reports, 138 ff.

go the way of Cuba. In the administration of Woodrow Wilson the Jones Act was passed, which gave dominion status to the islands as a first step toward independence. In 1933, over the veto of Herbert Hoover, Congress passed an independence act. But independence accompanied by the loss of trade privileges with the United States was not accepted by the legislature of the archipelago. However, satisfactory arrangements were eventually made, and on July 4, 1946, the Philippine Republic entered the community of free nations.

Others of the accessions of the period 1898–9 have had a different history. Hawaii, the most attractive of them, became linked to the mainland by ties of mutual interest and kindred population so close as almost to make her part of it. She had been "incorporated" into the United States by Congress as early as 1900.[43] Her population kept up a persistent agitation for admission to statehood in the Union. In 1959 she was offered statehood, and by an overwhelming vote accepted it. Puerto Rico, with a large Negro element in her population, became in 1952, with the consent of her people, a commonwealth associated with the United States. Guam, an advanced Pacific base, was administered by the Navy for a time. In 1950 the island obtained a civil government with a measure of local autonomy. Her function was that of defense, as was also that of other islands acquired at other times.[44]

In this remodeling of empire, there emerged a pattern indicative of the true temper of the American people. A few islands—those necessary for defense—were retained. Those that were useful chiefly for commercial exploitation, such as the Philippines, were freed. Commercial exploitation had lost favor. It had proved injurious to some interests on the mainland, even if advantageous to others. For instance, the agitation for the independence of the

[43] *Hawaii* v. *Mankichi,* 190 U.S. Reports, 197 ff.

[44] Other island possessions of the United States are eastern Samoa, taken as a protectorate in 1889 and annexed in 1899 in the imperialistic climate of that year, and the Virgin Islands, purchased in 1916. Guam, Samoa, and the Virgin Islands were transferred from the Navy Department to the Department of the Interior in 1950, 1951, and 1954, respectively. Local legislatures have been set up in Guam and the Virgin Islands, and are proposed for Samoa.

Philippines was led by some of the sugar interests in the United States. The archipelago may be said to have been shown the door by sugar barons. In separating functions which colonies served—commercial from defense—and renouncing the first, Americans were repudiating their imperialists of 1899 who had merged the two for the greater glory of both. The stage was finally reached where Americans boasted, in a war of propaganda, of not being a colonial power at all, and looked askance at expansionists of their past who had conceived of the possessions of their neighbors as apples to be gathered in a basket.

Chapter XII

Mission

It may be safe now to venture an opinion that continentalist and imperialist doctrines were never true expressions of the national spirit. They were the very opposite. In their espousal of the "outward look" in the Mahan sense of acquiring the property of others without consultation of the wishes of the owners; in their insistence on growth, regardless of the nature and manner of the growth; and in their reliance on divine favor for procedures that were amoral, they misrepresented the nation. They fooled a small part of the American people much of the time, another part some of the time, but never the mass all the time. A thesis that continentalist and imperialist goals were sought by the nation regardless of party or section, won't do. It is not substantiated by good evidence. A better-supported thesis is that Manifest Destiny and imperialism were traps into which the nation was led in 1846 and in 1899, and from which it extricated itself as well as it could afterward.

A truer expression of the national spirit was Mission. This was present from the beginning of American history, and is present, clearly, today. It was idealistic, self-denying, hopeful of divine favor for national aspirations, though not sure of it. It made itself heard most authentically in times of emergency, of ordeal, of disaster. Its language was that of dedication—dedication to the enduring values of American civilization. It was the language of Abraham Lincoln in the Civil War, on a great battlefield of the war, at a time when new meaning had been given to the war and to

American democracy by the Emancipation Proclamation. It appeared in the immortal phrases of the Gettysburg Address:

> It is rather for us to be here dedicated to the great task remaining before us—that from these honored dead we take increased devotion to that cause for which they gave the last full measure of devotion; that we here highly resolve that these dead shall not have died in vain—that this nation, under God, shall have a new birth of freedom; and that government of the people, by the people, for the people, shall not perish from the earth.[1]

Mission was a force that fought to curb expansionism of the aggressive variety. It did so with a measure of success at the time of the All Mexico movement. At the height of that movement Albert Gallatin sent to the press the first of his articles on the Mexican War, a section of which was a moving definition of "The Mission of the United States":

> Your mission is to improve the state of the world, to be the "model republic," to show that men are capable of governing themselves, and that the simple and natural form of government is that also which confers most happiness on all, is productive of the greatest development of the intellectual faculties, above all, that which is attended with the highest standard of private and political virtue and morality.
>
> Your forefathers, the founders of the republic, imbued with a deep feeling of their rights and duties, did not deviate from those principles. The sound sense, the wisdom, the probity, the respect for public faith, with which the internal concerns of the nation were managed made our institutions an object of general admiration. Here, for the first time, was the experiment attempted with any prospect of success, and on a large scale, of a representative democratic republic. If it failed, the last hope of the friends of mankind was lost, or indefinitely postponed; and the eyes of the world were turned towards you. Whenever real or pretended apprehensions of the imminent danger of trusting the people at large with power were expressed, the answer ever was, "Look at America!". . .
>
> Your mission was to be a model for all other governments and for all other less-favored nations, to adhere to the most elevated principles of political morality, to apply all your faculties to the

[1] The evolution of the phrasing of the address is recounted briefly in Basler (ed.): *Collected Works of Abraham Lincoln,* VII, 16–23.

> gradual improvement of your own institutions and social state, and by your example to exert a moral influence most beneficial to mankind at large. Instead of this, an appeal has been made to your worst passions; to cupidity; to the thirst of unjust aggrandizement by brutal force; to the love of military fame and false glory; and it has even been tried to pervert the noblest feelings of your nature. The attempt is made to make you abandon the lofty position which your fathers occupied, to substitute for it the political morality and heathen patriotism of the heroes and statesmen of antiquity.[2]

Again, in the 1890's Mission fought imperialism. It held its own in the fight until war brought an overwhelming force against it. It held the imperialists who sought Hawaii at bay until then. From the stronghold of Mission, old-school Republicans fought the imperialists in the Senate. So did the stalwart "Czar," Thomas B. Reed, in the House. Imperialists seemed to him betrayers not merely of a sacred American tradition but of the very life of the Constitution. Reed fought them till war overwhelmed him. He never recovered from the shock of the defeat.[3] Democrats fought from the same citadel. The annexation of the Hawaiian Islands seemed to Grover Cleveland in 1898 "a perversion of our national mission. The mission of our nation is to build up and make a greater country out of what we have instead of annexing islands."[4] Animating all defenders of the old faith was the sentiment of Daniel Webster admonishing expansionists of his day: "You have a Sparta; embellish it!"

Mission appeared in the twentieth century as a national sense of responsibility for saving democracy in Europe. It was an important force, among others, in inducing Congress in 1917 to vote entrance into the First World War. It did for democracy in the world, then, what it had not done for the newborn European republics in 1848. It inspired Woodrow Wilson, during the war and at its close, to take the lead in forming the League of Nations, which was designed

[2] Gallatin: *Peace with Mexico,* Section VII.

[3] William A. Robinson: *Thomas B. Reed* (New York, 1930), 357–71; Samuel W. McCall: *Life of Thomas Brackett Reed* (Boston, 1914), ch. 20.

[4] Allan Nevins (ed.): *Letters of Grover Cleveland* (Boston, 1933), 491–2. A mixed concept of mission is described in Edward M. Burns: *The American Ideal of Mission* (New Brunswick, N.J., 1957).

to save the future from wars precipitated by nationalistic states pursuing aggressive ends. The League had the support, probably, of a majority of the American people. But American membership in it was blocked in the Senate by a collision over the "reservation issue." Among individuals who blocked entrance the most influential were Republicans who had been nationalists and imperialists in 1899, the elements led by Henry Cabot Lodge, Theodore Roosevelt, and Albert J. Beveridge. Even louder and more fanatical were the isolationists, such as William E. Borah, Hiram W. Johnson, and James A. Reed, who had appeared in national politics after 1898.

In the tempestuous era following the First World War, Mission was a steadying force in an age of disaster. Disaster swept over the world in a succession of waves in the 1930's and 1940's. An economic tempest almost toppled the old order; then, before it had subsided, came the Second World War; and after that, the continuing crises of the cold war. In this era the hemispheric policy of the "Good Neighbor" was given effect; it was a truer expression of the American spirit than Manifest Destiny ever had been, and it quieted memories in Latin America which had persisted from the Mexican War. The concept of the Four Freedoms was framed by Franklin D. Roosevelt early in 1941, as the nation drifted toward involvement in the Second World War. The freedoms named were those imperiled by the war and the continuing depression—freedom of speech, freedom of religion, freedom from want, and freedom from fear. In defense of these freedoms Great Britain was given aid, the Fascist powers were checked, and were finally overthrown. Victory was followed by the framing of a new organ of internationalism, the United Nations, this time approved by the United States Senate and set on a course of peace.

National ideals are not simple. They are complex, and sometimes combined in mixtures as incompatible as oil and water. Manifest Destiny was sometimes mixed with a form of Mission of its own. It would be reckless to say that zealots of Manifest Destiny in the 1840's and in the 1890's had no sense of Mission. They battled for possession of the public mind armored in their own coats of idealism. They knew that in the United States a program armored in unrelieved materialism would lose the battle before a blow was struck or a shot fired. The public was usually able to detect differences between varieties of idealism, however, and to choose between them. The tests applied were the proportions found, in each variety, of aid to others and gain for self, of generous spaciousness and narrow parochialism, of enduring values and momentary appeal.

From the beginning programs of public welfare were identified with Mission. Programs of political, social, and economic change for the benefit of the underprivileged were fought for throughout the nineteenth century as phases of Mission. So were religious programs in which refreshment of the soul was sought in service to others. Philanthropy for public purposes was encouraged as part of the image of America. It reached dimensions in the United States unprecedented in the history of the world. At the end of the Second World War the same spirit appeared in the Marshall Plan for rebuilding the devastated areas of the world. It has appeared in recent programs, vast in scale, to help the peoples of underdeveloped areas.

Manifest Destiny, by contrast, seemed, despite its exaltation of language, somehow touched by a taint of selfishness, both national and individual. The sacrifices it asked were to be from others. Territory was to be taken, and all that was to be given in exchange was the prospect of American citizenship.

Manifest Destiny, moreover, seemed, on close examination, despite its breath-taking sweep, to be parochial. Its postulates were that Anglo-Saxons are endowed as a race with innate superiority, that Protestant Christianity holds the keys to Heaven, that only republican forms of political organization are free, that the future —even the predestined future—can be hurried along by human hands, and that the means of hurrying it, if the end be good, need not be inquired into too closely. Undeniably, some Americans were satisfied with such ideals. But a large majority appraised them—at least in periods when the nation was at peace—at their true worth.

Manifest Destiny and Mission differed in another respect—

durability. Manifest Destiny, in the twentieth century, vanished. Not only did it die; it stayed dead through two world wars. Mission, on the contrary, remained alive, and is as much alive at present as it ever was. It is still the beacon lighting the way to political and individual freedoms—to equality of right before the law, equality of economic opportunity, and equality of all races and creeds. It is still, as always in the past, the torch held aloft by the nation at its gate—to the world and to itself.

Index

Index

Index

A NOTE ABOUT THE AUTHOR

FREDERICK MERK is Gurney Professor, Emeritus, of American History at Harvard University, where he taught for thirty-nine years. Born in Milwaukee, Wisconsin, he took his A.B. degree at the University of Wisconsin, and his Ph.D. degree at Harvard in 1920. He served on the editorial staff of the Wisconsin State Historical Society for five years, and there developed an interest in American frontier history, through writing his *Economic History of Wisconsin during the Civil War Decade* (1916). This interest brought him to Harvard—to the great historian of the American frontier, Frederick Jackson Turner. He was associated with Professor Turner in revising the *List of References on the History of the West* (1922) and became his successor in teaching the Harvard course on the Westward Movement.

Professor Merk's most important writings have been series of articles on the Oregon question and on problems in other frontier areas, published in historical quarterlies. His writings also include *Fur Trade and Empire: George Simpson's Journal* (1931), *Albert Gallatin and the Oregon Problem* (1950), and, as co-author, *Harvard Guide to American History* (1954). He is former president of the Agricultural History Society and of the Mississippi Valley Historical Association. The holder of an honorary degree of Litt.D. from Harvard, he is a member of the Massachusetts Historical Society and the American Antiquarian Society, and is a fellow of the American Academy of Arts and Sciences.

VINTAGE HISTORY—WORLD

V-286 ARIES, PHILIPPE *Centuries of Childhood*
V-59 BEAUFRE, GEN. ANDRÉ *NATO and Europe*
V-44 BRINTON, CRANE *The Anatomy of Revolution*
V-250 BURCKHARDT, C. J. *Richelieu: His Rise to Power*
V-393 BURCKHARDT, JACOB *The Age of Constantine the Great*
V-391 CARR, E. H. *What Is History?*
V-67 CURTIUS, ERNST R. *The Civilization of France*
V-746 DEUTSCHER, ISAAC *The Prophet Armed*
V-747 DEUTSCHER, ISAAC *The Prophet Unarmed*
V-748 DEUTSCHER, ISAAC *The Prophet Outcast*
V-707 FISCHER, LOUIS *Soviets in World Affairs*
V-277 GAY, PETER *Voltaire's Politics*
V-114 HAUSER, ARNOLD *The Social History of Art* through V-117 (Four Volumes)
V-201 HUGHES, H. STUART *Consciousness and Society*
V-50 KELLY, AMY *Eleanor of Aquitaine and the Four Kings*
V-728 KLYUCHEVSKY, V. *Peter the Great*
V-246 KNOWLES, DAVID *Evolution of Medieval Thought*
V-83 KRONENBERGER, LOUIS *Kings and Desperate Men*
V-287 LA SOUCHÈRE, ÉLÉNA DE *An Explanation of Spain*
V-43 LEFEBVRE, GEORGES *The Coming of the French Revolution*
V-364 LEFEBVRE, GEORGES *The Directory*
V-343 LEFEBVRE, GEORGES *The Thermidorians*
V-92 MATTINGLY, GARRETT *Catherine of Aragon*
V-703 MOSELY, PHILIP E. *The Kremlin and World Politics:* Studies in Soviet Policy and Action
V-733 PARES, SIR BERNARD *The Fall of the Russian Monarchy*
V-285 PARKES, HENRY B. *Gods and Men*
V-719 REED, JOHN *Ten Days That Shook the World*
V-176 SCHAPIRO, LEONARD *Government and Politics of the Soviet Union* (Revised Edition)
V-375 SCHURMANN & SCHELL (eds.) *The China Reader: Imperial China,* I
V-376 SCHURMANN & SCHELL (eds.) *The China Reader: Republican China,* II
V-377 SCHURMANN & SCHELL (eds.) *The China Reader: Communist China,* III
V-312 TANNENBAUM, FRANK *Ten Keys to Latin America*
V-322 THOMPSON, E. P. *The Making of the English Working Class*
V-749 TROTSKY, LEON *Basic Writings of Trotsky*
V-724 WALLACE, SIR D. M. *Russia:* On the Eve of War and Revolution
V-206 WALLERSTEIN, IMMANUEL *Africa: The Politics of Independence*
V-729 WEIDLÉ, W. *Russia:* Absent and Present
V-122 WILENSKI, R. H. *Modern French Painters,* Volume I (1863-1903)
V-123 WILENSKI, R. H. *Modern French Painters,* Volume II (1904-1938)
V-106 WINSTON, RICHARD *Charlemagne:* From the Hammer to the Cross